WINDTOWER

WINDTOWER

Anne Coles & Peter Jackson

STACEY
INTERNATIONAL

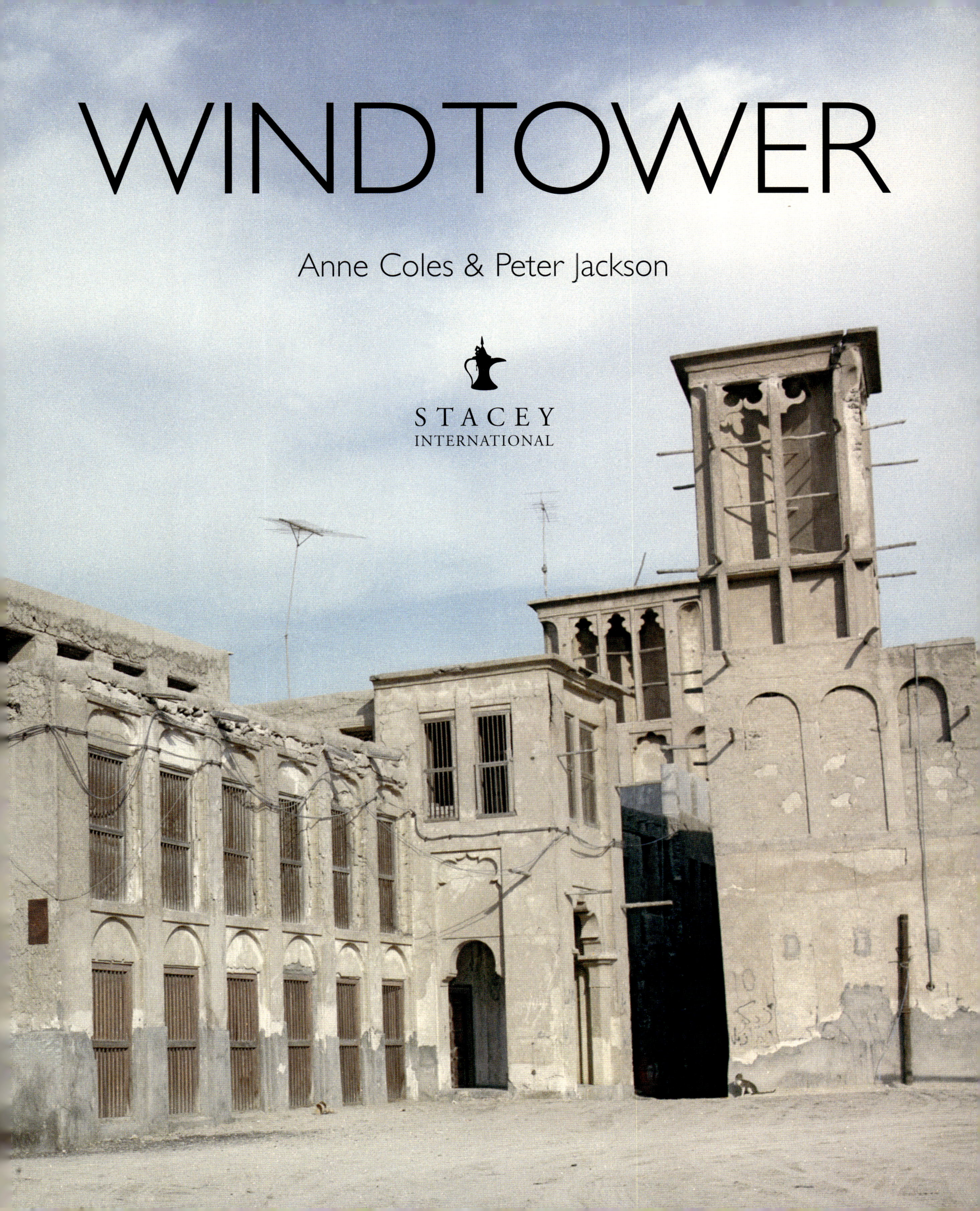

Editor
Christopher Ind

Design
Graham Edwards

Stacey International
128 Kensington Church Street
London W8 4BH
Telephone: +44 (0)20 7221 7166
Fax: +44 (0)20 7792 9288
Email: info@stacey-international.co.uk
www.stacey-international.co.uk

The publishers gratefully acknowledge the support of Joseph Tabet of Frayland LLC in the making of this book.

The authors would like to thank the National Bank of Dubai for their generous support for their research for this book.

ISBN: 978-1-9052992-4-9

CIP Data: A catalogue record for this book is available from the British Library

Printed by Oriental Press, UAE

Picture credits

The following photographers and institutions are gratefully acknowledged for their contributions. Images not listed here were taken by the authors.

Abu Dhabi Petroleum Company: 15*t*; Aerofilms: 2, 4; Mohammed Hadi Amiri: 98*t*; Ahmed Abdullah Al Bastaki: 118*b*; Eesa Bastaki: 58-60, 60*t*, 64; Ronald Codrai (© Justin Codrai): 16*b*, 45; Alison Collins: 130*b*, 177*t*; Kasra Eslachi: 161; John R Harris: 5; Mark Harris: 26; Historic Buildings Section, Dubai Municipality: 152*t*, 153*t*, 154*t*, 156*t*, 157*t*; Marcus Hope: viii, x, 12*b*, 60*b* (b/w); Hunting Surveys Ltd: 18, 19; Jutta Jackson: 115*b*, 154*b*; Oliver Jackson: 21, 56, 65, 138; Mohammed Noor Janahi: 141; Shirley Kay: 24, 100*t*, 129; Abdulkadr Salehi: 46*b*; Jennifer Scarce: 27, 31*t*, 69, 100*t*, 178*t*; Bibiya Shareefi: 106*t*, 107*b*; Wilfred Thesiger (© Pitt Rivers Museum, Oxford): 146; Vipac Engineering: 170*t*, 171, 173; Dariush Zandi: front cover, ii-iii, 22*b*, 25, 28*b*, 49, 79*t*, 158*c*, 162*t*, 163, 164, 177*t*, 180, 195*b*.

Contents

Foreword by HRH The Prince of Wales		vii
Preface		ix
Introduction		x
Acknowledgements		xii
1.	Historical Development	2
2.	House Form & Architecture	24
3.	Everyday Life	42
4.	House of Abdulrazak Abdulrahim Aminai Al Bastaki	56
5.	House of Mohammed Sharif Bukhash	66
6.	House of Mir Ahmed Mir Abdulwahid Amiri	96
7.	House of Sheikh Mohammed Shareef Abdulrahman Al Ulama	104
8.	House of Abdullah Mohammed Al Bastaki	116
9.	House of Mir Abdullah Amiri	128
10.	House of Sheikh Abdulraheem Mohammed Janahi Al Abbassi	138
11.	Construction	146
12.	Windtowers	160
13.	Decline & Regeneration	174
Appendix: Bastaki Families		186
Glossary		187
Bibliography		190
Index		192

'The heat is tremendous, and on that account their houses are built with ventilators to catch the wind. These ventilators are placed on the side from which the wind comes, and they bring the wind down into the house to cool it. But for this the heat would be utterly unbearable.'

Marco Polo (c.1254-1324) on wind-catchers in Hormuz

CLARENCE HOUSE

I recall visiting Dubai back in the 1980's and being struck, even then, by the rapid pace of development of this Emirate.

During the visit, I remember commenting upon one of the most remarkable features of the old city of Bastakiya, namely the traditional windtower houses. For me, they seemed to symbolize so much of the history and culture of this area, and the way of life of the people, and I felt it would be an absolute tragedy if they were demolished and lost to posterity.

Imagine my delight, therefore, to find that almost two decades later local wisdom had prevailed. Not only are these buildings still standing, but they now contain a museum and other uses have been found to keep them alive.

It is wonderful to see that other people have shared my enthusiasm for these buildings, with their remarkable natural air conditioning system and laid out in an urban form that enhances a sense of community and identity. I am delighted that Peter Jackson and Anne Coles have now produced this beautiful book celebrating the houses' continued existence.

I do hope this book will enable other people to join in appreciating the unique nature of these buildings and that it will encourage an awareness of how relevant many of their distinctive features are to the modern challenges of building sustainable communities in a way that maximizes the use of renewable energy and reduces the impact of the car. Learning such lessons from the timeless principles enshrined in the buildings, and appreciating that it is in fact possible to blend the modern necessities of life with ancient forms and patterns, could prove to be profoundly valuable.

Preface

My eyes were first opened to the profession of architecture in February 1974. I was 13 years old. An architect had been asked to survey my family's windtower house in Dubai's Bastakiya. Originally built in 1924 by my grandfather Mohammed Sharif Bukhash, it was one of the largest and most beautiful houses in the area. Every day for a month on my return from school I helped Peter Jackson measure the house and its features, trying to answer his many questions. The following day he would show me the sketches and drawings he was putting together, which instilled in me a lifelong love of historic buildings and architecture. That early survey by Peter Jackson, and his collaboration with Anne Coles, a geographer, would produce the first published record of a windtower house in Dubai.

I still remember that family home as being much more than just a house. Being large and spacious, it was also where I played with my brothers and sisters, cousins and neighbours' children. The house had secret places; for example I hid marbles in the opening of a windtower. I remember the ground floor room to which I accompanied my father daily to see my grandmother, and the first floor room that housed my grandfather's small library. Here I started to love books and reading; later I began my own library. My aunt's room was the most beautiful in the house, prepared for her marriage with the painted decoration and calligraphy on the walls and niches and with carved teakwood doors. The men's *majlis* became more important as I grew older; I would meet my friends there. I remember the annual migration within the house. At the beginning of each summer we would move all the main furniture from the warm ground floor rooms with their thick stone walls to the upper floor rooms with their windtowers and more openings in order to live more comfortably through the summer months. This was a suitable time to varnish all our wooden furniture and clean the carpets. During summer nights before electricity was introduced we would sleep on simple light wooden beds on the roof.

On leaving school, I left home to study architecture at Syracuse University in New York State, graduating in 1986. I joined the Dubai Municipality and worked on a number of planning and architectural projects, but a love for old buildings drew me to focus on this field. In 1991 I was given the opportunity to establish and develop a Historic Buildings Section within the Municipality.

For 12 years as Head of the Historic Buildings Section I have supervised the restoration and rehabilitation of more than 115 historic buildings in Dubai, including Al Faheidi Fort, Al Ahmadiya School, the old village of Hatta, and most recently, the Bastakiya. Since the 1990s the Municipality has sought to conserve the remaining 230 historic buildings: a heritage of which every citizen, expatriate and visitor will be proud.

During this time Peter Jackson remained in my memory as my first teacher in architecture. In 2002 we were re-introduced, and I asked him if he was the same architect who had surveyed my father's house. I told him, 'I was the boy who helped you measure it!' Since then we have met regularly to discuss architectural conservation, as well as our continuing interest in the Bastakiya.

Windtower is a further collaboration between Anne Coles and Peter Jackson. The authors have undertaken much additional research and conducted many interviews to bring it to its final form. They have extended their study of our family house to compare its form and use with others that have been or are being restored. Their historical and social perspective of the quarter provides an important record for future generations in Dubai. In describing traditional building methods and materials I am pleased that the information and experience gained by the Historic Buildings Section has been of special benefit. Their collaboration with engineer Ian Jones has resulted in a series of unique studies providing a better understanding of the effectiveness of windtowers, demonstrating the potential for adapting their principles to provide viable passive cooling systems for future buildings in the region and, indeed, elsewhere in the world. I believe that this book provides an invaluable reference for students to understand the links between architecture and social life.

Rashad Mohammed Bukhash
Director, General Projects Department, Dubai Municipality
March 2007

Opposite:
Classically elegant windtowers adorn this Bastakiya courtyard house in Dubai, 1975.

Introduction

The two authors of this book first became interested in the windtowers of Dubai over thirty years ago. In 1969 Anne Coles began to study summer migration patterns in the northern Emirates. Through her contacts and friendship with women of the Bastakiya whom she met through the local Women's Society, she came to realise that upstairs-downstairs migration within their windtower homes was an important response to summer climate in Dubai's urban area. So too was the erection of temporary windtowers in the less affluent parts of the town. Anne made preliminary measurements on the effectiveness of windtowers over the next few summers but with three small children, and, from 1970, working as a geographer in the Development Office, her time was necessarily limited. Late in 1971 she left Dubai after living there for three years.

Peter Jackson came to Dubai as a student architect in 1972 and subsequently joined a British firm of architects with growing interests in the area. When posted there for six weeks in 1974, Anne asked him whether he would make a drawing of a windtower for the Dubai Museum whose establishment she had enthusiastically supported during her time in Dubai. For the purpose she provided him with a letter of introduction to the Bukash family who lived in a particularly beautiful windtower house in the Bastakiya. Peter found this introduction to another culture and way of life so different from his previous experience, that he asked whether he might be permitted the time to survey the entire house. Over the next twelve months he was able to draw up a full set of measured drawings.

In 1976 we had the opportunity to collaborate in producing a short monograph 'A Windtower House in Dubai' published by Art and Archaeology Research Papers. It was printed in the Lebanon during a troubled period. An explosion scattered the pages with the result that some of the photos and captions were transposed. The copies sent to Dubai suffered water damage on the docks and had to be dried on the floor of the Museum. But, when Peter returned to Dubai in 2002, it was still available as a private re-print with the authors' names removed.

We initially planned to republish the monograph with an extended text and the full set of drawings, but with encouragement from some Bastakiya families, we made the decision to produce this completely new book. We have retained our interest in the architecture of the houses and how they were lived in, adding comparative chapters on six further houses that have been restored and can be visited today, although they are now no longer family homes. But we have also extended our study to include the history of the Bastakiya community and the neighbourhood as a whole, and expanded the information on house construction. We welcomed a generous offer by Ian Jones of Vipac to provide his environmental engineering team and laboratories in Australia to record and analyse in detail the way in which windtowers work.

We hope that this book will be easily accessible. Given its scope, we were aware, in writing it, that we were crossing many disciplinary boundaries. We have made maximum use of first-hand experiences and many of those who contributed information have also helped by checking our drafts. We record our thanks to all who helped in the Acknowledgements. Any mistakes or omissions that remain are ours.

Throughout the project we have benefited greatly from the interest and generous hospitality of the Bastakiya families. As outsiders we have felt privileged to share the personal memories of some of those who lived in the area, to hear stories of their grandparents' time and of how their predecessors came to Dubai. Genealogy and place of origin were important in how the families perceived themselves. We have attempted to set these oral accounts in the broader context of Dubai's recorded history. An attractive feature of these memories was the importance of being 'first' – the first to own a football, a refrigerator, or a television. To have owned one of the oldest houses in the Bastakiya was the best 'first' of all.

The families were keen that we should commit to paper their recollections of a former way of life, one unknown and therefore little appreciated by the children of today, so rapid has been the pace of change. While they recalled the hardship of life in Dubai before the introduction of modern health care, education, communications, as well as, not least, air conditioning, there were rosy memories as well, especially of childhoods which seemed less complicated than those of today.

In our account of how windtower houses were occupied and the life that went on within them, we have recognised that women and children spent more time than men in these family homes. We have made a particular effort to reflect the perspectives of women, who traditionally were much less visible than men, and who, in as much as they engaged in public, did so largely through men. Many provided lively and valuable accounts of life in the past.

When families moved out of the Bastakiya prior to its partial demolition they left many of their old possessions to be bulldozed along with their former homes, moving into modern villas and apartments. For a time it seemed that only a few professionals and westerners were interested in the old buildings and artefacts of Dubai. Today, the same families take pride in the heritage of the windtowers, which are as much a part of Dubai as the dhows that ply the Creek and the imaginative modernisation that has transformed the Emirates. Modern Dubai exploded into the late twentieth century but began to look back just before it was too late: enough of its earlier material culture remained to be restored. The authors hope that this book will help to preserve memories of a traditional past. It is therefore dedicated to the present and future children of Dubai.

Anne Coles and Peter Jackson
March 2007

Opposite:
A fine view across the Bastakiya – the old quarter – towards the Creek, taken in the mid 1970s.

Acknowledgements

This book would not have been possible without the tremendous assistance and support that we have received from a very large number of people. Individual acknowledgements are included for each chapter, but broader acknowledgements are also necessary, especially to those who have put up with our interminable queries and questions over a year and a half, and have spent considerable time reviewing and checking our draft manuscript. To those whose names may not appear, we are no less grateful. Every small piece of information we have recorded has assisted us to understand the story that we endeavour to tell, whether or not it has been possible to include it here. Indeed there remains much more still to be told, and we hope that our small start will encourage others, more able, to do so.

Architect Rashad Bukhash rallied both his family and the Historic Buildings Section of the Municipality on our behalf. This book could not have been produced without his personal support, and the considerable assistance provided by his department at the Dubai Municipality.

During the course of this project we have made some close friends, which has made the making of this book all the more worthwhile. Dr Eesa Bastaki and his wife Layla Jani, his father Mohammed, Mohammad Abdulrazak, Dr Hadi Amiri, Bibiya Shareefi, Mahmoud Al Bastaki, his parents Ahmed and Haleema, and Mohammad Noor al Janahi have all offered their extensive support and encouragement. Each contributed personally to this research and our understanding of the Bastakiya.

Anne, particularly, would like to acknowledge the friendship and fellowship experienced through membership of the Women's Society in 1968-71. The memories of those times together have inspired this book. Through visiting members in their homes she became entranced by their architectural heritage. Some were good enough to allow her to take preliminary measurements of windtower effectiveness in their homes. Sadly not all are still with us but it has been marvellous to meet up again with several, including Bibiya Shareefi, in the course of the book's preparation. We would also like to thank those women who provided us with memories, anecdotes and information but who prefer to remain anonymous.

Through their hospitality and friendship, the members of the Areesh Majlis club in the Bastakiya have made us feel a part of their community: Mohammad Ahmed Al Bastaki, brothers Abdulrahman and Abdullah Mohammed Sharif, Saeed and Amin Ahmed Al Awadhi who have all shared coffee, meals, boat trips and a multitude of memories with us. Ahmed Buijsaim has patiently talked to us about the Bastakiya in the broader context of Dubai, with stories of his father and grandfather in Shindagha. Farook Bin Ahmad Al Awar, Saeed Al Hasmi, Younis and Yousif Mohammed Sharif, Abdullah Haj Rashidi, and Muhsin Fahad Haza, among others, have all provided information and encouragement for the project.

The support given to us by Brian Johnson, following his introducing us to Max Scott of Stacey International, cannot be underestimated. Assistance was provided by a number of staff from Godwin Austen Johnson Chartered Architects, in particular Eduard Juliano for the sketch of the cradle, William Macaloyos for drawing the floor plans of the houses, and Kasra Eslahchi for patiently ensuring the best reproduction of the original survey drawings.

Dariush Zandi who made considerable efforts to save the Bastakiya generously provided us with a number of his fine photographs, especially that on the cover. Shirley Kay, Marcus Hope, Jennifer Scarce, Phil Iddison, Abdulkadr Salehi in Bastak, architects John R Harris and Mark Harris have also freely given us access to their photographs. (John Harris had also supported our original publication in 1975.) The Historic Buildings Section of Dubai Municipality permitted us to use a number of their photographs and provided us with copies of archive images, maps of the Bastakiya and reconstruction drawings of individual houses, on which were able to base our own. Aerofilms Ltd and Hunting Aviation kindly permitted us to use early aerial images of Dubai. Mick Pilcher flew specially from Lusaka to assist us with diagrams, maps and graphs. Simon Gray of Llewellyn Davies kindly provided details from their 1994 report, and gave permission for reproduction from it.

Joseph Tabet has taken great pains to ensure that publication might be commercially attractive and has enthusiastically supported its preparation from the outset. His confidence in our book cannot be underestimated.

The enthusiastic support of our respective families has been huge. Sir John Coles reviewed the manuscript at various stages, Jutta Jackson uncomplainingly put up with the many weekends spent by her husband over a computer, and looked after the authors during joint-working sessions. Her assistance in interviews proved invaluable, while Karsten Jackson often provided transport for Anne. Oliver Jackson took a number of new photographs for the book, and cleaned many scans of old photographs for us.

Chapter 1: Dr Ron Hawker, who prepared a paper especially, and with his wife Laila most generously shared ideas with us and whose work also contributed to Chapter 12. Dr Farhad Farjam for facilitating Peter's trip to Bastak with Dr Eesa Bastaki; and while there Ismael Mohammed Noor Aminai and his family for their generous hospitality. Dr Eesa Bastaki, Ahmed Abdulrazak Abdulrahim, Kamal Hamza Alhassan, Dr Mohammed Hadi Amiri, Munira Khalil and Mark Harris.

Chapter 2: Rashad Bukhash and Dr Eesa Bastaki. Jennifer Scarce for her considerable help, particularly on this chapter, but also elsewhere in this book. Carolyn Heath for her thought-provoking contribution.

Chapter 3: Khaleed Zaroony and Nabila Al Awadhi at Al Dar Al Nadwa Wafa Al Hamed of the Sheikh Mohammed Centre for Cultural Understanding, Ameena Al Attar, Abdulla Al Jasmi, Mariam Benham, Layla Jani, Norah Ghalib, Bibiya Shareefi, Munira Khalil, Mohammad Abdulrazaq Al Bastaki, Phil Iddison, Ruqaya Abdulrazzak, Farida Abdulrazzak, Dr Nabil Bastaki for translating.

Chapter 4: Mohammed Abdulrazak Abdulrahim and his son Dr Eesa Bastaki

Chapter 5: Rashad Mohammed Bukhash, Mohammed Shareef Bukhash, Dr Aqeel Fikree, Farouk Fikree, Fuad Mohammed Bukhash

Chapter 6: Dr Mohammad Hadi Amiri and his brothers

Chapter 7: Bibiya Shareefi

Chapter 8: Mahmood Ahmed Al Bastaki, and his parents Ahmed Abdullah Al Bastaki and Haleema bint Abdulraheem Janahi

Chapter 9: Alison Collins, Ali M R Amiri, Ali Abdullah Amiri

Chapter 10: Ahmed Abdullah Al Bastaki and Haleema bin Abdulraheem Janahi, Mohammed Noor Janahi

Chapter 11: The late Ostad Mohammed Ahmad Al Banna in 1974, his son Ostad Aqeel Mohammad Al Banna, and grandson Ahmad Aqeel Al Banna for patiently translating for us. Rashad Mohammed Bukhash, Amrik Singh Plaka, and Abdulqader Saleh Albanna.

Chapter 12: The manager of Dubai Airport Meteorological Office, Dave Thomas for providing us with extensive data, and to Clive Stevens for his facilitating. Andrew Henderson for his early discussions on the climate and for introducing us to Vipac. Enormous gratitude is due to Ian Jones and Vipac Engineers and Scientists Ltd for their original research carried out for this book, with Dr Seifu Bekele in Melbourne and Dr Neihad Al Khalidy in Sydney. Professor Susan Roaf, for sharing her earlier work on windtowers in Yazd. Alasdair Coles and Oliver Jackson for their help with graphics.

Chapter 13: Rashad Bukhash, Dariush Zandi, former Consul-General Jolyon Kay, and former Director of Dubai Municipality, Kamal Hamza Alhassan, Simon Grey of Llewelyn Davies architects and planners, Dr Mike Ziegler, Mahmood Mohammed Noor, together with the men of the Areesh Majlis club.

Appendix: Abdullah Mohammed Sharif, Dr Eesa Bastaki, Ahmed Abdulrazak Abdulrahim, Rashad Bukhash, Mohammed Shareef Bukhash, Dr Aqeel Fikree and Dr Mohammad Hadi Amiri.

General

Abdullah Saleh, Chairman of the National Bank of Dubai for his early encouragement and generous support. Ahmad Mahmoud Ahmad and Khalid Mohammed Ahmad of the Historic Buildings Section for access to records and houses, and for arranging the opening up of two windtowers for experiment. Geoff Sanderson for advice on tree species. Julia Wheeler for advice, encouragement and sharing ideas. Abdin Nasralla (manager of Bab Al Shams resort) for a marvellous weekend escape from the computer. Last and not least, Max Scott and our editor Christopher Ind and their team at Stacey International for their skill, patience and confidence in the book.

To all of you, we express our enormous gratitude.

AC & PJ

1

Historical Development

The first Arabian windtowers were built in the late nineteenth century, and are associated with the immigration of merchant families from southern Persia, many from Bastak. The far-sightedness of Dubai's ruling family provided conditions under which these merchants and others could establish flourishing businesses. With this new prosperity, Dubai rapidly developed its own distinctive architecture, the most striking feature of which was its windtowers, which were to fill the skyline by the middle of the twentieth century.

Left:
This early air photograph of Dubai in1950 shows trading vessels anchored in the shallow waters of the creek, with smaller boats pulled up on the shore. Courtyard houses – many with windtowers – are closely built, separated by narrow lanes. *Areesh* (palm frond) buildings lie beyond the masonry dwellings. Behind these are scattered palm trees and the outline of garden plots. The fort is on the far side of the Creek in the centre of the photograph.

Characteristics

The basic physical elements that underlie Dubai's geography and history – its climate, land, geology and position, tell only a small part of the story. The economic and social possibilities they offered changed over time, as international politics and technology defined their importance. In the case of Dubai, the harshness of the land focused attention on the resources of the sea. Its geographical position in the Middle East gave it a potential but fluctuating importance depending on global trends. When technological changes led to exploitation of oil, Dubai later became a participant. What flowed from this was increased wealth to transform the state. Desalination has partly greened the urban landscape. Air conditioning has not only totally altered the micro-climate in which people conduct their lives but has made possible the promotion of tourism. Investment in ports, repair facilities and airports has enabled Dubai to capitalise on its geographical location to become a major regional communications centre.

Opposite:
This 1950 photograph of Dubai looks north-east. It shows a small town divided into distinct areas, much as described by Lorimer half a century earlier. The ruling family lived in Shindagha, at the head of the Creek. Separated from it by a stretch of low-lying saline flats (*sabkha*), but still on the far side of the Creek, is the main settlement of Dubai. The distinctive quarter of the Bastakiya lies immediately beyond and adjacent to it. Deira lies on the near side of the creek in the foreground.

Below:
The waterfront of the Dubai souq in 1960 had been developed to allow boats farther inland to unload their cargo. The single bays on these relatively small windtowers signify the modest scale of these commercial buildings.

The United Arab Emirates is situated at the southern lower end of the Gulf; only Oman's rugged Musandam peninsula separates it from the narrow straits of Hormuz which overlook the Gulf's entrance. The Hajar ranges, running roughly north-south into Oman, influence the climate and affected the area's earlier history. Over 90 per cent of the Emirates' land area is desert, merging into the formidable Rub Al Khali (Empty Quarter). Its 750 kilometre Gulf shoreline is low-lying, sandy and often saline, with numerous islets in the west and inlets towards the east. Beyond the mountains a narrow 75 kilometre strip of coast faces the Indian Ocean. The heat is such that over 70 per cent of the scanty, variable rainfall is lost through evaporation; only a bare 15 per cent infiltrates the soil. Oases are few. The oilfields lie both off and on shore; the earliest to be exploited and the most productive are in Abu Dhabi.

Dubai is the second most extensive Emirate with 5 per cent of the land; Abu Dhabi has 87 per cent. Dubai's agricultural resources were (and are) minimal and it lacked a tribal hinterland. People looked to the sea for their livelihood, for fishing, pearling, and maritime trade. Dubai's Creek offers one of the few natural harbours on the Arab coast, although, like neighbouring creeks, its entrance was vulnerable to sand bars created by the north-south currents. In the first part of the twentieth century, Dubai benefited

commercially from stability in the area resulting from Britain's presence in India and the Gulf.

Climate

The Emirates have a dry climate – maritime desert in type – with mild, warm winters and hot summers. Despite the lack of rain, a characteristic of the coastal areas is their high humidity. In summer, the combination of high temperatures and high humidities created oppressive, uncomfortable conditions which windtowers were designed to alleviate.

January is the coolest month, with an average (mean) maximum temperature of 24°C and an average minimum temperature of 14°C. Temperatures gradually rise with 'spring-like' conditions in March, April and early May. Then the long summer sets in. From May to September inclusive average maximum temperatures exceed 37.5°C. It is hottest in August with average maximum temperatures of over 41°C and an average minimum of 30°C. Air temperatures begin to fall from September onwards. From April to September the average monthly figures show at least 10 hours of sunshine per day. The diurnal temperature range is 9-13 degrees, depending on the season.

Throughout the year, the main winds are from the north-west or north. In winter the general flow is interrupted and the weather becomes unsettled when mid-latitude disturbances penetrate into the area. Then the wind veers

Below:
This view from 1974 looks north across the western end of the Bastakiya. It highlights the close relationship between the Creek, trading dhows and the merchant houses.

Above:
In-shore fishing boats in the shallows of Dubai creek with their lateen sails unfurled to dry after rain. Sailing boats with palm-stem built-up sides were becoming less common by 1974.

to the south-east ahead of the north-westerly *shamal*, which sweeps down the Gulf through the winter months. Most of the annual rainfall (of barely 90mm) falls during this period, typically as short-lived showers. May and June mark the beginning of summer. Low pressure over Iran and high pressure over Saudi Arabia can result in strong north-westerly winds which bring hot and sometimes sandy conditions, but from July onwards the pressure gradient declines and winds are less.

Land and sea breezes come to dominate the air flow in the summer months and their characteristics are immensely important in terms of human comfort. Those living without air conditioning are very sensitive to the resulting diurnal patterns and fluctuations in climate. In Dubai the land breeze is predominantly from the south-east and the afternoon breeze from the north-west. Generally the land breeze blows offshore at night and in the early morning. As the land heats up rapidly after sunrise, it is very hot by mid-morning. The onshore breeze, which is slightly cooler, but more humid, sets in towards noon and blows until late afternoon. In the evening and at night the breeze is light and averages around 5-6 knots; there may be patches of calm. The breeze picks up after dawn and by late morning and particularly in the afternoon winds average 12 knots. As summer progresses, sea temperatures rise and the warm humid afternoon wind can produce some of the most uncomfortable conditions. Throughout the summer, the average daily maximum humidity is over 70 per cent, rising to 80 per cent in September.

Left:
Al Faheidi Fort, together with a fragment of the old town wall, are the oldest structures in Dubai, dating from the late eighteenth century. The wall and fort were described in 1822 by Lt J N Guy, commander of *HMS Discovery*: 'The town is a simple assemblage of mud hovels surrounded by a low mud wall in which are several branches and defended by three round towers, and a square castellated building, with a tower at one angle, much dilapidated. . .'

History

The history of the Bastakiya is the story of how the people of Bastak and Lingeh came to migrate from southern Persia to the small port of Dubai on the Arab side of the Gulf and how many of them built an architecturally coherent neighbourhood and created a community that was to contribute both commercially and more broadly to the subsequent development of Dubai. It involves the story of how the far-sightedness of the ruling family of Dubai provided the conditions under which these merchants and others could establish flourishing businesses that have responded to and even anticipated changes in the regional and global economy.

At the end of the eighteenth century Dubai was a small fishing town under the overall suzerainty of Abu Dhabi, although it was a separate signatory to the General Treaty of Peace, which the individual sheikhs of the Trucial Coast made with Britain in 1820. Al Faheidi Fort, the oldest surviving building, was first mentioned in 1799.

Dubai's fortunes changed in 1833 when about 800 people from the Al bu Falasah sub-section of the Bani Yas revolted against the new Sheikh of Abu Dhabi, left there and settled in Dubai. Maktoum bin Buti, one of their leaders became Ruler, and all the subsequent rulers of Dubai have been his descendants. Dubai was positioned uneasily between the territory of Abu Dhabi and that of the Qawasim sheikhs, who controlled Ras al Khaimah, Sharjah and most of the area in between. In the sometimes unsettled decades that followed, Dubai maintained its independence and by the late 1870s had overtaken the city of Abu Dhabi in size and emerged as the principal port of the Trucial States.

Like the other coastal settlements in this desert region, Dubai had few natural resources, not least because its land area was limited and its date gardens few. It had an important pearling fleet with over 300 boats. Dubai's only exports during the nineteenth century were pearls, mother-of-pearl and dried fish. Its merchant fleet engaged in general trading, and was considerably larger than those of the other states.

Writing early in the twentieth century, Lorimer, in his *Gazeteer of the Persian Gulf*, describes Dubai as an embryonic city state with a population of 10,000 or a little more. The town lay astride a shallow creek, with a difficult entrance, and had a small quay for vessels able to go inside. It consisted of three main quarters. Deira, the largest lying on the north side of the creek, had a mixed population of Arabs, Persians, Baluchis and others. It contained about 1,600 houses and the main bazaar, with some 350 shops. Both Shindagha and Dubai were on the south-west side of the Creek. Shindagha with some 250 houses was the closer to the sea and was the base for the Bani Yas, the ruling Arab family. Dubai itself contained about 200 houses and 50 shops, and was where the Indian merchant community lived. Here, too, was the principal mosque; *abras* (ferry boats) crossing the Creek were free to the inhabitants of Deira on a Friday. When the people of Bastak began migrating to Dubai, they were to settle beyond the Indian community along the Creek further inland. In the nineteenth century, this area was known as Hamriyah, after the red fruit of the date palms growing there. A century later, the quarters forming this early urban pattern can still be seen in the present city landscape.

Below:
The original Shindagha palaces of the Maktoum family were some of the finest examples of masonry architecture in Dubai. Construction of the Sheikh Obaid bin Thani house began in 1916, but by the 1970s like most early buildings was in a poor state of repair. Demolished in 1991, this house has since been reconstructed. Windtowers can be seen on the neighbouring house of Sheikh Saeed.

The Gulf

The Gulf was a source of common resources and served as a highway, a communications link, for the communities of the surrounding lands. However different their administrations, the coastal peoples were brought together by a common economy. Backed by inhospitable deserts and mountains both to north and to south, the sea had been for centuries a major focus for their existence. There has long been a fluidity of movement among the Gulf peoples; to this day migration has responded to economic opportunity at least when political circumstances have permitted. The culture of the area reflects the complexities of tribal and sub-tribal distributions, common ancestry, place of origin and religious affiliation.

The warm shallow waters of the Gulf had provided ideal conditions for the pearl oyster and for centuries pearling was a mainstay of the Gulf economy. Pearls were not valuable per se; the market for them depended on the demand for luxury goods. They were widely valued by the Indian elite but in the nineteenth century imperial concepts of an exotic east created a booming fashion for pearls in Britain, and France, a demand which spread throughout Europe and then to the United States. Most of the pearling banks lay on the Arab rather than the Persian side of the Gulf, but they were freely available for boats from all the coastal sheikhdoms. The main pearling season was from June to September. The boats from each town would set out and return together led by their port's 'admiral'. The main season lasted about 120 days but there was also a shorter 40 day 'cold dive' earlier in the year which some boats took part in. Equipping a boat for the season needed considerable finance and merchants engaged in the trade often advanced the necessary sums or provided supplies in lieu. Captains were responsible for selling the pearls and dividing the proceeds between members of the crew. Bombay was the main international market for pearls. However, prior to transhipment to Bombay, the pearls passed through a series of traders and merchants, with Bahrain and Lingeh acting as the main collection and distribution centres in the Gulf.

Apart from fishing and pearling, there had for centuries also been a lively carrying trade. While Bushire at the head of the Gulf was an important nodal point for goods destined for the Mediterranean and Europe, places such as Bandar Abbas and Lingeh provided Indian goods to the cities of the Persian heartland and beyond. To the south, on the Arabian side, demand was less, for the interior was generally more sparsely populated. While smaller boats traded locally, within the Gulf, to the Batinah, Muscat and the Makran coast, larger sailing dhows undertook longer voyages to the Red Sea, India and the east coast of Africa, moving with the seasonal monsoon winds. Aden (at the southern tip of Arabia) was an important staging post, particularly after the coming of steam ships and the completion of the Suez Canal in 1869.

Lingeh and Bastak

In the second half of the nineteenth century parts of the coast of southern Iran were in Arab control. Although Muscat's lease on Bandar Abbas ran out in 1868, the Qawasim were established in various places including Lingeh, which was administered as a tribal principality. The Persian government

Above:
Motorised fishing boats moored in the shallows of the Creek, c.1970. The middle vessel is laden with wire netting traps: fish was a staple foodstuff, eaten almost daily.

Below:
A typical Creek scene in about 1970, with a fishing boat in the foreground.

Above:
The map shows the town of Bastak and the surrounding villages from which families settling in the Bastakiya originally came. It also shows Lingeh and the ports on the Arabian side of the Gulf. The largest remaining clusters of windtowers are in Dubai and Bahrain.

increasingly involved itself in the area until, in 1889, the Sheikh was deposed. The governor of Bushire was subsequently put in charge of Lingeh, which was incorporated in the administration of Persia's Gulf ports. Troops were garrisoned on the town and most of the Qawasimi's family property was confiscated. In 1898 there was a failed Qawasimi attempt to retake the town and the situation seems to have been rather unsettled for several years.

Nevertheless Lingeh seems to have been at the height of its prosperity in the last decade of the nineteenth century. Curzon, writing in 1892 described Lingeh as the 'prettiest and most attractive of the Gulf ports.' Both the Gulf trade with India and the pearling industry grew rapidly in the second half of the nineteenth century. Lingeh, Bandar Abbas and Bushire were the main ports serving the interior of Persia, with the mainly Sunni merchants of Larestan not only controlling the overland trade from Lingeh to Shiraz and Lingeh to Yazd, but also maintaining commercial offices in India and sometimes elsewhere.

The Larestan merchants included many from the town and district of Bastak, which lay on the trade route some 130 kilometres inland from Lingeh. It is this area which has given its name to the Bastakiya and from which most of its families originally came. Given the town's position it was natural for its enterprising families to become merchants, who became increasingly involved in the maritime entrepot trade and pearling, many basing themselves in Lingeh.

At the turn of the century, Lingeh had a thriving shipping trade between India and Bahrain and the rest of the Arab coast. Lingeh and Bahrain were the two main centres for the pearl trade; over half Lingeh's imports by value were pearls, which were then re-exported to Bombay. Its merchants also traded with Oman, Aden and Zanzibar. Lingeh's population, which numbered about 12,000 in winter, was ethnically mixed. Like that of many of the Gulf ports it was partly Arab, partly Persian, and partly African, this last group including both the enslaved and the free.

In 1899, in an attempt to increase the Qajar government's revenues and put them on a more modern basis, the Persian customs administration was reformed, placed under the organisation of Belgian officials and run on a European pattern. (Before this income from customs had been obtained by a system of tax farming.) Lingeh merchants regarded this as a serious blow, for much of the transit trade was included in the new duties. The imposition of the new system was a major cause of merchants transferring business to the other side of the Gulf, particularly to Dubai, Bahrain and Kuwait. As Lorimer wrote, 'To save themselves from utter ruin, most of the leading merchants of Lingeh have established agencies in Trucial Oman, by means of which they hope to retain a part of their former businesses…'.

While customs reform may have been the final straw, there had been a trickle of migration from along the coast of the Gulf for some time, including some provoked by Sunni-Shia disruptions in the 1850s and the economic hardship of that period. The few early merchants leaving Lingeh seem to have gone initially to ports in Qawasimi territory: to Umm al Qawain, Ras al Khaimah and Sharjah.

Above:
The house of Haji Mohammad Falakhnaz immediately faced Sheikh Rashid's old residence. In this 1970 view crated goods are being hand portered from the customs sheds to the souq.

Below left:
By the 1970s, despite its run down condition, the house of Abdul Kareem Farouk still possessed a grandeur befitting the creek-side home of one of the wealthiest Bastaki merchants.

Pioneers

The first of the big merchant families to establish themselves in Dubai were Al Awar, followed by Abdulrazaq, Kazim and Farouk. Abdul Kareem Farouk was the wealthiest: he often visited Paris on pearling business, and had his own yacht. The son of Kazim, Al Haji Ahmed bin Mohammad Aqil Kazim, is pictured. Not all Bastaki merchants moved to Dubai. Communities grew up in other ports of the Gulf, most notably in Bahrain, but also in Qatar and Kuwait.

Social hierarchies in Bastak were replicated in the society of the Bastakiya. The highest strata were the Abbassi family, the khans. Important too were the *mirs*, descendants of the Prophet through the maternal line, and *sayyids*, descendants of the Prophet on the male line. Then came the sheikhs, both traditional secular leaders and those sheikhs who were religious men, followed finally by ordinary Bastakis. Intermarriage between adjacent social strata was acceptable but it was rare between groups further apart on the social scale. Men with high social status could marry anyone but they did not give their daughters to men of a lower rank. Social status was not immutable. Family alone was not enough. Intellect and education, wealth and character all contributed to the respect in which a person was held.

The extended family was the main social unit. Houses, with their large enclosing courtyard walls, were flexibly designed to accommodate several generations. Families were also extended geographically. Today, many still have distant or even close cousins in Bastak or Lingeh. Relatives headed branches of family businesses both in other Gulf cities and further afield, particularly in Bombay but also in Karachi, Calcutta, Aden and elsewhere. Family links and the integrity of dynastic business 'empires' were strengthened by inter-marriage. Bastakis also travelled widely, maintaining commercial links with the Red Sea and East African coasts and even with Europe.

The Bastakis were important to a Maktoum vision for the growth of Dubai. As energetic traders they were the principal links between the Gulf and India. In the 1920s the wealthiest Bastaki merchant, Abbas Abdullah Abbas (*right*) settled permanently in Dubai. He was the first to charter and fill an entire cargo ship belonging to the British India Steam Navigation Company, sending it straight to Dubai from Bombay in 1928. This was the start of regular cargoes being shipped directly between the two ports.

Although maintaining family connections on the other side of the Gulf, the Bastakis severed all political, though not family, links with Iran and transferred their loyalty to Dubai. Despite being incomers the Bastakis and other Iranians were not discriminated against and several individuals, including Abdul Kareem Farouk, Abdulrazaq Abdulrahim Al Bastaki and Abdul Kader Abbas, were close to Sheikh Saeed and Sheikh Rashid. Mohammed Shareef Sultan al Ulama provided advice on legal matters. These community leaders maintained regular *majlises* and would be visited by the British political agent at the Eids as well as on other occasions. When the Dubai municipal council was established in the late 1950s, two of the members were of Persian and one of Indian origin, in recognition of their role as prominent citizens, committed to the political and commercial future of the city.

Above:
An evening view from Deira in 1972, looking across to the warehouses which front the Bastakiya. Its windtowers are already lost against new low-rise blocks of flats beyond. The minaret of the Friday Mosque still dominates the skyline.

Immigration

Dubai offered particularly attractive opportunities for commerce. From 1904 steamships began to call weekly at its port. Most of its rulers were to show themselves remarkably shrewd and keen that the state should prosper. Under Sheikh Maktoum bin Hasher Al Maktoum, who ruled from 1894 until 1906, there was not only an absence of official harassment but newcomers were welcomed. There was a liberal tax policy with initially no, but later low, customs duties. Land for building was made available for a modest sum. Nevertheless, in the early days life in Dubai was considered hard and uncomfortable for women and children – there was little fresh food or water – so most remained in Bastak or Lingeh, where living conditions were better. Since businesses were often run by brothers, they would take it in turns to spend time with their families.

Tradition records that during the rule of Sheikh Maktoum, the community previously settled in Hamriyah in *areesh* houses was moved to land in Shindagah. Hamriyah was then set aside for the Bastaki merchants who initially lived in rooms above their shops in the nearby souq. The area's proximity to the fort, the commercial area and the Creek was important.

When a building plot was purchased from the Ruler, either he or his representative would go to the site and allocate the piece of land. Old deeds indicate that plots were originally allocated to an owner only for as long as he

Above:
Sheikh Rashid's palace was designed and built by Ostad Mohammed Al Banna during the 1940s.

Below:
The distinctive porch of the house of Haji Qaed Ahmad Al Attar, which was demolished in 1985.

remained resident in Dubai, and could not be sold. Upon departure from Dubai the land would revert to the Ruler's estate.

Sheikh Maktoum's policies were continued by his successors for Dubai's rulers shrewdly perceived the advantages that the merchant community would bring to the prosperity and power of the state. In the years that followed Dubai's trade continued to prosper; the newcomers brought their pearl business with them, local Arab markets grew and even goods destined for Persia were passing through its port. In contrast, by the 1920s the economic restrictions affecting commerce on the Persian coast remained firmly in place. Moreover, unsettled political conditions in Persia, notably the instability in the wake of the 1909 assault on Bastak, and later drought and food scarcity following the 1918 flu epidemic, resulted in merchants who had thought of themselves as living only temporarily in Dubai for trading purposes, beginning to bring their families across to settle permanently. Constitutional reforms in Persia, particularly after the accession of Reza Shah in 1926, became more irksome. In 1936 when the Shah abolished the traditional veil for women and required men to wear modern trousers, many Sunni families were appalled and many left for good.

The wealthy families of the Bastakiya were joined by other merchants and many more smaller scale traders, tradesmen and shopkeepers who crossed the Gulf in this period to settle both in Dubai and in the other Arab coastal towns where economic opportunities were available. Those from certain places came to dominate certain occupations, for example, immigrants from Minab, Bastak and Khamir ran Dubai's *abras*.

When Dubai was primarily a pearling and fishing settlement, the majority of its domestic buildings, were constructed with *areesh* (palm fronds). Its early masonry buildings were principally fortifications: the fort, the residence of the ruler, the town walls and watchtowers. When merchants came from Persia and obtained plots of land, they brought with them builders and craftsmen who introduced a monumental style of residential architecture from Bastak and Lingeh. It was with the immigration of families from southern Iran that windtower courtyard houses became a distinguishing feature of Dubai and also of Bahrain. These houses provided an effective response to the summer heat and humidity. Importantly, the rulers of both states adopted this architecture. As Ron Hawker observes in *The Windtower Houses of Iran and the Iranian Gulf*, 'The obvious comfort and impressive architectural designs of the house style, echoing classic Safavid shapes and lines, gained popularity among the Arab ruling classes as well. Both the Sheikh Issa house in Muharraq and the Sheikh Saeed house [in Shindagha], residences of the rulers of Bahrain and Dubai respectively, follow similar design lines and utilize the windtower as a cooling device. The acceptance of the house style by the ruling Arab elite demonstrates the value of these houses as an indicator of high status in the Gulf's complex social hierarchy.'

The Sheikh Saeed House was started in 1896, at about the same time as the first Bastaki houses, well ahead of the main development of the quarter. These masonry windtower buildings, soon also to be found in the souqs on both sides of the creek and scattered throughout Shindagha and Deira, came to typify the transformation of Dubai from a village to a town, providing a

Left:
A large sea-faring vessel is repaired at the shipyard a little upstream from the Bastakiya.

Opposite top:
Sheikh Rashid was ruler of Dubai from 1958 to 1990. His vision was responsible for Dubai's remarkable progress during his lifetime: a development which never relied solely on revenues from oil but was an enormously successful attempt to diversify the economy of the Emirate.

Below:
Sheikh Saeed, the father of Sheikh Rashid was ruler of Dubai from 1912 to 1958 and fostered the immigration of merchants and traders, craftsmen and artisans from southern Iran to contribute to the development of Dubai as the main commercial centre on the lower Gulf.

sense of permanence and stability. The windtowers dominated the skyline, giving Dubai an architectural identity and presenting an image of prosperous urban development to approaching ships. They would come to symbolise Dubai's role as an emerging international commercial city.

A much more difficult economic climate set in at the start of the 1930s. The world economic depression inevitably affected the Gulf States, causing dislocation and hardship. The pearling industry on which so many people depended was badly hit as Japanese cultured pearls arrived to compete in a market where demand from Europe and the United States had become uncertain. In 1929, sixty pearling boats from Dubai had been unable to set out because they lacked funding. Nevertheless as people adjusted to the new trading conditions some signs of increasing affluence appeared.

The first motorcar was imported into Dubai in 1930 although there were no roads. By the late 1930s however there was a limited taxi service between Dubai and Sharjah. Facilities along the Creek were developed, wooden platforms were built as landing points for *abras* and to enable boats to offload goods more easily. Gray Mackenzie, shipping agents established in Dubai since the 1890s, organised lighterage and other facilities.

Dubai's prosperity was by no means evenly shared. Friction between various groups combined with dynastic disputes led to a political crisis in 1938, the outcome of which was that the ruler accepted the establishment of a *majlis* with reforming ambitions. It was dissolved after a few months, and was followed by armed confrontation, during which the merchant community remained unwavering in their support for Sheikh Saeed.

Shortly before 1940 a number of families within the quarter pooled their resources and labour to reclaim a portion of the creek at the north-east end of the Bastakiya to provide a jetty. For this they were rewarded by being given full title to their land by Sheikh Saeed. In the 1940s a substantial palace for

Sheikh Rashid and a Customs House were built immediately to the north-west of the Bastakiya. By 1950, a series of aerial photographs reveal over 50 substantial buildings, nearly all with windtowers, and 40 or more areesh compounds, some with masonry boundary walls. At its greatest extent in the mid-1960s the Bastakiya covered an area of approximately four hectares, with an east-west frontage of about 250 metres, and 150 metres deep.

The Second World War dealt a major blow to the region as a whole. Much trading business was sharply curtailed. There were serious shortages of essential food imports, such as sugar and rice. In parts of the Emirates there was a risk of starvation but this was largely avoided when the British government organised food supplies. However, during the war, the merchants of the Bastakiya found themselves fully occupied, sourcing and shipping essential commodities, particularly those needed to alleviate the hardship being experienced in the region.

Development and oil

The 1950s brought new opportunities to Dubai. It became clear that oil exploration in the Trucial Coast would intensify and that the port which offered the best import facilities for heavy equipment and other supplies would benefit considerably. In 1954 the British firm Sir William Halcrow & Partners was asked to advise on the deepening of the silted-up entrance to Dubai creek. In 1955 the British Bank of the Middle East, which had been

Below:
A rig is towed down the Creek to be positioned offshore. Oil, while never found in the same quantities as in Abu Dhabi nevertheless provided revenue to spur on modernisation. Dubai already had an established maritime commercial economy.

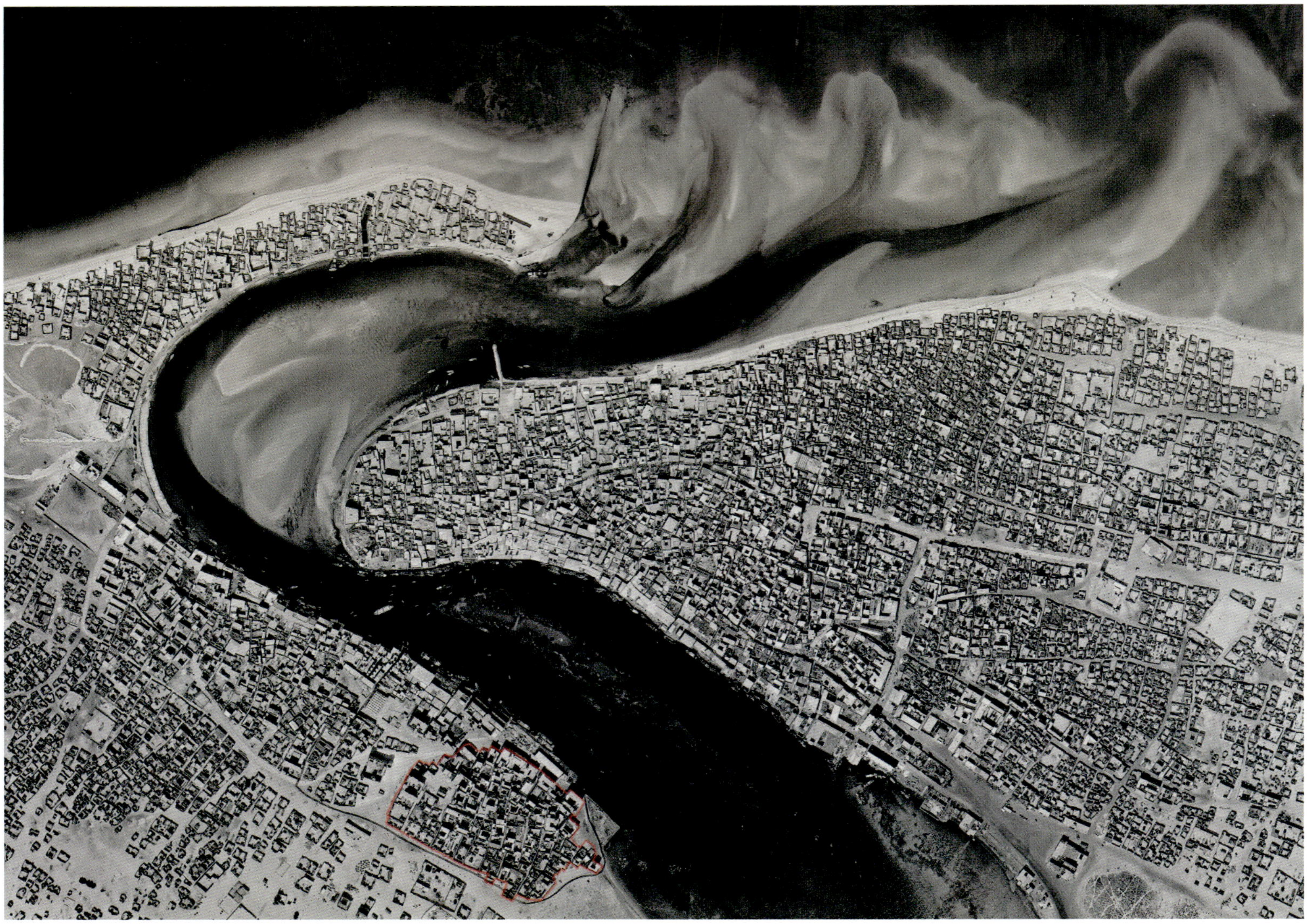

established in Dubai since 1946, was given a role in the collection of certain duties. By the time Sheikh Rashid succeeded his father in 1958 Dubai was becoming the port of preference in the Gulf. Commerce continued to flourish in the 1960s with Dubai as the centre of the gold trade.

The city began to develop rapidly. A municipal council and a police force were established. The Creek and its facilities were further developed. A land department was set up in 1959 to deal with the increasingly pressing issue of land management. An airstrip was completed in 1961 but was soon extended in 1965 to provide for international flights. A bridge across the Creek, linking Dubai and Deira opened in 1963. Schools and health facilities now increased rapidly, admittedly from a very low base, to ensure a population able to play a full part in the modern world.

The Bastakiya quarter, too, was part of this urban development. In the past there had been two fires that caused severe damage to the Bastakiya in the days when many of the houses were still made of *areesh*. The first was in 1940. Witnesses described the second in September 1955. People said that it was caused by a woman putting sand on her paraffin stove to extinguish the flames and somehow sparks flew up and set her *areesh* house alight. The fire then spread from house to house along the canvas windtowers. No one was

Above:
In 1960, silting of the Creek's estuary was becoming a major problem, causing larger vessels to be off-loaded at sea. Although the development of Dubai is already underway, there was still a clear defensive area around the fort (just visible between the Bastakiya and the souq).

Above:
By 1970, Dubai has developed considerably. There is a new deep-water harbour, the Creek has been widened and deepened, and land is being reclaimed, especially on the Deira side. A modern road network is clearly visible, and the Bastakiya is now encircled.

killed though one man was badly burnt. Children were gathered by the beach for safety. Some waded into the Creek. After the fire occupants from the masonry houses that had escaped substantial damage took in some of the homeless; so did one of the sheikhas. Relatives helped too. Prominent families in the Bastakiya, the Bastaki community in Bahrain, the Ruler and Saudi merchants all donated funds for re-building. Community leaders compiled an inventory of the losses and within a week families had received assistance. Masonry houses were becoming more numerous. Sand-lime blocks were by now being used (see Chapter 11). Cement was imported from India as early as 1950, and the first reinforced concrete building was erected in 1956. Cement, being relatively cheap, spelt the end of construction in coral and gypsum.

Expansion of the port facilities in the 1960s led to the former palace being replaced by a modern two-storey building containing the Ruler's office overlooking the Creek, a new customs building and extensive warehouses. These buildings, together with new roads constructed around the Bastakiya, isolated the quarter from the creek. Modern buildings extended the Bastakiya on its southern and western edges. By 1961 Dubai Electricity Company had power stations in Deira and Dubai, which provided the first permanent supply to the Bastakiya. Originally drinking water was brought from a well near Al Faheidi Fort. Later it came from a large high level storage tank located to the south of the quarter. In 1963 a new permanent piped water supply from the artesian wells at Al Awir was extended to include the Bastakiya. In the early 1970s a piped sewage system was connected, but never extended to some houses in the north and north-east of the quarter. However, the modernisation of Dubai and the provision of basic services would also indirectly contribute to the decline of the Bastakiya, and eventually, its partial demolition (see Chapter 13).

However, the most important advance in Dubai's economy was to come. In 1967 work began on a deepwater harbour to cope with expanding trade and to anticipate that oil, discovered in 1966, would soon be available in commercial quantities. The project was extended from four to fifteen berths and opened in 1972. By 1969 Dubai was producing half a million tons of petroleum a year (though this would always be much less than in Abu Dhabi). The additional labour required (both skilled and unskilled) came mainly from Iran and the Indian subcontinent.

Below:
The plan shows the Bastakiya quarter at its greatest extent in 1978, shortly before the western portion was demolished. It covered an area of approximately 7 hectares, with an east-west frontage of about 320 metres, and 220 metres deep. The numbers refer to the family owners (see Appendix). The first masonry houses were built along the Creek edge at the end of the nineteenth century. The largest houses were concentrated in the north-west.

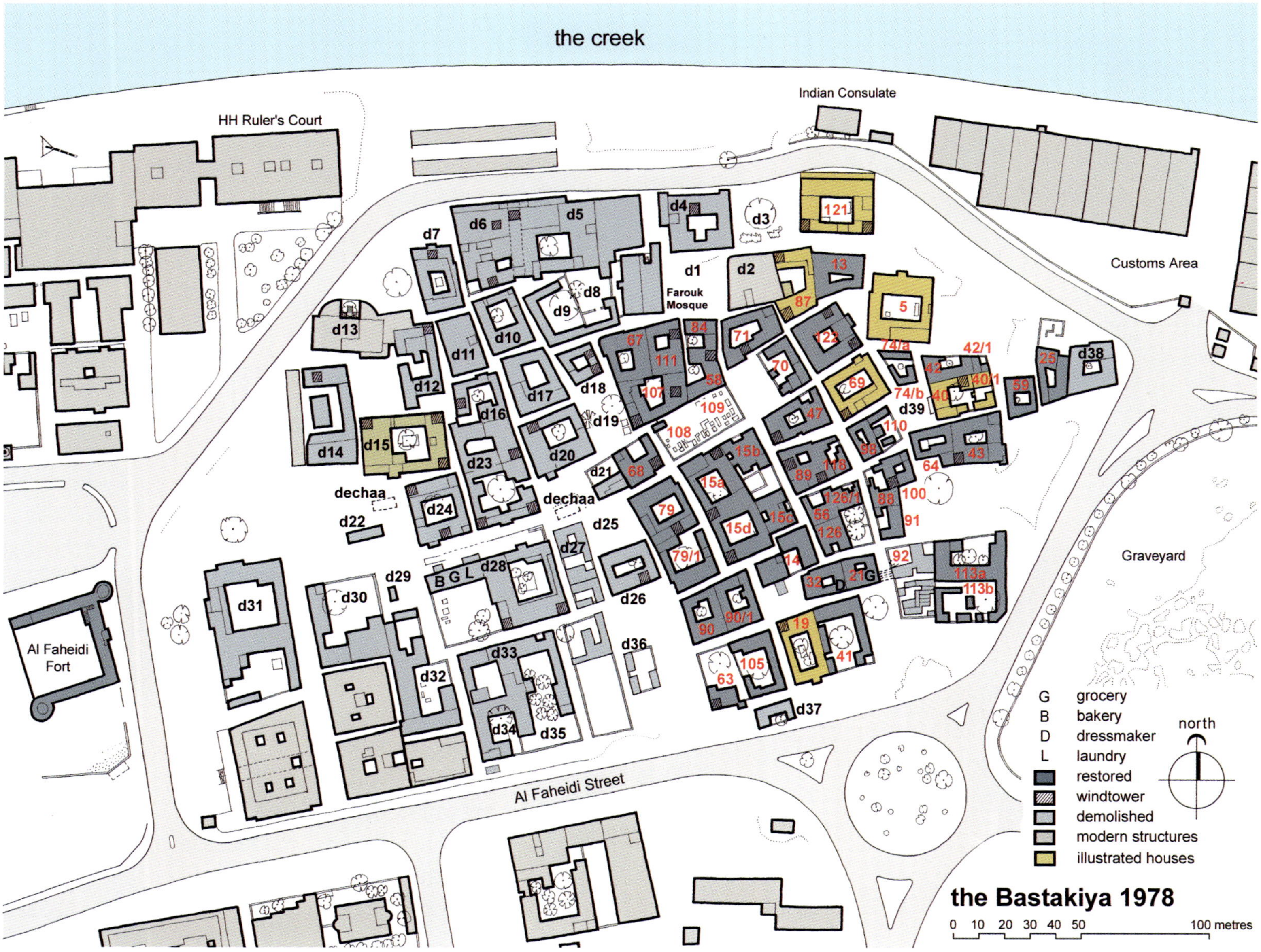

Above:
A small Iranian trading vessel manoeuvres into the Deira wharf, opposite the windtowers of the Bastakiya, today merged into the modern skyline. Behind, modern (non-operational) towers adorn a multi-storey building, illustrating the importance of windtowers as symbols of Dubai's architectural heritage and history.

Economic change was accompanied by political change. In the late 1960s it became clear both that there were strong economic and political arguments for the Trucial States to establish a basis for closer co-operation, and that the treaty arrangements by which Britain had a protective role would shortly come to an end. Long and sometimes difficult negotiation led to the proclamation in December 1971 of the United Arab Emirates with Ras al Khaimah joining the original six members a few months later.

By the time of his death in 1990, Sheikh Rashid's vision for Dubai had also seen the development of dry docks, an industrial port and a free zone at Jebel Ali, together with a comprehensive urban infrastructure, supported not only by oil but a wider, stable trading economy. Education and health care were established as important priorities. These developments were to provide the framework on which his sons would develop today's modern state, with its investment in financial services, property development, aviation and tourism.

The Bastakiya once provided the defining image of Dubai. Today it is all but invisible on a satellite image of the fastest growing commercial city in the world.

Bastak

The families that lived in the Bastakiya originated from the town and region of Bastak in southern Iran. Sited in the hills of the Zagros ranges, its name suggests a barrier or perhaps a place of security. After the sacking of Baghdad by the Mongols at the end of the fifteenth century, some members of the Abbassi dynasty took refuge in Bastak. For several centuries the Bani Abbassi family were khans – local hereditary rulers – and despite changes to political regimes, were prominent in successive administrations until well into the twentieth century. Other Sunnis came to Bastak as religious refugees, the first early in the sixteenth century when the Safavid rulers began to impose Shiite Islam on the population of Persia. Bastak became a centre of learning, renowned for its philosophers and religious scholars. Enterprising merchant families became increasingly involved in maritime trade and pearling.

Bastak today is a district in the province of Hormozgan. The town itself has a population of some 10,000. The surrounding area is largely rural encompassing some eighty villages, and home to a population of about 18,000. There are still monuments reflecting the lives of its wealthy families in the past, not least the house of the late Khans, and their court (*Diwan*). While

Right:
The Great Mosque stands deserted after the collapse of its central dome.

Opposite top:
Nineteenth-century painted medallions, in an enormous variety of floral designs, are set into the walls of the Great Mosque. These carved and painted art forms were replicated in the windtower houses of the Bastakiya.

Below:
Octagonal columns and corniced stone beams frame multi-foliate arches and verandah balustrades in a geometric design that inspired the finest architecture in the Bastakiya.

Opposite bottom:
The town of Bastak is sheltered by the southern ranges of the Zagros mountains. 'Bastak' suggests a place of security, or a barrier.

much of the mud-brick court is disintegrating, the original throne room and its anteroom are reasonably intact, providing a tantalising glimpse of the former grandeur of nineteenth-century Iran. Mirrored panels are embossed with faded historic sepia photo portraits. Much of the mirroring has fallen away, replaced by white gypsum. Other framed portraits line the alcoves behind the hanging throne. Mizahudin Khan Abassi, brother of the last Khan, had offered to sell the palace to the government if they would restore it, but there was no interest. The nearby Khan's *hammam*, a semi-subterranean bath complex built around 1840, has been restored to become the town's museum, below a conglomerate of mud brick domes rising from the ground.

The little that remains of the old architecture of Bastak town is sufficient to demonstrate the source for the architectural design of the Bastakiya. There are no longer any windtowers extant in Bastak; these have all collapsed or been demolished, following an earthquake fifty years ago and two major floods in 1977 and 1992. The large timber entrance doors into fortress-like houses of the Bukhash and Kazim families could be in the Bastakiya. The nineteenth-century Kazim house follows the same plan of inner rooms and outer verandahs, on two storeys around a courtyard, in the proportions and style that characterise the Bastakiya buildings. The timber doors and barred and shuttered windows are identical. The principal building material is rendered mud brick, with all the architectural detail carved in Indian sandstone. Octagonal columns and corniced stone beams frame multi-foliate arches and verandah balustrades in a geometric design of floral inspiration. Distinctive carved gargoyles above each column are in stone rather than timber. Delicately carved screens show the same artistic tradition as their heirs in the Bastakiya.

The Great Mosque stands deserted after the collapse of its central dome, plans for its reconstruction still awaiting a benefactor. Rows of parallel arches supported on simple square columns combine to form the spacious prayer hall, and within each arched recess of the enclosing walls are three stencilled and painted recessed circular medallions, in an enormous variety of floral designs, like an array of ancient decorated bowls set into the walls. Here the original carved and painted art forms of the Bastakiya can be seen.

2

House Form & Architecture

In the Bastakiya, in contrast to so much of the contemporary built environment, the influences of tradition and extreme climate interacted to create a distinctive architecture entirely of its time and place. The closely built windtower houses help foster a sense of community, while enabling residents of the quarter to observe the laws of Islam.

Above:
A young girl stands framed in the wicket within the main door of the house of Abdulkareem Mahmoud Hamal Barshi, since demolished. This small door was used for everyday access.

Opposite:
An exquisite palm frond archway frames a characteristic pair of massive teak entrance doors to the demolished house of Abdullah Abbas. The main doors would only be opened fully on special occasions such as weddings and funerals, on the anniversary of the birth of the Prophet and at Eid al Fitr, which marks the end of Ramadan.

Characteristics

The most dramatic feature of the Bastakiya houses was their windtowers, which gave Dubai its distinctive skyline. The windtower (*baadgir* in Persian, meaning wind-catcher, locally known as *barjeel* in Arabic), is a sophisticated architectural adaptation which takes every advantage of the daily on and offshore breezes. The origins of the windtower and how it functions efficiently are covered in Chapter 12.

In the Bastakiya all the houses were built up to the edges of the plot, with rooms around a central courtyard. This would usually contain a small garden and a tree. Houses were generally large, both single and double storey, with flat roofs. First floor rooms and loggias were provided for occupation during the summer. Each house was the home of a number of closely interrelated couples and their children. Each family unit within the extended family would have a suite of inner and outer rooms (*jaadumee* and *teedumee*) opening onto the courtyard, as far as space and resources would allow. Additional rooms were added as families grew, resulting in what could seem to western eyes to be an unfinished external appearance. The external façades were largely devoid of visible openings. Repeating patterns of recessed

Above:
This view from the east over the Bastakiya in 1978 clearly shows a quarter characterised by inward-looking courtyard houses with windtowers separated by narrow lanes. The Farouk Mosque, with a roof-top prayer hall, can be seen towards the top right on the edge of the image.

panelled wind-scoops ran the length of rooms and along the parapets above. The *majlis* was the only ground floor room that had a series of large windows opening on to external public space.

There were usually two entrances to a house. The main formal entrance was almost exclusively used by men. The women used a smaller, more discreet door which opened directly into the narrow lanes around the house. The large double door of the principal entrance was framed within a projecting porch containing masonry benches, which created a semi-private space within the public lane.

On two-storey houses, projecting wooden balconies were not uncommon. These sometimes provided access around the edge of a courtyard, but they usually overhung the public lane, effectively extending the area of the house. The sides were enclosed with louvred or carved perforated timber panels up to above head height.

Similar principles of construction are not only widespread on both sides of the Gulf coast, but are also seen in the coastal architecture of Oman (Muscat, Salalah), Yemen (Aden, Mukallah) and the Red Sea (Suakin, Jeddah), and along the Swahili east coast of Africa (Zanzibar, Kilwa, Mombassa, Lamu).

The houses are heavy masonry structures built on the column-and-beam principle of irregular coral and laminar shell-stone slabs, these being the most readily available materials in a marine-desert environment. Continuous walls

Below:
The *majlis* windows of the dramatically decorated house of Haji Ahmed Arshi (since demolished) provide the only large openings visible from the street. When the barred shutters were open during the *majlis*, its activity was visible, encouraging others to enter, join in and contribute.

Left:
The house of Mohammed Saleh Mohammed Fiikree was constructed around the perimeter of the plot to create a courtyard, onto which all rooms of the house face. This house is to be converted into a coin museum.

Below:
This photograph shows the coral and shell-stone blocks and the column and beam technique used in the construction of these houses. Gypsum floors and flat roofs are supported here by closely spaced mangrove poles. Their limited length results in rooms, which though spacious and long are relatively narrow.

are some 50-60cm deep, the inner face of the wall made lighter with alcoves and recesses that articulate the framed nature of the buildings. Foundations are minimal, being no deeper than they are wide, which significantly limits the load that the sand will bear. The dimensions of the square columns, rising to a maximum height of 4 metres, and spaced with about one metre between them, were determined by experience.

Where first floor rooms were built these would be of lighter construction to reduce the load on the foundations. Windtowers in particular had to be built with masonry as light as possible, if differential settlement was not to occur, and the tall towers lean and break away from the main structure (see Chapter 13).

Closely spaced mangrove poles, or *chandals*, to support the flat gypsum floors or roofs above, were imported from the East African coast. The mangrove grows to a limited height, and its relatively short poles determined the width of rooms. Typical spans range from 2.7m to a maximum of 3.5m. After the Second World War, squared hardwood beams imported from India were more commonly used. These could have achieved greater spans, but by this time empirical rules for construction were established. This construction system favoured long narrow rooms and verandahs, averaging 3m wide and up to 4m high, planned on a regular module of piers alternating with recesses.

Islam and the Bastakiya

The planning and architecture of the Bastakiya quarter reflects the culture and religion of its Sunni Arab residents. Islam is strongly orientated towards the family and the wider community, promoting a high degree of active social interaction and strong neighbourly relationships. Social injustice has no place in the religion, and discrimination or segregation on the basis of status or wealth is not permitted. At the same time, an emphasis is maintained on the segregation of men and women, to encourage modest behaviour. These traditions evolved through a combination of Middle East custom, with its patriarchal hierarchy, and Islamic tradition.

From its beginnings as an expansionist movement, Islam fostered urbanisation and a settled urban way of life, in contrast to the traditionally nomadic existence of the Arab. The traditional Islamic urban environment closely mirrors the social framework of the community, and is seen in the built environment of the Bastakiya.

At the heart of any neighbourhood is the mosque (*masjid*), a place of prostration and prayer. The Friday Mosque was in Dubai's Grand Souq and was within easy walking distance. However, the growing population of the Bastakiya needed a mosque of its own to create community harmony with God and among its members. Practically, it also enabled the muezzin's call to prayer to be heard throughout the neighbourhood. The Farouk Mosque was centrally located, close to the northern (Creek) edge of the Bastakiya. Rebuilt and enlarged in about 1945, it could accommodate 150 worshippers inside and a further 150 on the roof. The roof was used in summer, accessed by

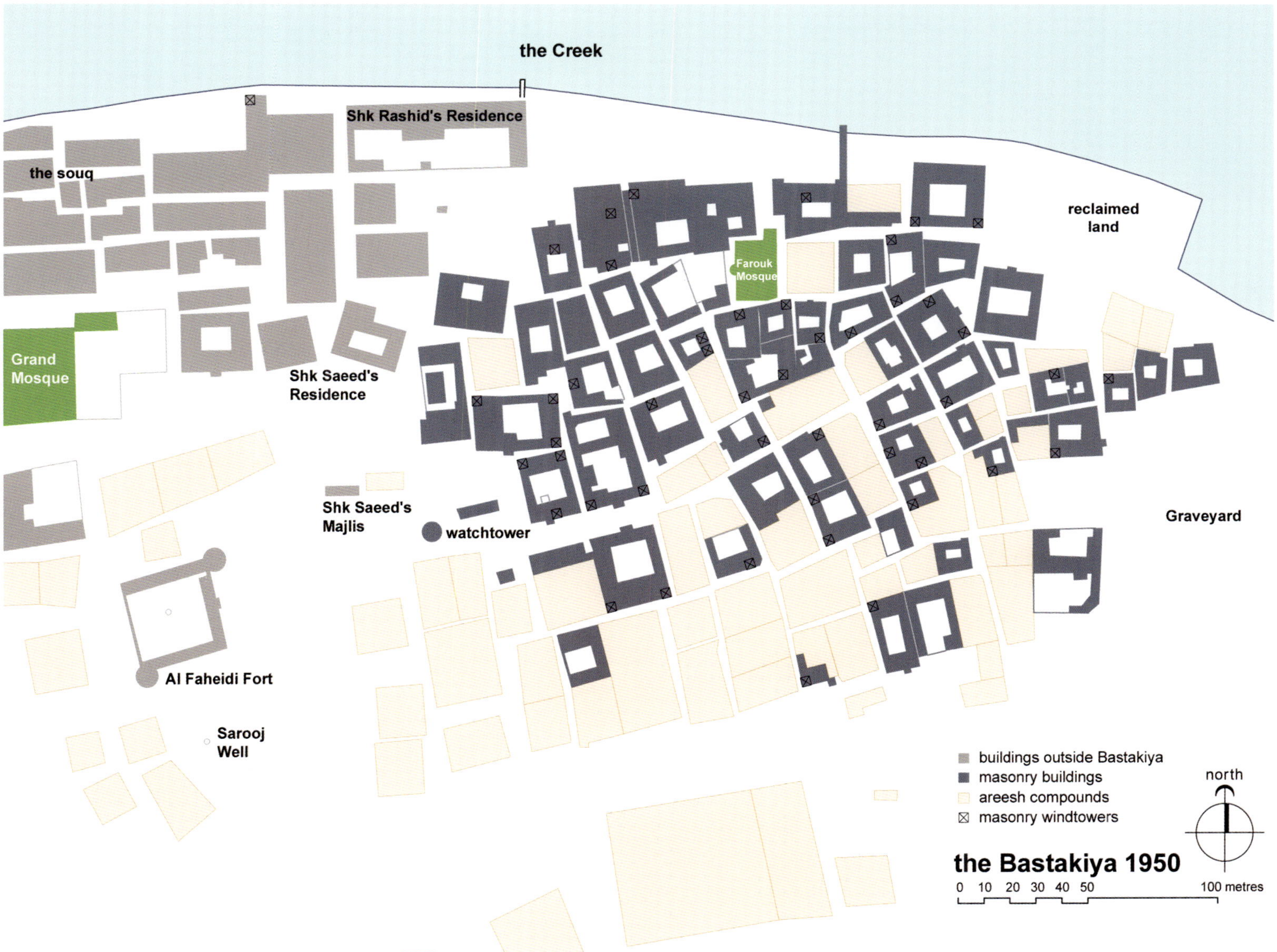

Below:
The street pattern of the Bastakiya shows that the building plots and lanes immediately to the north of the Farouk Mosque share its orientation. This map, dating from 1950, includes the area of the Bastakiya that was later demolished. It demonstrates the close relationship of the quarter with Sheikh Rashid's Palace, the Customs House and the souq.

Above:
Seen from the perimeter of the Bastakiya, the massive anonymous outer walls of the houses presented a fortress-like appearance. The house of Abdulrazaq Abdulrahim is on the right (see Chapter 4).

steps on one side. For male Muslims prayer in the mosque is preferable to private prayer, in that it unites rich and poor, weak and powerful without distinction. The mosque is traditionally a place not only for prayer but also for teaching the Qur'an, and for rest. The women of the Bastakiya, while no less devout than the men, prayed at home; in those days there were no separate prayer halls for women.

Mosques are oriented to the *qibla*, towards the Kaaba in Makkah; all prayers are made facing in this direction, which in the case of the Bastakiya is approximately 12 degrees south of west. Many mosques are built at distinct angles to the street pattern to achieve this orientation. However, within the Bastakiya, the building plots and lanes immediately to the north of the Farouk Mosque share its orientation and it would seem that the early houses were aligned to it. As the lanes run south from the creek they orient more towards the south or south-east.

The size of a community was traditionally determined by its members all being within easy walking distance of each other. The close proximity of houses encouraged social interaction, reinforcing social cohesion and unity. The compact physical layout is an expression of strong social relations, defined by the shared spaces between individual private houses. The shady lanes between houses were only as wide as they needed to be to permit the easy passage of individuals passing each other, and the movement of donkeys

Right:
Goods being transported on barrows between storerooms *(godowns)* in the Bastakiya and the nearby souq. The rolla tree was a local landmark and a place for many children's games.

Below:
Overhanging balconies on the houses of Mohammed Tayeb Al Khoory (left) and Ahmed Qasim Al Sadiqi House (right), today the XVA Gallery and Hotel.

and small carts. Their irregularity and narrowness helped women move discreetly between houses.

From its beginnings the Bastakiya neighbourhood was culturally distinct, with all of its original families having migrated from Bastak, and a high degree of intermarriage. The community can therefore be seen as a group of closely interrelated families, of common geographical origin. They share a common religious and cultural background, as well as mutual business interests, reinforced through family alliances.

Seen from the perimeter of the Bastakiya, the massive anonymous outer walls of the houses presented a fortress-like appearance, concealing a liveliness within. Young men were employed by the community to act as sentinels to discourage strangers or thieves. In the 1960s Faisal Amiri and four friends would protect the privacy of the lanes at the eastern end of the Bastakiya, and Salim Ismail with a similar group at the Al Faheidi Fort end. They would each discourage unaccompanied male strangers from venturing too far into the neighbourhood.

The need for high defensive walls and heavy timber doors should not be underestimated. There are many stories in the Gulf region of local inter-clan strife, and of Bedouin raids from the desert, as for instance the seizing of the town of Bastak in southern Iran by force.

Islam and privacy

Islam stipulates a strict demarcation between public and private life, which is reflected in the inward-looking form of the courtyard house. The house is a sanctuary, providing protection from the elements and from the pressures of society, as well as being a place of rest for body and mind. Particularly for a Muslim, the house is a symbol of strong family relationships.

Proscriptions against casual mingling between men and women further emphasise the requirement for privacy. From the earliest days of Islam rules were established to govern the relations between the sexes, for the protection of women, and in particular to reinforce the value of the family unit. Building around a courtyard or series of courtyards enables the number of openings onto public streets and alleys to be minimized, providing a secluded environment for family life.

Traditionally a private house should not overlook another, nor should it be overlooked; a far cry from the dense apartment blocks that dominate contemporary cities. Nowhere in the Bastakiya would windows overlook those of another house, unless they were obscured by a screened balcony. House entrances would never be built close to each other, or directly facing each other across a lane (*sikka*). They would always be constructed a reasonable distance apart, so that there was no possibility of looking from one house into another while doors were open to receive guests or if goods were being taken inside.

The distinctive character of the Bastakiya is an environment of windowless walls, at least at street level. It follows that the emphasis for architectural detail and decoration was principally found on the inside of the house, particularly around the courtyard. The Qur'an describes Paradise as a garden that is promised to believers. The garden in an inhospitable desert environment is an especially relevant symbol of the Paradise that is to come. Courtyards provide the opportunity to plant a garden sheltered from the wind. Most houses of the Bastakiya contained a small fenced or walled garden, with one or more trees. It would generate its own microclimate, adding to the cooling nature of the courtyard, thus reinforcing its symbolic qualities.

As a house was home to several nuclear families, seclusion within the home was as necessary as separation between the home and the streets and houses around it. Inner rooms, outer rooms and verandahs were arranged parallel to each other.

Islam encourages humility and moderation. It expects wealth to be displayed modestly, and without ostentation. As demonstrated, for example, in the fine products of Arab and Persian potters and calligraphers, beauty and restrained elegance are very important, and are significant elements in Islamic life and culture. The relatively elaborate and formal entrances to the Bastakiya houses, particularly set against the plain undecorated walls that otherwise dominated the lanes, gave identity to each house, and reflected the importance of the owner in their size and degree of decoration. The entrances and the windtowers of the Bastakiya formed the principal external distinctions between the homes of more wealthy families and more humble masonry homes. Benches within a semi-enclosed porch provide the house with its most public of private spaces, marking the beginning of a transition from neighbourhood to household.

The smaller arched door, or wicket, within the main door was that normally used. Being about half a metre above ground level, the dust from the street was kept out and inquisitive toddlers were kept in. Any stranger would have to lower his head on entering, to avoid striking it, and to watch his step over the threshold. Thus a visitor entered in a posture of respect, which also offered an appropriate opportunity for any woman in the vicinity

Right:
The handsome entrance porch to the house of Abdulkareem Mahmoud Hamal Barshi, Head of Port and Customs. A small room within the porch, above the doors, was his lock-up for offenders. Abdulkareem was also a noted healer, and patients would wait on benches either side of his door. The Bukhash house is visible beyond, to the right (see Chapter 5).

to turn away her face or cover it with a veil. Internal doors between rooms were always provided with a shallow threshold, also requiring a person to look down while entering or leaving in order to avoid tripping. The threshold completes the fourth side of a framed opening, carefully defining the integrity of the spaces on either side.

The outer door always opened into a lobby, usually with the inner and outer doors offset so that it was not possible to see directly into the courtyard from the street. In only a few houses did the main entrance lobby open centrally into the courtyard beyond. It was more usually placed so that the family courtyard was entered from a corner. This offered greater privacy and less visual exposure of the courtyard upon entering. Located within the

Right:
Pairs of prancing peacocks provide an unusual form of windtower decoration on the house of Sheikh Mohammed Shareef.

Opposite:
From a distance windtowers add a series of strong vertical accents to an otherwise predominantly horizontal and windowless architecture of walls. Within the quarter a windtower's individuality not only distinguishes particular houses, but also acts as a landmark, offering orientation as one moves through otherwise undistinguished alleys. This windtower is on the house of Abdulrahman Farouk, today Dar Al Nadwa.

Below:
A typical stained glass fanlight, in the building of the headquarters of the Architectural Heritage Society, the former house of Abdullah Yousuf Al Khoory.

house, the lobby provided a mid-point in the transition from public space into the home, with refreshments being prepared here for visitors.

Generosity and hospitality towards guests are essential parts of the spirit of Islam, perhaps deriving from the inhospitable nature of the desert, which so dominates much of the Arab world. A separate guest and reception room, close to the entrance, is therefore a basic requirement in any traditional Muslim house.

As the most intimate of the transitional spaces between the household and the community, the *majlis* was always directly accessible from the main entrance lobby, allowing no glimpse of family activities beyond. The *majlis* was where the men of the family received visitors. Apart from the house of Sheikh Mohammed Shareef, this was always a ground floor room with windows opening on to the outside. These were deep windows starting just above the floor, barred for security and timber-shuttered for shade.

Islam and decoration

A further influence of Islam on the architecture of the Bastakiya can be seen in the nature of its decoration. While there is nothing specific within the Qur'an that forbids the depiction of human figures, it does explicitly forbid idolatry. The prohibition on the representation of living forms probably comes from a tradition that the Angel of Mercy will not visit the home of an idol worshipper. Islam has therefore acted as a restraint on decorative forms. Over time the absence of figures became a principal characteristic of Islamic art, leading to the development of complex repetitive geometric forms emblematic of the pervasive presence of the one God throughout his Creation. Representations of plants and animals continued in the eastern parts of the Islamic world, and are found especially within Persian art. The subjects for decorative screens, and stencilled painting to be found in the Bastakiya fall into three categories: geometric, floral, and birds. The most beautiful screens in the Bastakiya are those of intricately hand-carved

gypsum, which form balustrades at first floor level around courtyards and as fanlight panels over external doors opening onto verandahs. The screens diffuse the bright glare that reflects from the courtyard walls, and permit natural ventilation and the escape of hot air. There are many different screen designs, in contrast to the greater regularity of western architecture, and the motifs are varied. Birds are a common feature, but the most dominant design is the geometric representation of flowers and foliage arranged in a vase. The birds that are depicted are either peacocks or doves, seen in ventilation screens over doors, or incorporated into the decoration of windtowers in gypsum or paint. We might interpret the birds and flowers both as symbols of a promised garden Paradise, and of a cultivated humanised world distinct from the harsh, untamed desert.

Glass fanlights were often provided over internal doors, in either clear or coloured imported glass, or as a mixture of both. These might be rectangular, or often semi-circular with a delicate symmetrical geometry. The rich effect of glowing colour must have seemed positively luxurious and a delightful relief from the harsh glare of bright reflected sunlight. The panels of internal doors were often intricately carved. When combined with glass fanlights they could be particularly beautiful. Rooms were named after the number of pairs of doors into it. A three-door room was called a *sideri*; a five-door room a *panjdari*.

Above:
Finely carved ventilation screens *(panjara)* depicting a variety of elegant flower-in-vase motifs from the house of Sheikh Mohammad Shareef.

Below:
A combined floral and geometric design within a small ventilation screen.

Climate and house form

The architecture of the Bastakiya had to respond to the especially aggressive climatic conditions of the Gulf Coast. With very low rainfall in the region, masonry buildings are constructed with characteristically flat roofs. Pitched roofs only occur on *khaimah*, the *areesh* (barasti) houses used in winter (see Chapter 11: Construction).

In a dry desert environment the houses are usually built tight up to each other, presenting few exposed faces to the street. The houses of the Bastakiya were mainly detached, with lanes around all four sides. There were exceptions, where two, three or sometimes four houses shared a sub-divided plot of land, or where three or four larger houses were in common ownership,

Right:
Ornate geometry of a semi-circular arch in the house of Abdul Rahman Farouk, with flower-in-vase perforated and painted screens behind.

Below:
Peacocks and flowers-in-vases were a favourite subject for paintings in merchant family homes.

and in one case where two houses were linked across a covered passage. The narrow, high walled alleyways between are particularly appropriate in a hot and humid coastal desert climate, providing very significant environmental benefit, through shading and through the funnelling of cooling breezes. The many lanes of the Bastakiya running predominantly north-northwest to south-southeast, and west-southwest to east-northeast, successfully capture and channel the cooler offshore creek breezes between individual houses. This makes them more pleasant to walk in during the afternoons and evenings in the hottest months, also benefiting the *majlis* and those first floor summer rooms opening onto them.

Air movement in the lanes is much greater than the wind speed outside the built up area, whether it is a hot wind from the land, or a cooler breeze off the sea and the Creek. The wind is deflected between and over the buildings, increasing its speed where it is forced into the narrow alleyways that serve to act as funnels. In a hot environment, any increased air movement over the skin provides relief through the cooling evaporation of perspiration.

Research has shown that restricted penetration of solar radiation within narrow lanes will result in air temperatures within the lanes being up to 5 degrees cooler than the ambient air temperature at rooftop level. The narrow shaded lanes receive limited direct sunlight and therefore retain their store of coolness well into the day benefiting both the lanes and those rooms immediately on the inside of the walls which line them.

Above the street, at the level of the first floor summer rooms, the extremes of temperature and humidity of the Gulf summer climate necessitate large openings that catch every breeze, to offset the acute discomfort of summer shade temperatures at midday, which may exceed 40°C, and relative humidities rising during the evening, often to reach well over 80 per cent before dawn.

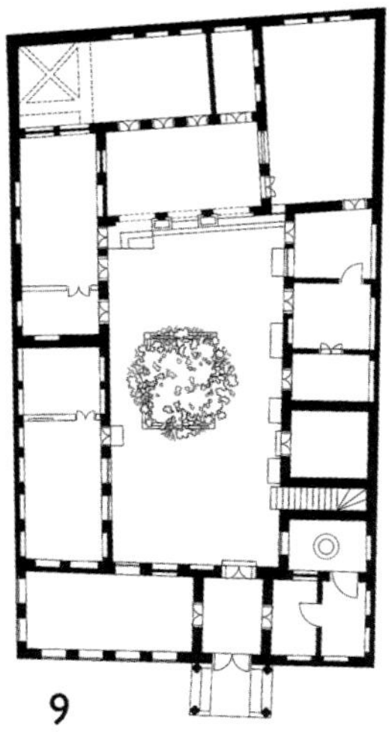

9

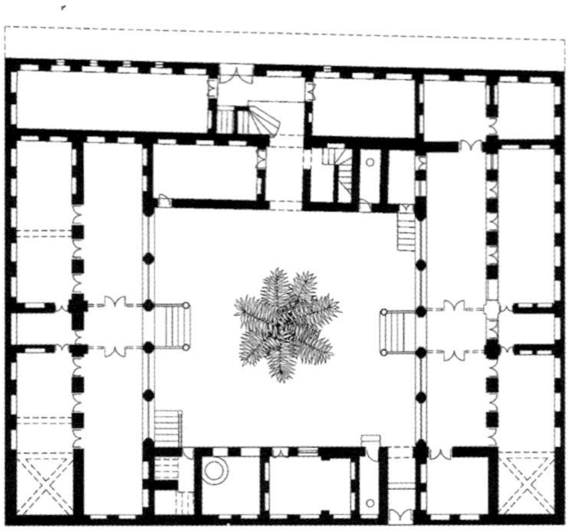

7

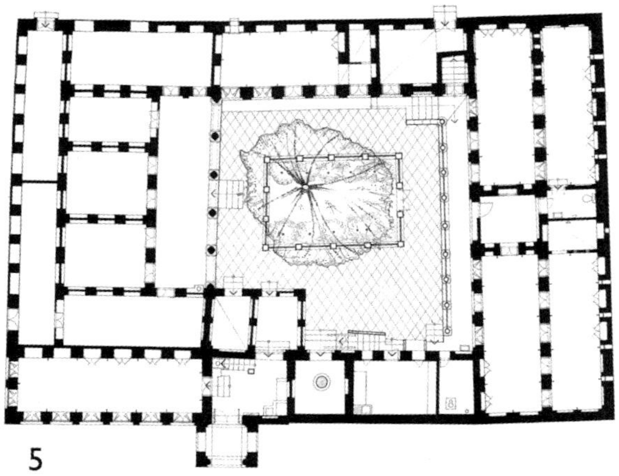

5

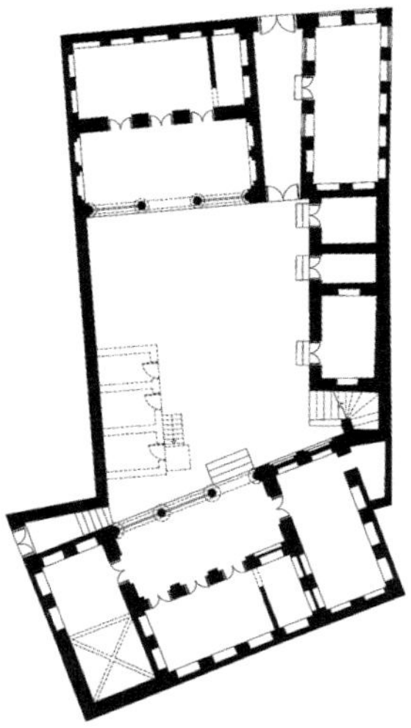

6

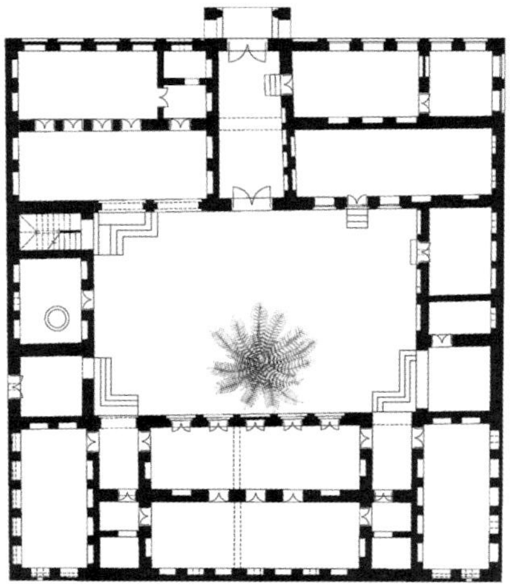

4

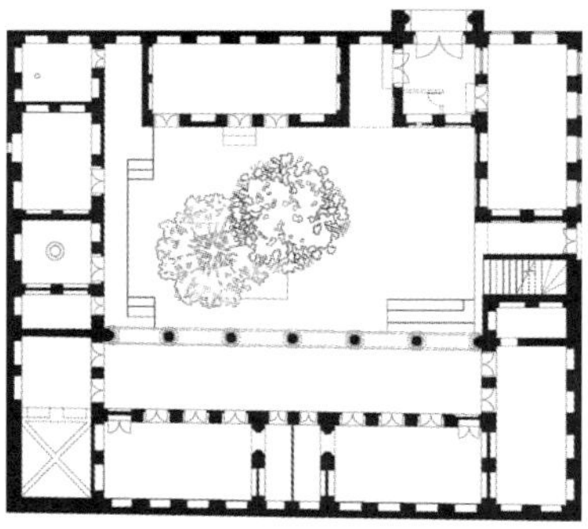

8

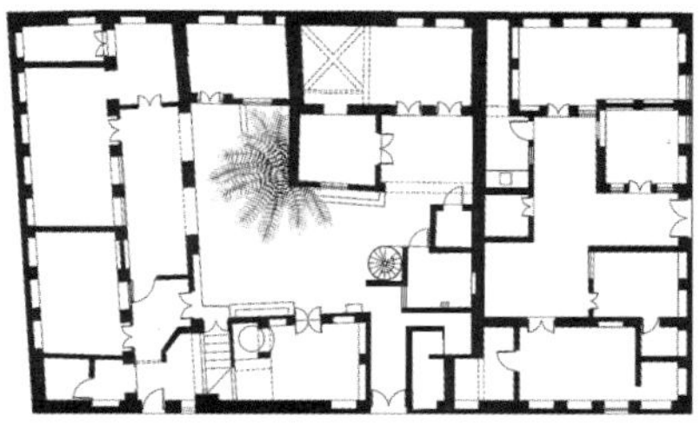

10

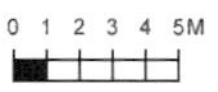

Left:
The seven houses illustrated in this book differ markedly in size and shape. They do however share a characteristic courtyard form, with rooms arranged around it, and parallel rows of outer and inner living spaces. The courtyard is a protected environment providing shade from the desert sun, and shelter from hot, dust-filled winds. During the day it is slowly heated by the sun and in turn by the increasingly hot walls around it. The warm air it contains rises, as external air temperature falls and evening progresses, to be rep aced by cooler night air. The cooler air accumulates in the courtyard in laminar layers, and seeps into the surrounding rooms, cooling them. Cool air remains in the courtyard until the next day when the sun is high enough to shine into and warm it. By midday, eddies gust into the courtyard from the strong sea breezes.

These floor plans are numbered according to their respective chapters:

4. Abdulrazak Abdulrahim Aminai Al Bastaki
5. Mohammed Shareef Bukhash
6. Mir Ahmed Mir Abdulwahid Amiri
7. Sheikh Mohammed Shareef Al Ulama
8. Abdullah Mohammed Al Bastaki
9. Mir Abdullah Mir Amiri
10. Sheikh Abdul-Raheem Mohammed Janahi Al Abbassi

Above:
The verandah of the former house of Abdullah Yousuf Al Khoory surrounds family rooms facing a central courtyard. These rooms would normally comprise the verandah (*sabaat*) as a day space, and an inner private space (*jaadumee*) used for sleeping, with a screened space for washing at one end. In some larger houses the verandah would be replaced by an outer room (*teedumee*), with pairs of doors that could be closed in cold weather.

In the Bastakiya courtyards varied considerably in both size and proportion. Many are less than six metres wide. Some in the larger two-storey houses are up to 14 or 15 metres across, for example in the Bukhash and Shareefi homes. Both these courtyards are nearly square. Others are long and narrow, giving the greatest benefit when orientated with their longest walls on the north and south sides to minimize direct solar exposure of the east and west facing walls. In the Bastakiya, most long courtyards seem to have been well orientated, though a few of the youngest houses, on the southern edge of the Bastakiya, have long courtyards running north-south.

It would appear that a majority of the houses in the Bastakiya had main living rooms on the south side of the courtyard. This meant that the inner room was relatively shaded, with its back to the narrow *sikka*, and was protected on the inner side by the verandah (*sabaat*) or a parallel day room (*teedumee*). The houses of Abdulrazaq Abdulrahim Al Bastaki and Abdullah Mohammad Al Bastaki both show this well. The north facing *sabaat* faced the prevailing cool afternoon breeze in summer. In both homes as well, the majlis faces north toward the creek. Kitchens and storerooms would ideally be placed on the east and west sides of the courtyard, as they are in both these examples. It is interesting that the very fine Bukhash house seems to break all the rules, with west-facing dayrooms, and the kitchen, well and latrine on the south side, facing north.

In high rooms the radiation from conducted heat through the roof would be little felt. Screened window openings at high level would allow the hotter air to escape. Traditionally, glass was never used externally. External windows were barred rather than glazed, and closed with sets of internally opening timber shutters. These insulated a room against the extreme heat of the day, and when open let in cooling afternoon breezes.

Screens enhanced natural ventilation and also created a degree of privacy between different family zones, breaking up shapes and movement into a network of light and shade. Windscoops, *baadkash*, captured breezes through a double section of wall, directing air into the room at low level, to cool people sitting on the floor. There was a timber closer that could be slid across the gap to eliminate the draught and blowing sand if necessary. As with windtowers, these were closed during winter. Other openings were screened with perforated decorative gypsum panels. Timber louvres (*dustandaaz*) gave privacy to the women in their household tasks, and provided shade with good natural ventilation, and a very pleasant subdued light. They were found on

Above:
Decorative screens were characteristic of Bastakiya houses, combining good through-ventilation in summer with privacy. These examples are in the summer *majlis* of the Amiri home (see Chapter 6).

Right:
Rooms were always relatively high, never less than 3.2 metres, and often closer to 4 metres. High ceilings enhanced air circulation, allowing hotter air to collect near the ceiling where its effects would not be felt. Note, however, the fan and air conditioning unit replacing a sealed windscoop.

Below:
Windscoops (*baadkash*) provided a means of achieving ventilation while maintaining a visual barrier. This example is from the house of the Bukhash family.

Opposite left:
A tree in a courtyard assisted cooling through the introduction of shade, by the reflectivity of the leaves, and by the effects of photosynthesis and transpiration of the foliage. The greenery added colour to the buff browns of the house, with dappled, moving patterns of cool shade. In the courtyard of the Bukhash family a low perforated screen wall protected an Indian almond tree entwined with bougainvilia.

the openings to the first floor kitchen in the Bukhash house, and enclosed the projecting balconies that sometimes overlook the lanes.

While the form and detail of the Bastakiya houses can be seen to have been very carefully configured to maximize cooling in summer, in winter it can be relatively cool, with average minimum temperatures in January and February around 14°C, dropping to as low as 7°C at dawn. The thick sea-stone walls of the ground floor rooms would provide effective insulation against the chill nights and cold winter winds, particularly the north-westerly *shamal*. Small charcoal braziers for brewing tea and coffee were also used as room heaters. When Ramadan occurred in winter, *sohoor*, the meal taken before sunrise, before the daily fast began, would invariably be eaten around a bracing fire in the kitchen.

3

Everyday Life

The architecture of the Bastakiya comes alive in the way in which the houses were used and the patterns of everyday life within them. The information and stories gathered here come from recollections collected for this book and from notes compiled in 1969-71.

Above:
Little girls play in the shelter of the Bastakiya lanes.

Opposite:
Women moved comparatively freely within the Bastakiya quarter. Visiting was an important part of social life, and children usually accompanied adults. The proximity of the houses lent a degree of seclusion to the narrow lanes between.

Left:
The courtyard of a windtower house served many purposes. Here, an empty packing case provides shade for the family's goat, while dishes and pans dry in the sun. This photograph, taken in 1970, shows one of the Bastakiya houses demolished in 1985.

Courtyards and wells

Courtyards provided secluded outside spaces where women could move about freely. Depending on the time of day and the season, courtyards had multiple uses – for domestic tasks (particularly the messier ones), for children's play, for animal pens, and occasionally for overflow storage of business stock. While courtyards themselves were not necessarily tidy, their small centrally placed gardens gave a sense of order. The verandahs that opened on to the courtyards had the additional advantages of being better shaded and less dusty: here women carried out domestic tasks and socialised.

The gardens were watered from household wells and with domestic waste water. Fruit trees would be widely grown, in particular date, tamarind, citrus, pomegranates, henna and fig. There are still sidr trees and Indian almonds (*loz*) which bear small fruit popular with children. Some trees may be as old as the houses themselves, but comparatively few remain.

The houses of the Bastakiya all had wells either in the courtyard or in a small well-room near the kitchen. These were shallow, and the water was brackish from infiltration of creek water into the subsoil. They were lined to prevent them collapsing, and had raised rims to prevent dirt entering. The water was used for bathing, for washing clothes, dishes and household utensils and for irrigating plants in the courtyard. Before piped water became available, fresh water for drinking was delivered by water-carriers, using a donkey or a yoke. The water would be stored in a large clay pot, becoming cool as a result of evaporation.

Food and fuel

Most food in the Bastakiya had to be imported, much of it from India or Iran. Many items could only be bought cheaply immediately after harvest, and vagaries of the weather could affect the arrival of supplies by sailing dhow. Considerable storage space was required. Mezzanine stores, found over entrance halls, in stairwells or over the kitchen itself were often used. Dry goods such as wheat, rice, spices, sugar and tea that were needed all the time

Below:
A woman uses a leather bucket to carry water from a shallow well. A donkey could carry four containers, two on each side. Carriers 'sold' water by the 20 litre tin or jerrycan. The water itself was free; the charge was for its delivery, which was usually daily. Although the water was sweet, it sometimes contained grit or worms.

Left:
This kitchen was typical of the Bastaki quarter. In the corner, unleavened bread is being heated on a traditional iron griddle. Large aluminium pots and trays were needed for communal meals. (Heritage House.)

Below:
A traditional bread oven in Bastak, of the same simple type which was used in the Bastakiya.

would be kept accessible. Fresh food was bought on a daily basis. In these very hot conditions fish would be caught before dawn, bought in the early morning and eaten at mid-day, often with a sauce. There was a traditional taboo against eating it later in case it deteriorated in the heat of the afternoon. (Dried and salted fish were standbys; in summer there was a period when fish moved to deeper water offshore; in the winter bad weather might reduce the catch.) Meat, usually goat, was more of a luxury, often eaten only on a Friday.

Fresh vegetables were always in short supply (and largely unobtainable in summer), but after rain certain wild herbs would be eaten with pleasure as a salad garnish or in cooked dishes. Formal meals ended with tea, then coffee and dates. Dates came in many different varieties and, not only were they an important source of energy, but they also had symbolic value and were always served to guests. Fresh fruit was a luxury and when a family received some from overseas, it might be carefully shared with neighbours or a single fruit divided among the children. As convenience food became available, children might be given cereal at breakfast or canned food at the evening meal. There were many different kinds of bread. Not all houses had ovens. Some bought bread from the baker, but all households cooked certain types of thin flat bread on a slightly convex iron sheet or shallow pan placed over the fire. There was not a distinct Bastaki cuisine: many dishes were common on both sides of the Gulf. Families with strong connections with India often served dishes such as *biriani*, and a stall in the souq sold Indian sweetmeats.

Not all women could cook; some relied on the family's matriarch supervising servants in the kitchen. In many cases the women of the house would share the cooking themselves. One type of traditional stove was made of clay with an open space or spaces for pots to sit on. Kerosene burners were also common but other families simply cooked over an open fire, with stones to support the pots. Wood was the main fuel. Much of it came from Oman or Iran, since the natural vegetation of the area was inadequate. Charcoal for portable braziers for preparing tea and coffee came from Oman and later from the extensive mangrove swamps at Khamir on the Iranian coast.

Above:
The first floor kitchen of the Bukhash house was rebuilt in concrete blocks but in the traditional style.

Below:
The roof was also used for food preservation. Here, small fish are preserved in pots to make *mehyawa*, a fishpaste, eaten with bread.

Traditionally men and women ate separately, men sitting on the floor around a common dish. Customs changed comparatively slowly; although cooking might still be done communally, individual nuclear families often ate separately in their rooms. Later, when modern cookers could be sited flexibly within the house, these families might cook for themselves. Cooking pots and dishes were dried in the sun on a raised platform or masonry table in the courtyard. Every evening, servants or the women of the house cleaned the paraffin lamps and lanterns before they were lit.

Animals

Many families kept a few goats for fresh milk. In some cases the goats lived entirely in the courtyard, perhaps in a pen in the shade of a tree; in others they would bound out of open doors in the morning to follow a shepherd who would herd them all day while they grazed on whatever was available locally, dropping them off in the evening. Any animal that failed to return to its owner was put in a pound in Al Faheidi Fort and a fine had to be paid for its release. Cows were less common, but those with a dairy cow might provide milk to their neighbours. A man from the Bani Yas who lived in Shindagha began with twenty cows in his courtyard – they were let out daily to swim and cool off in the sea! He sold milk, as well as yoghurt and *laban*, which kept better. The milk was put in empty spirit bottles, obtained from the Indian community, and sterilized in the sun.

Chickens were kept for eggs rather than their meat. In a large household a goat might be brought home alive, to be slaughtered. Sheep lived temporarily in courtyards before being slain for the Eid. Pets were also kept: cats, green parrots, and even a monkey that escaped down the creek.

Furniture

Each nuclear family had a suite of rooms in the house. The inner room contained mats for the children to sleep on, and sometimes a bed, usually a carved Indian four-poster, for the father. His wife would often sleep on the floor with the children. There were pegs (*gulmeekh*), for hanging lamps and clothes, sets of hanging mirrors were popular, and there was sometimes a portrait of a family elder. Shelved alcoves (the lower alcoves called *baalak* and the upper arched recesses *taakheechah*) were built into the thick outer walls and were used to display vases, china and other decorative items. More valuable ornaments would be higher up out of reach of young hands, while the lower shelves would be for objects in daily use. Some washrooms had mezzanine stores above, which were used for bulky items. In the absence of cupboards, personal possessions were kept in wooden or painted metal chests. There would be mats or carpets for the floor and piles of mattresses and cushions that could be used in either the outer or inner rooms. These traditional furnishings had a simplicity and flexibility that facilitated seasonal and daily movements within the house.

In the very early days people, particularly the men, relieved themselves below the high tide line on the Creek shore. Bastakiya houses usually had one, perhaps two, long-drop latrines, which were barely adequate for families of more than twenty. Mahmoud has childhood memories of his family's 'long-drop'. There was no door, and at night it was difficult to tell if it was occupied. It was very scary for a toddler; he was always afraid that he would fall down the dark hole.

Servants

These large houses were not easy to run, particularly before the coming of electricity and mains water, although there might be several nuclear families living in them to help with the work. Most families had several servants, both men and women. Some came from poor families in Bastak, Lingeh, or other parts of southern Iran including Baluchistan. Some stayed a few years; others for many more. Servants were not usually paid a regular salary but were treated more as members of the family and provided for in kind. If one wanted to get married, for example, his or her employer would arrange and pay for the wedding. Relations with servants were often close and personal – though much would depend on the household's dynamics. Some were from poorer families in the neighbourhood, who wanted their daughters to benefit from working in an educated household; these girls did not usually live in.

Left:
Laundry dried rapidly on the roof, in the sunny, less dusty environment, where breezes were particularly strong. This view, from a Bastakiya house in 1970, shows modern buildings on the Deira side of the Creek. A camp bed is just visible beneath a pile of clothes.

Weddings

Weddings were very much women's affairs: while women were fully able to take part in the day-long events, men's dancing and eating largely took place only after work.

Norah described a typical wedding in the 1950s from a female perspective. Preparations started some days in advance when women gathered at the bride's house to clean the large amounts of rice provided by the groom's family. Next, invitations were issued. This was traditionally done by ten or twelve ladies visiting the bride's relatives, neighbours and friends, offering cardamoms tied with silver thread and covered with a green cloth on a decorated tray. For three days the women would come to eat at the bride's house for breakfast, lunch and dinner, and in the evening there would be dancing and music with drums and tambourines. Often the bride was in seclusion in her own room.

About a week later came the wedding itself and the bride was adorned with henna. A close female friend or relative would apply a thick henna paste in patterns to her hands and feet, designs that would only fade about three weeks later. Again all the women came to support her. (The bride's family usually paid for the festivities that day.) Each evening when the bride appeared she wore a different dress in luxurious, glittering material with splendid jewels.

On the fourth evening, the bride and groom would finally come together in public, before leaving to spend the night at her family home. The next afternoon the newly weds would sit with the women guests, who would shower them with coins and sweets to wish them well. After about two weeks, the groom's family held a party to welcome the bride, who would thereafter live in her husband's home. If the bride was young or her new home some distance away, she might be accompanied by a relative or servant who would stay with her until she was settled.

Ruqaya recollected how, as a child, she had witnessed her uncle's wedding. Because of her young age she was able to move freely about the groom's and the bride's houses to experience all that took place. Once a girl was older she would not be allowed to mix with the married women and when a wedding occurred she and her peers would have to watch the dancing in their *abayas* from an adjacent room. A professional woman prepared the bride, plaiting her hair and attaching gold tassles to the ends. It was traditional to wear three gold necklaces: a choker, one of normal length and a long piece with a pendant attached. Two items were only worn on the final wedding day. One was a gold cap sewn with coins, the other a nose ring with a crescent shaped piece suspended from it. Brides were not supposed to look happy, so should she smile, the crescent would conceal it. On the final night, the bride appeared with the groom on a decorated throne. Their heads were knocked together to show that they were man and wife.

There were no special servants' quarters; manservants slept in the *majlis*, maids often with the women and children. Abdulrahim's house had bars on the arched opening above his main door; he had slaves, and there were others who kept them too.

One reason that servants were needed was because many visitors would stay. Before there were hotels, business clients would be put up by the merchant concerned, particularly if they had come from overseas. Moreover, members of extended families paid prolonged visits to cousins in other countries, for social as well as commercial reasons, though often the two motives were intertwined. The early families in the Bastakiya might also have to provide accommodation for relatives in the process of moving permanently to Dubai, until such time as they found their own housing.

Childbirth

Once a woman's contractions began she carried on for a while with normal household duties. Women feared long labours, so they were advised not to go to sleep and, if necessary, the process was hurried along by a companion encouraging her to run about. For the delivery, the woman went to a separate room, accompanied only by female relatives who had themselves borne children. She sat on a hard sack of sand with the local traditional midwife, who had been summoned, sitting in front of her. She would clutch the midwife by the shoulders to help bear the pain of the contractions. Another woman sat behind and pushed against her back. Although the mother was exhorted not to scream, it was not shameful to do so and, as the door was shut, no one would hear. The midwife took the baby's head as it emerged but made no other effort to control its birth and it lay on the sack until the placenta was delivered before the cord was cut. The sack was then thrown in the creek and the placenta buried privately in the compound. For it to be seen by anyone from outside was to ensure future sterility.

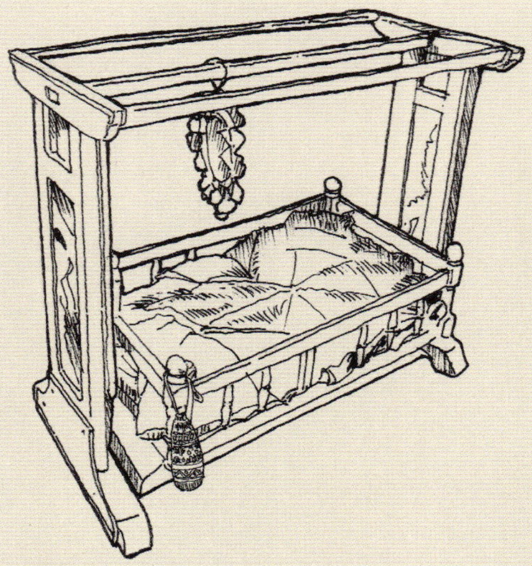

The lying in period in theory lasted forty days, though this was usually impractical. After delivery the vaginal canal was packed night and morning with a small piece of salt. Twice a day a hot brick, wrapped in cloth, would be placed on her abdomen. In theory she was allowed nothing to drink for several days but sometimes she was desperate and she would be slipped a half glass of water or permitted small cups of tea. For three days she had no food other than halva, rich with butterfat and spicy with pepper and ginger. After that she received specially strengthening meals that included lots of chicken. She was supposed to lie still on her back for at least two weeks. Both she and the baby were massaged with oil.

The baby was swaddled and fed on demand, sleeping beside its mother. During the lying in period the husband could only peep through the door to exchange a few words with his wife.

Above:
Haleema (see Chapter 8) has a cradle that has been in the family for over 40 years. The wooden cot hangs in a frame with painted glass ends showing Persian landscapes. It had a brightly coloured cloth toy suspended from it, and a little cloth packet of incense. Mother could use a string tied to her foot to rock it while she worked. It is still used, made up ready with bedclothes.

Given the uncertainty of the weather and shipping, it was rare to know in advance exactly when visitors would arrive, let alone depart.

Summer migration

Traditionally, throughout the Emirates, many people would migrate in summer to escape the worst of the heat and humidity in the towns. They built summerhouses of palm fronds (see Chapter 11) which were designed to allow as much air as possible to pass through their walls. Some families moved inland to where temperatures might be higher but humidities around 20 per cent lower than near the coast. Others moved into the shade of their date gardens; labour was required for the date harvest around this time. Some, particularly those with regular work in the towns, simply moved nearby to an exposed area of the coast.

In the case of Dubai, some local families left their town houses and moved to Jumeirah or the coast behind Shindagha where they erected summerhouses on the dunes, where they would benefit from breeze blowing directly off the sea and the sweet water available at shallow depth beneath the sand. Generally Bastakiya families did not engage in this migration but one mother took her children to her fisherman uncle's *areesh* house near the seashore. The

Right:
The alcoves in this well-furnished inner room hold decorative and precious objects. There are family pictures on the wall, and a radio. The well-stuffed cushion on the left served as a backrest. A ceiling fan was especially useful as this room had no windtower. (Photograph 1970.)

children loved swimming though she, herself, was afraid of the ocean. The practice of summer migration to Jumeirah died out in the 1960s.

The normal migration for wealthy Bastakiya families was from their downstairs winter rooms to airier summer quarters on the first floor. However, not all houses had first-floor rooms and, even when they did, as the years passed homes might become too crowded for migration to be possible. Windtowers were effective during the day, particularly so in the afternoon when the north-west sea breeze blew strongly. After lunch, families would gather in rooms with windtowers to rest, the senior male members receiving priority under the windtower itself, where the air movement was greatest. At night, people would sleep on the roof, or occasionally on first floor verandahs. The part of the roof where people slept was always surrounded by walls at least chest high so that neighbours did not overlook each other.

Left:
A woman prepares food in the courtyard of a windtower house. Families would often keep large volumes of basic ingredients in storage.

Below:
In wash rooms, washing was carried out with water heated with a charcoal burner beneath large metal samovars. There were no showers, just the samovar and pails

Opposite below:
A scoop enables water from the large pot to be thrown over the body. The ewer is important for general hand-washing, being economical to use. There is a small drain to the outside in this example of a washroom from the Heritage House in Deira.

There were other ways of passing the summer months. Some women and children spent the time visiting cousins; perhaps enjoying the fresher, drier, upland climate of Bastak, Shiraz and Tehran or perhaps the city life of India.

Family welfare and education

Marriage between cousins was the norm, although since the early 1980s some young people have married outside the Bastaki community and a few have married foreigners. Cousin marriages kept wealth within the family, and avoided possible later disputes over inheritance. The compatability of the young people concerned could be better assessed. Ideally the couple shared

Qur'an School

The *maktab* was for boys and girls; they started when they were five years old. Children usually stayed for two years, but the duration depended on when the child could pass its exams. As many as fifty or sixty children, including some from the Maktoum ruling family, attended the *maktab*. In Haleema's time, fees were 5 rupees per child per month but Sheikh Abdul-Raheem was compassionate and orphans were taught free.

Subjects included reading and writing (in Arabic), arithmetic, and the Qur'an, beginning with the last chapter. Pupils learnt the Islamic rules of daily life and prayer. They also were taught parts of the Divan of Hafiz, a collection of famous Persian poetry. Haleema assisted her father, taking over lessons when he went to prayers. She also taught one group in an adjoining *areesh khaimah*, while her father taught another in the masonry house.

Classes were every day except Fridays, throughout the summer and throughout Ramadan. There were no school holidays, apart from the two Eids and the Prophet's birthday, or on the passing of one of the community elders. The school day was long. Classes began at sunrise. After an hour the pupils went home for breakfast. Lessons then continued until lunchtime, some pupils attending afternoon classes until sunset prayers (*Magreb*). In the early days, the children wrote on rough paper with a bamboo pen (*left*).

Ruqaya remembers children arriving in the mornings clutching little porous pots of drinking water, although later the school sold iced milk to its pupils. Rashad remembered that at the end of class the Sheikh would distribute sweets, but not until the children had held out their hands to receive a flick of his cane – perhaps a lesson in there being no pleasure without pain!

common ancestors on both their maternal and paternal sides. Several husbands joked about how, 'Her mother is my aunt and my mother is her aunt,' and similar complex relationships. Girls married in their teens; young men typically in their early twenties.

The first step was for women to sound out possible partners informally, one woman suggesting that a son might make a suitable groom for another's daughter. If the potential bride's mother gave encouragement (and it was perfectly possible for a girl to turn down a potential suitor), the two fathers would meet formally in the presence of a senior member of the bride's family to discuss the contract. Once agreed, the marriage was legalised when the contract was signed by the groom, the girl's father and two witnesses in the presence of an authorised religious leader. The bride might wait in an adjacent room to be asked separately by the sheikh (*mullah*) whether she agreed.

The contract was an important, binding document. The groom's family settled a sum of gold on the bride and this became her inalienable property, even in the event of a divorce. (Payment of the whole or part of the sum could be deferred if the bride's family agreed.) His family was also responsible for paying for at least most of the festivities and for providing the newly-weds with accommodation and furniture. The groom gave the bride a gift of expensive clothes and jewellery.

Weddings would take place within a few days, after several months or even longer. Conservative families ensured that the young couple did not see each other between the contract and the wedding. Other families would treat this period like an engagement, allowing the pair to spend time together in the presence of other adults.

Weddings were major social events. In the 1950s they might last for a week. Later they became more modern, with the bride wearing a western bridal gown on one of the days. Ceremonies also became shorter; five, three, or even two days. The celebrations, which used to be held at the bride's house, were then increasingly held in hotels. Men and women always celebrated separately until the final evening when the groom and bride would appear together in front of the assembled guests.

Bastakiya families welcomed the arrival of babies whether they were boys or girls, although there was a preference for sons. The stories of these families, however, show only too clearly the impact of the lack of health services. Children died, not simply in infancy, but later, too, from lack of medical care and medicines. Women died in childbirth, partly because there were only traditional midwives to assist and no specialist care was available if there were complications. Those with the wealth and family connections would often arrange to have their babies in India in modern hospitals. The Indian government provided a dispensary in Dubai with a doctor in 1939 but it was not until 1950 that the British-run Maktoum hospital opened with 38 beds to serve the whole Trucial States. Soon afterwards other health facilities were established provided by a range of donors.

Death was followed by rapid burial but the period of mourning when friends and relatives offered condolences lasted longer. The body was washed at home, though a man's might be washed at the mosque. It was laid out in the mosque for prayers before burial. Then men took it in a procession to the nearby Sheikhs' Graveyard.

Some women were economically active, perhaps needing to make a contribution to family income after the death of a father or husband. One young woman, who had lost her parents, loved embroidery. She not only made her own white wedding dress, but also took orders for sewing from others, including the sheikhas. If a woman lacked capital, stitching, which could be undertaken at home, was often her most accessible source of income. But other women, like their menfolk, had a shrewd business sense, even although they usually worked in public through a male agent or relative. Munira Khalil's mother, who was one of the few women to own a house in the Bastakiya, had a business, initially financed with gold received under the terms of her contract on her divorce. She imported sewing materials, especially silver thread from India. She ordered materials using catalogues and pattern books and a nephew helped with the external formalities. She had a monopoly in this particular niche trade, selling to women on both sides of the Creek.

The education and socialising of children began in the home, where toddlers would mix with adults of all ages. Children learnt social skills through visiting with their mothers. Girls, in particular, would help with household tasks, as well as learning traditional skills such as embroidery. Informally, children absorbed and then took part in the religious life of the family, learning from the behaviour of the adults around them. Boys and girls

Below:
The Bastakiya provided an ideal environment for children to grow up in. With several families often sharing one courtyard house children were rarely short of playmates. Inside young boys and girls played together.

Above:
Boys playing marbles, a popular pastime (Heritage House). They played in the lanes and at the edge of the Creek, trying to catch crabs, fish or even seagulls, and learning to swim. *Mistaa* was a game played with a bat and ball. *Horeed*, hide and seek, was played by older boys on Ramadan evenings.

also attended the Qur'an school in the Bastakiya.

The families of the Bastakiya had a high regard for education – Bastak and Lingeh had been long known for their philosophical and religious learning. Although Al Ahmadiya boys' school in Dubai, founded in 1912, survived, many other schools were forced to close during the early 1930s due to difficult economic conditions. This meant that, effectively, access to higher education was restricted to those children who had relatives in India who would care for them during their schooling, as day pupils or boarders. The situation changed in the 1950s, when Britain, Kuwait and then other countries established schools or supplied teachers to newly established government schools.

The schooling of girls was more challenging. The formal education of the women who talked to us was very varied. Some, through great determination, had achieved much in their lives against the odds. There were no girls' schools in Dubai until the 1950s, and even then, in some cases, social norms and family responsibilities might restrict their access to higher levels. One girl brought up on the Batinah coast was taught the Qur'an, some reading and writing by her father, a religious teacher. A convent educated girl of thirteen, brought up in Karachi, taken to Dubai by her grandmother after the death of her mother, felt the frustration of having no more access to learning. In contrast, another, who lost her mother in Dubai, also went to live with her grandmother but this time in Bombay. She went on to achieve an MA. Munira, born and brought up in Dubai, completed her Qur'anic course in a year, studied on her own, despite losing her trunk of precious books in the fire of 1955, then, when the opportunity arose, attended evening classes. She went on to work at the Rashid hospital. Sisters Bibiya and Mariam spoke of how liberating it was to go to school in India, and both thereafter became committed to passing on their knowledge to other women, whether in Iran or the UAE.

Right:
Football was a favourite game in the Bastakiya's open spaces. Here the Al Shibl Club team (see Chapter 13) pose in front of the Bukhash and Al Attar houses in a photograph taken by a tourist in 1981.

4

House of Abdulrazak Abdulrahim Aminai Al Bastaki

This house is a reconstruction of one of the earliest dwellings in the Bastakiya. Abdulrazak's family was one of the first to settle in the quarter and he is regarded as one of the community's founding fathers. He placed great importance on learning, a value that characterises the family today. Sadly the family's story also reflects the high incidence of death at a time when medical facilities in the Trucial States were scarce.

Left:
The floodlit *majlis* and entrance of this carefully reconstructed early house today provide a dramatic night-time entry to the Bastakiya.

The well-to-do Aminai family was one of the original four that emigrated to Dubai from Bastak before the twentieth century. Trading between Lingeh and Dubai in the later part of the nineteenth century, general merchant Mohammed Amin Aminai (born 1876) with his younger brother, Abdulrazak Abdulrahim Aminai (born 1882), settled in Dubai at the invitation of Sheikh Maktoum bin Hasher in about 1890. Their trade in those days was in textiles, tea, coffee, rice and spices which were brought from Bombay and Calcutta to be sold in the Gulf.

The brothers first lived in rooms over the old Dubai souq. Abdulrazak Abdulrahim had begun work before he entered his teens, as was usual in those days. He came to be held in such high regard by the Sheikhs that he was the only merchant given the opportunity to own a plot of land outside the old town wall, at the eastern end of what would become the Bastakiya.

The family is confident that construction of the house took place from about 1896, on a rectangular plot 28.8m long by 23.5m deep. Initially there were only the *majlis* wing and main entrance gate on the north side. A kitchen and toilet wing lined the east side, with two parallel living rooms on the south side. A wall enclosed the rest of the site on the north and west, providing a secure and private courtyard, with a well at its western end. Soon after Abdulrazaq Abdulrahim married his second wife, Fatima in 1919, she planted a date palm in the courtyard.

The house was planned with future extension in mind, the main entrance, unusually, being centrally placed. At the end of the *majlis* was a special room, apparently unique to this house: a library, where Abdulrazaq Abdulrahim kept his collection of books and papers. Several generations on, the family still shows a keen interest in learning. The southern rooms comprised a central sleeping room (*jaadumee*) and outer dayroom (*teedumee*), with door height shuttered openings. On each side was a small verandah with a washing area behind a lobby, and a side room, sometimes used as a bedroom and sometimes as a store.

Abdulrazaq Abdulrahim, and later his sons Mohammed, Ahmed and Sharif, continued as wholesale general merchants, with stores in the old Dubai souq, Souq Banyan, as Souq al Kabeer was then known. There were already quite a number of shops belonging to Bastaki traders. Abdulrazaq entered the pearl business rather late in about 1928. When the pearl market crashed after 1929, a great deal of money was lost but Abdulrazak survived, pearls being only a part of his business.

Abdulrazaq's son Mohammed was born to his first wife, Shamsulqamar, in the house in 1916. After her death, Abdulrazaq married Fatima. Mohammed's half-brothers and sisters were Khadija, Ahmed, Fatima (who died aged 16), Fatima and Ruqaya (who both died in infancy), and Sharif. After Mohammed Abdulrazaq married his bride Fatima, the house was extended in 1937, completing the wings on the north and east sides of the courtyard. A central entrance lobby was provided with a covered entrance porch and large timber doors both externally and into the courtyard. A new sleeping room (with its adjoining washing area) with a south facing verandah were built on the north-west corner of the house for the newly married couple. Above this a summer sleeping room was also provided together with

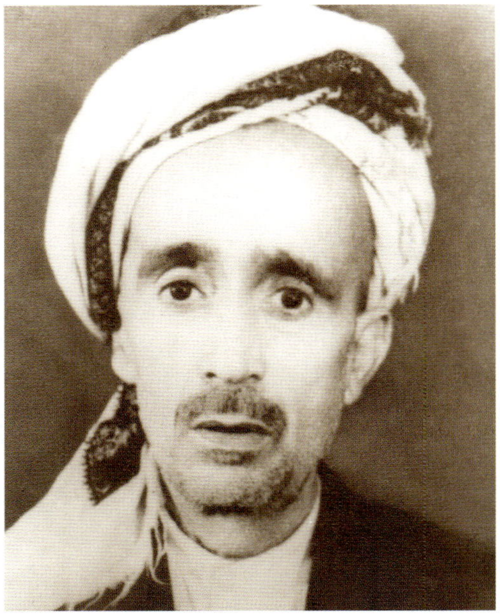

Above:
Abdulrazaq Abdulrahim, Mohammed's father, in a photograph taken in 1940.

Below:
Mohammad Abdulrazaq is wearing a turban and his gold braided fine woolen *bisht*, in a 1934 photograph by Abdulla Qambar.

Above:
18 year old Eesa, still studying at school. Some of the majlis windows are blocked up.

Above right:
Nabil as a 9 year old in front of Mohammad's verandah.

Below:
Ahmed, Mohammed's younger brother standing outside the main door in the courtyard.

Below right:
Mohammed's daughter Najiba and Ahmed's daughter Shafiqa playing on the roof - an ideal place for drying clothes.

a summer rest room over the main entrance, which would sometimes serve as a ladies' summer *majlis*.

A new kitchen was added on the west side over the original well. The old kitchen became a store room. The new buildings were joined up to the southern family wing with a ladies' entrance door and lobby opening into the corner of the courtyard.

In the early 1940s one more bedroom was added centrally on the roof to the south side of the building, over the sleeping room below, for brother Ahmed Abdulrazaq and his wife Ziba. Mohammed's son Eesa was born in 1955. He was the fifth of ten children, five girls and five boys, Abdullah (who died aged 2), Ruqaya, Farida, Salim, Yusuf, Nabeel, Nailofar, Najiba and Manal. As a child he slept in his parents' room, and sometimes in his grandmother's room on the south side. The plan of the house is as he remembers it. After his grandfather's death the southern wing was subdivided

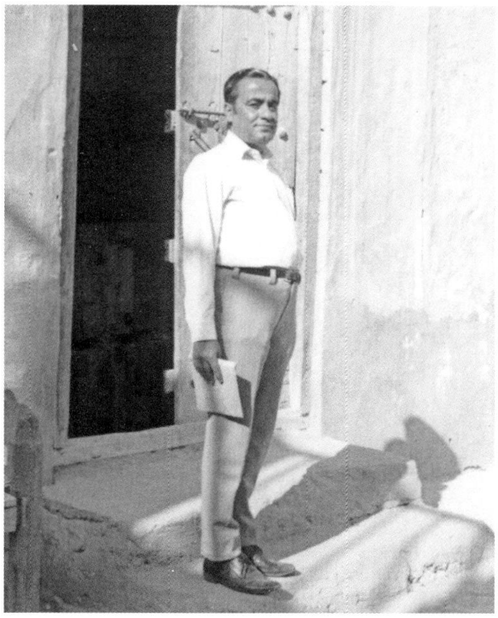

Left:
A view of the house from the north in 1974. The *majlis* windows are barred and shuttered, within the tall arched recesses that give form to an otherwise plain ground floor façade. The regular pattern of windscoops around the roof above contrasts with the screened openings of the summer room that are on the opposite side of the entrance porch.

Below left:
The same view of the reconstructed house in 2005. A shaded area on the roof seen in aerial photographs was included in the reconstruction.

Below:
These photographs give a good comparison of the differences between the original building, and the recent reconstruction which has been faithful to the screens, but the roof edge is now thicker without any exposed timber or stone.

into two pairs of rooms, the east side used by his grandmother Fatima, and the west side by his uncle Mohammed Sharif. The south-west corner room became the ladies' *majlis*, and the south-east corner room was occupied by his great grandmother, Mullah Fatima. Long before Eesa was born, his father's uncle Mohammed Amin lived in the room parallel to the *majlis*, that opened into the courtyard.

Summer migration from the ground floor up to the summer rooms on the roof was possible from 1936 when the extensions were built until about 1962, when the house again became crowded, and the rooms were occupied throughout the year. At some time a shaded *areesh* area was constructed on the north-east corner of the roof, providing valuable shade for rest during the day. This was particularly necessary as there was no windtower.

Dr Eesa takes great pride in the story of his old home, and gives lectures on his experiences as a boy growing up in the Bastakiya. His memories are not dissimilar to those of others, though few can have been born in a taxi! His mother, being in labour, crossed the creek by *abra*, on her way to the hospital in Sharjah. It was 25 December, 1955, and he was named Eesa, the Arabic name for Jesus. For three years from the age of 3 he lived with his mother in

Right:
The plan of this early house shows a simple symmetrical formality. The rooms shaded in grey indicate those added to the house in 1937. The subdivision of the southern wing (shown dotted) took place in the 1950s.

1. Entrance lobby
2. Ladies' entrance
3. *Majlis*
4. Library
5. Verandah
6. Sleeping rooms
   a) Mohammad Abdulrazaq
   b) Mohammad Amin Tawfiqi (later a storeroom)
   c) Abdulrazaq Abdulrahim
   d) Sharif
   e) Great Grandmother Fatima
   f) Ahmad
7. Wash rooms
8. Day rooms
   a) Ladies' *majlis*
   b) Sharif
9. Lobby
10. Kitchen
    a) Old kitchen
    b) Well, and kitchen after 1937
11. Latrine
12. Courtyard
13. Stairs
14. Summer sleeping room of Mohammad Abdulrazaq
15. Ladies' summer majlis
16. Sleeping roof
    a) *Areesh* shelter providing shade

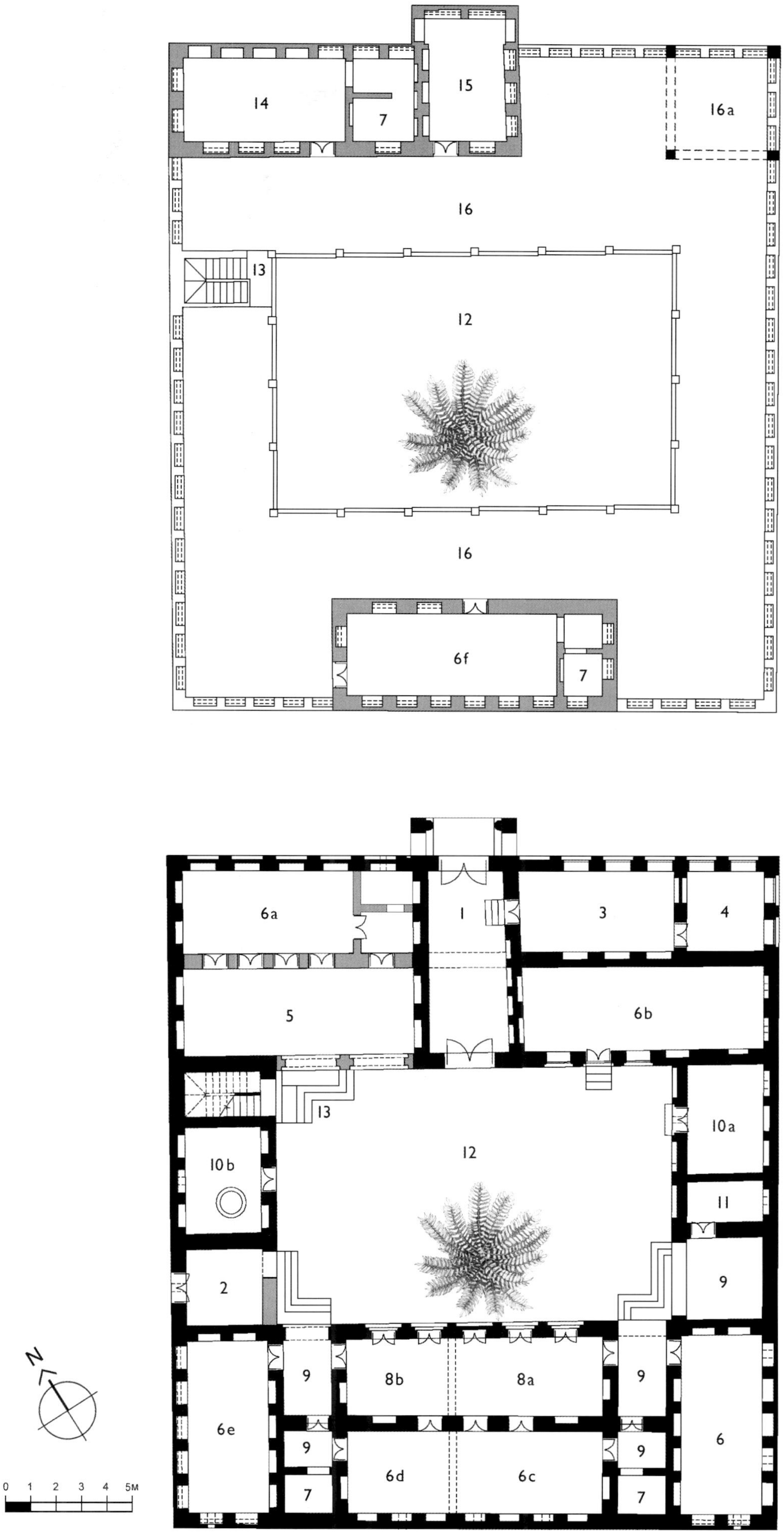

Kuwait. Shortly after this, he was sent to school in Bombay for four years. He returned to Dubai in 1966, and continued his schooling at Al-Shaab Primary and Intermediate School, located close to the Shindagah watchtower. He would walk to and from school, through the narrow Bastakiya lanes and past the souq, some thirteen kilometres daily, six days a week. He then went to Jamal Abdulnaser Secondary School in Satwa, graduating in 1976.

Left:
An evening view of the courtyard from the roof, with Uncle Ahmed's room to the left. The rooftop provides restaurant seating which is used except in summer. The windtower behind is on Al Dar Al Nadwa.

Below:
One of the dining rooms. the *teedumee* of the south wing.

Above:
The reconstructed verandah to Mohammad Abdulrazaq's former sleeping room.

Below:
Dr Eesa, his wife Layla and their sons Mohammed, Yahya and Marwan at Eesa's family home.

The open spaces in front of the house were popular places where boys from the neighbourhood would gather to play after school and on Fridays.

In the Bastakiya, women often came together in the morning and afternoon at the house of the most senior family member, in this case Eesa's grandmother. They usually met in her room, bringing their handwork with them. This was often 'talli', the bands of gold and silver thread embroidery that were attached to the bottoms of trousers, the edges of sleeves and around the neckline. Since women did not go to the souq, their menfolk would bring bales of cloth to the house for them to choose from. The women would meet once the men had gone out to work, returning home to cook the mid-day meal. Small children would go with them, learning early to play together and to behave in the company of a group of adults.

The day was structured around prayer times. After *Asr* (afternoon prayers), the women would go out again, returning before their men came back in the evening. After *Isha* prayers at the end of the day neighbours, friends and prominent members of the community would meet in the men's *majlis* to discuss business, trade, and social issues. Literature, politics and science were favourite topics of debate. Women would meet in their own *majlis* within the house, to relax together; to discuss family affairs, forthcoming weddings, and health; maybe to sew or embroider if the light was good enough, or to smoke the *qadou*, also known as *qalyoon* ('hubble-bubble').

Different gatherings took place following a death in the family, when friends and other relatives would come to support and share in the grief of the bereaved. Eesa remembers the loss of his cousin and very close friend Faisal Amiri in a car accident on their way to the cinema in Deira, over the recently opened Maktoum Bridge. Eesa was also hurt. Women were gathered in the room behind the *majlis*. It was the only occasion that his future wife Layla visited the house, when her family came from Sharjah to offer their condolences, but she was soon whisked away from the grieving to play with the other children on the roof. It would be many years later after their respective studies that they would meet again and become engaged.

Premature deaths were not uncommon in the Bastakiya. Eesa's father Mohammed lost his first wife in 1940, as well as experiencing the deaths of two sisters when they were still young. Although Mohammed visited the house during reconstruction with Eesa to advise on its authenticity and accuracy, he feels no longer able to visit his former home. The deep wounds left by the losses of his first wife and sisters, while they were still children, have never healed.

At the beginning of the 1960s the house was connected to a mains water supply and electricity, though it never had water borne sewerage. This particularly early example of a Bastakiya house was interesting in that it was constructed with thinner walls (not more than 40cm thick) than those of later houses. Perhaps this may be one of the reasons why it never had a windtower. By 1975, probably as a result of its age, its less substantial structure, and its close proximity to the tidal creek, it was in very poor condition and increasingly uncomfortable to live in. Sharif moved to a rented villa in Satwa. In 1976 Eesa travelled to the United States to study electronics and was away when the family moved out. In 1977, on the day that the family finally left, the palm tree that had been planted by Fatima in 1919 fell of its own accord. They temporarily moved to four flats in a block owned by Mohammed and Ahmed who then built and occupied adjacent villas in Jumeirah. In 1985 the structure was considered to be dangerous, and the only remaining example of a very early Bastakiya house was demolished by the Municipality.

In 2001, as part of the restoration and reconstructions plans for the Bastakiya, the original foundations were exposed, and plans were drawn up for the house to be reconstructed using the same materials as those used in the original building. Family photographs and memories of how the house had been were assembled by Dr Eesa. Reconstruction proceeded, with Dr Eesa providing regular advice to Khaled Al-Zarouni and architect Khaled Al Hammadi, of the Historic Buildings Section. Work was completed in 2004.

While the house was entirely traditionally re-built, some changes were introduced during the reconstruction. The existing foundations were reinforced and the thickness of the walls was increased, to ensure stability and durability. The later partition dividing the day and sleeping rooms in the south wing was omitted. The flights of the staircase were incorrectly built the wrong way round, while the architect and Dr Eesa were both away from the site. Parts of the external walls have been left un-rendered, to expose the attractive herringbone pattern of coral stone construction. The courtyard was paved, and new toilets, a commercial kitchen and a built-in bread oven were all added, to serve the house in its new role as a restaurant. The former *majlis* has become a curio shop. The Bastakiya Nights restaurant is now illuminated at night to show its original features, providing a special attraction for tourists and other visitors.

Above:
Dr Eesa and his father Mohammad visit the site and monitor the accuracy of the reconstruction work.

Below left:
Restoration using traditional coral and shellstone bedded in a gypsum mortar, underway in 2003.

The Pearl Trade

This is the story of how Abdulrazak Abdulrahim and and his son Mohammed entered the pearl business. A customer who owed Abdulrazak 30,000 rupees offered to settle his account in pearls, which, he said, were worth 80,000 rupees. Abdulrazak paid cash, less the 30,000 rupees he was owed, and sailed off to Bombay to sell them. But there he was offered only 30,000 rupees for the whole stock. So he decided to hold onto the pearls and in the meantime bought more. Only after two to three years was he able to cover his loss. Although it was during the depression, pearling continued on a modest scale. His son Ahmed remembers that as a boy of 8 or 10 it was fun to watch the hard bargaining between buyer and seller. Pearls deteriorate if left too long before they are drilled, after which they last forever. Abdulrazaq kept them in a bowl of water in a safe, to keep them looking fresh, and as was the custom in the trade, always displayed them against a fine red cloth. His son Mohammed recounted the story of visiting a house in Deira with his father when he was twelve.

Abdulrazak had heard of someone selling a *hasbaa*, the highest quality and most expensive pearl. The pair were treated to rosewater, and delicious tea, and a sum of 6,000 rupees was mentioned. The pearl duly arrived, wrapped in layers of cloth. When the final layer was opened and the pearl revealed, Mohammed looked long and carefully at it, before suddenly insisting to his father that they must leave. His father was very puzzled, but once outside, Mohammed said that he couldn't talk in front of their hosts, but the *hasbaa* was very old and was cracked. No-one else had seen this flaw, but as a result the pearl was worth only a couple of hundred rupees. Because of his sharp eyesight, Mohammed became known as 'Johari Sagheer' (little pearl merchant), becoming his father's right hand in business.

Importing wholesale from overseas and selling retail in the local market required considerable capital. In comparison the pearl business did not require such extensive foreign contracts or such capital outlay. Abdulrazak would go once a year to Bombay to sell his pearls, the only place that pearls could be drilled for stringing. There were other Persians as well as Bastakis engaged in pearling, but the Bastakis were the most numerous, and the ones with some wealth. The pearling business was unusual in that a great deal of cash was needed to finance the boats. The ship owners were local Arabs. The lending of money for interest is not permitted by Islam but the captains needed to finance their boats and crews for the season. Many merchants would purchase large quantities of rice in India and provide it to the captains, who would then sell it on to raise the funds they required.

Pearl diving

Sheikh Abdulraheem Al Janahi (see Chapter 10) would go pearling for up to four months in at a time throughout the summer. When they were at sea, the men would look to him to lead prayers, and would ask his advice. He became a respected leader and latterly the captains, *nokhada*, used to tell him not to dive too much, but he insisted on doing his job. He became an excellent navigator, and knew all the Gulf routes by the stars. He knew the locations of all the pearl-fields *(al maghasat)*, which were richest around the Abu Dhabi islands, the locations of each of the islands themselves and the distances between them and the shore.

Occasionally when divers went down they saw *jinn*, and would come to the surface screaming. The only treatment was to read to them from the Qur'an. On one occasion, there was an Omani magician on board, who could deal with the *jinn*. One evening a diver said he really would like some hot Omani *halwa*. The magician said he would get him some. Everyone stared in surprise, when, having gone to the front of the dhow, he returned with a container full of hot *halwa*, which they all shared. Sheikh Abdul-Raheem kept the container!

He would tell his grandchildren the story of when he was diving early one morning in very murky water. Unable to see much, he suddenly felt something soft beneath him. He had landed on the back of a large shark, and, while he remained absolutely motionless, a second shark appeared. To his enormous relief, they swam away without attacking.

A goat-horn nose clip (*above*) was worn by pearl divers.

5

House of Mohammed Sharif Bukhash

Since demolished, this was the original house studied and surveyed by the authors in the 1970s. Its many fine decorative features were recorded in extensive photographs and architectural drawings, reproduced in the following pages, which recreate a rare and poignant picture of a vanished way of life.

Above:
Mirrored leaf forms combine to create a robust Persian arched opening in the south-east wing, in contrast to the intricate timber fretwork balustrade it framed.

Opposite:
The north-east windtower was the largest and most substantial, rising 7.5 metres above the roof, with six narrow openings into each vent. The fins created a security screen as well as an effective shade against sun penetration into the tower.

This was one of the finest houses in the Bastakiya. Built on two floors around a central courtyard, it had three windtowers descending into first floor rooms. In two-storey houses many ground floor rooms would be duplicated on the first floor with the ground floor being occupied during winter, and those on the first floor in summer. This was a particular feature of the Bukhash house.

Mohammed Sharif Bukhash (1871-1946) came from the town of Bastak. He began trading in Dubai from the turn of the twentieth century. In 1909 while he was on a trip in Dubai, a large gang of bandits from Mistan attacked Bastak. To save lives, the Khan evacuated the town and retreated to the port of Shibkooh. On the night of the Eid al Fitr at the end of Ramadan, he returned, capturing the aggressors and freeing the town. Soon after this battle the family joined Mohammed Sharif in Dubai.

From 1913 until 1923 Mohammed Sharif lived in Bombay, a key port for the family's trade in garments, fabrics, rice and tea. (Later, in the 1950s, his son, Mohammed Bukhash, would move the business into electrical goods:

Above:
The entrance porch to the family home in Bastak.

Left:
Looking along the lane to the west of the house provided a rich image of the repetitive pattern of the *majlis* windows, an oblique view of the decorative arches and gypsum screens enclosing the summer *loggia*, terminated by the elegant proportions and details of the south-west windtower.

Above:
The most visible part of the house offered an elegant rhythm of tall shuttered *majlis* windows on two floors, strongly expressing the building frame. Two bell-headed pilasters columns supported a Bastaki style arch, framing the pair of handsome high teak doors behind.

radios, fridges, portable fans and televisions). Together the Fikree and Bukhash families had agencies in Lingeh, Karachi, Bombay, Aden, and in Kalba and Buraimi, both on the Omani border. The Fikrees owned dhows which sailed as far as Zanzibar and Madagascar, where they collected mangrove *chandals*. Dhows from Lingeh would sail with various nuts, dried game meat and salt, to Bombay and Karachi. From there they would be loaded with timber, cloth, rice, sugar, spices and pepper destined for Dubai, Bahrain and Kuwait. From Dubai dried lemons were exported; in Basra dates were loaded. Mohammed Sharif had a house and office in Buraimi, with a Fikree as his agent there. Camel caravans from the coast would carry rice and cloth to the oasis village, returning with fruit.

In 1929 Mohammed Sharif's wife Fatima gave birth to a son, Mohammed, the only one of his children to be born in this house. Five years before Mohammed was born, in 1924, Mohammed Sharif bought the eastern half of the Bastakiya plot from the Ruler. A walled compound with a number of small rooms had previously been built by Mohammed Khonji, who unfortunately fell into disfavour with Sheikh Saeed, and had to leave the city, thereby losing his land.

The size of the original plot was approximately 22.5 by 33.5 metres, but excluded an 18 by 2.7 metre strip along the west boundary. Mohammed

Sharif immediately demolished the existing rooms and began anew. The house was designed and constructed in its various stages by Ostad Mohammed Al Banna. In about 1944 Mohammed Sharif was able to purchase the previously excluded strip, before proceeding to re-build the north and west wings of the house. The sequence of building originally explained by Ostad Mohammad in 1974 was not as Mohammed Bukhash remembered it. He described this in detail, often in relation to family events. The house was built in two phases.

Construction of the living rooms on two floors began in 1924. These form the classic east wing of the house, with a steep curving staircase up to the first floor in the central lobby. The southern kitchen and bathroom wing, including the main entrance and *majlis* were also completed at ground floor and first floor levels. At this stage the room above the *majlis* was built to provide another family room. Mohammed recalls a single storey L-shaped wing that was built along the original west and north boundaries. It was not so well constructed as the other wings, but it provided two living rooms on the west side of the house with a storeroom along the northern boundary, and a ladies' entrance at the north-east corner of the courtyard. Masonry columns around the outside edge of the roof supported *areesh* screens. (These were removed during the fire of 1940 although in the event it did not reach as far as this house).

In 1945, after Mohammed Sharif acquired the western strip of land, the entire west and north wings were re-modelled and extended. Two long thin storerooms with external access were built on the western edge of the house, while the western rooms were re-built to provide five stores opening off a new verandah. The north room was shortened, and the walls vividly decorated. A ladder was added in the north-east corner to give access to a first floor shaded roof area above.

The first floor part of the west wing was never completed. The windtower that descends into a bedroom in the north-west corner was never rendered.

Above:
The main door was opened fully on festive occasions or when large objects were being brought in, otherwise the wicket was used.

Below left:
Three distinctively different windtowers set off the corners of house in this aerial view from 1974.

Below:
The main entrance was locked with stout wooden bolts that would slide in response to a hidden mechanism.

Right:
The south wing of the house contained the kitchen, well and lavatory on two levels. The first floor suite was for use in summer, and was entirely screened from the courtyard by timber louvres which created privacy, and in conjunction with the windscoops on the outside wall of the house provided a good degree of cross ventilation. A masonry table was just outside the ground floor kitchen, and the house's garden was particularly fine (see Chapter 2).

Below:
Carved gypsum balustrades along the first floor west elevation of the summer *loggia*. The carved decorated face with the most elaborate detail is placed facing outwards, the plainer side facing into the house.

This room was intended for Mohammed's then elderly parents, but Mohammed Sharif passed away in 1946. Plans to enclose a summer room with sets of doors between the inner pillars of the wide shady verandah were abandoned, even though the doors had been purchased.

As part of the next phase, 1951-52, a covered verandah was built on the north side (the two little rooms here are much later additions). A permanent stair was built from the north-east corner of the courtyard, replacing both the earlier ladder and the former central staircase in the east wing.

In 1968 the old first floor kitchen was demolished, and a new kitchen was constructed using cement blocks. At the same time the old bread oven on the ground floor and its chimney were done away with. The north-east bedroom was modernised in 1972-3, by stripping out the old doors and replacing these with modern steel framed windows and a pressed steel doorframe and painted flush door.

The coming of electricity enabled fans as well as lighting to be installed in nearly all the rooms. Air conditioning units were fitted in two first floor sleeping rooms and in the north-east ground floor sleeping room. With the advent of water and sewage infrastructure, the opportunity was taken to modernize and to rearrange washing and lavatory facilities.

The most decorative element in this house was its carved gypsum balustrades. The beautiful designs were variations on a geometric representation of flowers and foliage in a vase, arranged in pairs along the first floor west elevation of the summer loggia. The finest were located centrally in the classically proportioned east elevation within the courtyard. A series of simple geometric patterns was also used, particularly at the first floor on the north side of the courtyard.

The house had an impressive presence on the edge of the Bastakiya, in the corner of the clear area in front of the fort. The most visible part of the house offered an elegant rhythm of tall shuttered majlis windows on two floors strongly expressing the building frame. This pattern terminated at an

Left:
The finest gypsum screens were located centrally in the classically proportioned east elevation within the courtyard.

Below:
Finely carved hardwood panelled doors with arched fanlights of stained glass gave life and colour to the main rooms.

elegantly proportioned entrance porch, punctuated by the windows of a small summer rest room above it. Two bell-headed columns supported a Bastaki style arch, framing the large pair of handsome high teak doors behind. Finely carved hardwood panelled doors with arched fanlights of stained glass gave life and colour to its main rooms.

The three windtowers were each quite different. That on the south-east corner was a typical Bastakiya windtower in size and design, 6.3m high above the roof finish, with its vent divided into three bays each capped with a floral crown formed of intersecting circles. The north-east windtower over Mohammed Sharif's summer room was 7.5m high above the roof, and considerably more substantial, with six narrow openings into each vent with a smaller and more delicate version of the same floral crown above. Strong

Above and below right:
A special feature of the Bukhash house was its 'painted room'. Built in 1945, and painted by Abdulrahim Al Banna, the stencil applied paintings were lively in their viv d colours.They did not appear anywhere else in the house. Colourful vases of flowers alternated between arched recesses, each containing a geometric courting peacock displaying his fan of tail feathers, within a floral roundel. The images were framed between two painted borders running around the room; the upper cornice had a repetitive pattern of alternating black circles and red ovals; the lower one in red, below a narrow black band, was inscribed with verses from the Qur'an.

chamfers on the corners of both towers curved outwards to meet the horizontals at its base, at the division between base and vents and at the cornice, and assisted to unify the different designs. As a composition, the towers break the otherwise symmetrical balance of the classically

proportioned courtyard elevation below. The third, north-western tower appears to be the tallest, but this is an illusion, it being as tall as the south-east tower, but rising from a higher roof level. It was also a metre narrower in diameter, its width seems to have been be determined by the breadth of the additional strip of land that was acquired to extend the west wing of the house.

The house, built by Mohammed Sharif and his wife, would be home for their son Mohammed, and his wife from Lingeh, together with his sisters and their husbands Abdullah Fikree and Zubair Fikree. The oldest sister moved to her husband's house when she married. The house was occupied as soon as the first phase of the building was complete. Mohammed Sharif and his wife used the rooms in the south-east corner. Later, when his oldest daughter married, the newly weds were given the north-east suite. The two couples each had a set of rooms both on the ground floor and on the first floor, and were thus able to practice seasonal migration. When his youngest daughter married, additional ground floor accommodation was built on the north side. Eventually, when Mohammed married Mariam Fikree in 1953 they occupied the north-east ground floor rooms, where they brought up three sons, Sharif, Fuad and Rashad and two daughters. Thus, at one point, the house was home to the elderly grandmother, three of their married children together with their young families: a total of seven adults and seven children. By the time of our detailed survey in 1974 Grandmother Fatima had recently died and one of the three families had moved out. Zubair and his wife were living in the painted room.

In the 1940s and 50s there were usually about 15-20 family members and servants living in the house. Maids would sleep with the women and children. About seven menservants slept in the *majlis*, as well as several employees from the family shop. There would inevitably be up to half a dozen guests staying in the *majlis* for two to three months at a time. Thus,

Above left:
The entrance to the wash room in the south-east (Rashad's) bedroom behind an embroidered curtain. Above it is a screened mezzanine storage area. There are Persian carpets on the floor.

Above:
The sleeping end of the same room had two beds immediately below the windtower, with an imported western style chair. Sunlight glints through the open slot of the recessed windscoop.

Below:
On the ground floor, outer dayrooms were enclosed by three pairs of timber doors opening into the courtyard. This view of the south-east dayroom shows the doors opening into the bedroom with leaded coloured glass fanlights. The pegs between used to support oil lamps. Furnishings include Persian carpets, a wall clock and a marble topped table.

there would regularly be as many as thirty occupants.

From the 1960s, because more people were living in the house, there was inevitably a marked decline in the practice of migrating from the ground to the first floor in summer. This had been an important feature of the conceptualisation, architecture and use of the house in its early years.

The Bukhash family also had a summer house in Kalba on the east coast beyond the Hajar mountains. It was built in the 1960s, on a small farm of 150 trees, planted by Rashad's grandfather Abdulwahad Fikree, who was passionate about horticulture. The house remains, but as fresh groundwater disappeared, the trees progressively died. The men and boys of the family would go there in summer for two to three days, at least once a year, together

Above:
The narrow triple conjoined circular pilaster at the corners of the north-west windtower, with one similar central column dividing each vent gives this tower particular grace, style and individuality, making it the most elegant of the three towers.

Right:
The framed nature of the building is again visible on the north side of the courtyard. A series of screens with simple geometric patterns edge the first floor passage.

Above:
An attractive series of simple geometric patterns were used for the gypsum balustrades along the first floor on the north side of the courtyard.

Left:
The airy, shaded first floor verandah was ideal for children's games and as a place for women to sit during the summer.

Below:
The ground floor verandah was used as a storage area for goods from the family business.

with friends from the Bastakiya, in their Land Rovers. The journey took all day through Masafi, after which the track followed the wadis. Rashad described the fun when the Land Rover required two or three attempts to climb up a particularly steep path through the wadi. The trees planted were palms, papaya, banana, oranges, pepper, fig, lemon, vines for grapes, and 'chicu', a very sweet fruit with three or four seeds. On holiday they would eat kebabs every day, skewered on the green stems of palm fronds. They slept on the roof from midnight until they were woken by the sounds of birds. There were mango trees, which the children would deplete in between swimming in the pool. In the afternoon they would go to the sea, and watch the fishermen empty their nets.

In the Bastakiya house, two sets of inner sleeping and outer day rooms occupied the main wing of the building. A well, kitchen and lavatory together occupied a separate wing of the house, in this case the south side. There were two kitchens, one above the other. Since traditionally wood was used as fuel, the roofs of older kitchens (*matbakh*) were black with smoke. Holes in the wall to the lane let smoke escape up through a chimney on the roof. In 1968 the kitchens in the Bukhash house were modernized, with sinks, bottled gas and primus stoves. Although the open shelves and work surfaces were traditional in design they were tiled for easy cleaning. The well was only a few metres deep and because of the proximity of the creek the water was brackish. Well water could be raised to the first floor overhead by a pulley.

The main entrance doors (*dahreez*) opened into a lobby with direct access to the men's reception room or *majlis*. The lobby was staggered in plan, so that it was not possible to see directly into the courtyard. Prominent families in Dubai traditionally 'sit' or hold open house in their *majlis* in the evening, but in the house we are describing the practice ceased in 1971. The floor of the *majlis* was a few feet above ground level, and at the same height as the

Above:
The well could be accessed both for ground floor winter accommodation (pictured) and for use on the first floor in summer.

Below:
Traditional bell-shaped columns, capitals and floreate brackets contrast with the western classicism of imported artificial Indian sandstone columns which lined the summer veranda edge overlooking the courtyard.

bottom of the tall shuttered windows on two sides, so that guests seated on the carpets were assured of maximum breeze. To make it easy to serve visitors the lobby was equipped with a sink and a work surface for the tea urn and with what was once a hatch giving direct access to the well room.

From the lobby, wooden steps ascended to an airy, first floor room with a painted board ceiling. Until the alterations of 1945 this had been a private family room, accessible only from the interior of the building. It then became a summer *majlis* – a feature that only a few houses possessed. (The Amiri house had a semi-enclosed room on the roof which served the same purpose).

In the middle of the open space outside the house was a slightly raised area or *dechaa* (high place), built by the family – something prominent citizens would do to bring together their neighbours. It had wooden benches and was a place where men of the community would meet after evening prayers and dinner, for an hour or so. It was mainly used in summer, or when there were too many to sit within the majlis. It would also be used on the 26th and 27th nights of Ramadan, for farewells to the Fast, where between 50 and 200 men might gather for discourse and the recital of poetry. The main entrance of the house faced this open area, clearly visible from the road. In contrast, the back door *(takhee)* opened on to the shaded, narrow alleys of the quarter.

The courtyard was paved and drained towards the centre. Here the owner of the house had personally created a small garden (*baaghcheh*), bringing sweet soil from an oasis fifty miles away and protecting his Indian almond, papaya, vines, green peppers and bougainvilia with a low perforated wall. The family took particular and justifiable pride in their garden. These trees were dying by the 1970s, probably because they were watered with brackish well water (often by Rashad). The courtyard was especially clean because the family, unusually, did not keep chickens or goats.

The last windtower to be constructed was on the north-west corner of the house, and after the death of Mohammed Sharif, it made a pleasant summer room for his widow Fatima. Mohammed purchased the old building immediately to the north so that he could demolish and clear the area in front of the future windtower room. In winter Fatima would move into the south-east ground floor suite. The summer room with its open shutters was fully exposed to the marvellous sea breeze from the Creek in the early afternoon.

The house was unusual in that on the first floor there was a wide roofed area which was used for family gatherings. The airy, shaded place was also ideal for children's games and as a place for women to sit in during the summer. Only part of the roof was available for use as a summer sleeping place; several beds were kept permanently up there, accessible by stairs and screened and made safe by a wall of windscoops.

The Bukhash house had particularly generous storage facilities used for both business and domestic purposes. This was essential in a situation where both household provisions and trade goods became available only when ships arrived. The ground floor verandah was used as a storage area for goods from the family business. The two stores with external access could be let to other merchants or used for stock destined for the family's shops. The large storerooms on the west side were originally used for fuel, wood and coal

Left:
By 1974 the north-east bedroom doors had been replaced by steel framed glazed windows and a flush door.

Below:
Each of the internal stores had a different purpose: one for old household goods, coffee pots, sets of doors, antiques, flour and sweets, another for family trunks and business papers. Here the decorative screened openings for ventilation are covered during the winter months.

(*zoghaaldun* and *khajahdun*). By 1974 most were unused and empty, although later the verandah was enclosed and more storage space added, with some storerooms being rented out to other merchants.

The house had a mezzanine store, in this case for onions which were spread out on its floor. Just within the main entrance was a date store, *qandeel*. Here, fresh dates were piled up in wicker baskets on a sloping floor with projecting plaster ribs with channels between. The weight of the piles caused their juice to run out and along the channels into a small pit in the floor. When the dates were eaten the juice would be mixed with them. The juice was also eaten on *chebab*, a type of bread, used as a sweetener on *blelalit* (a fine pasta), and on Fridays with an omelette.

The family moved out of the house at different times up until 1978. Mohammed moved into an apartment. He was given a plot on which to build in Mankhool, close to the Ramada Hotel. Rashad's elderly aunt and uncle Zubair stayed in their painted room up until demolition was due, cared for by servants. When they did leave, they moved into an apartment. Thus, unusually, members of the family remained there until eviction notices were issued in 1984. The house was never entirely empty or occupied by labourers.

In February 1985 this beautiful house was demolished to make way for construction of the new Ruler's Diwan. Mohammed Bukhash and his sons had hoped it might become a museum but that was not to be. Its destruction was filmed and photographed by Dariush Zandi. The largest windtower was so well built that it had to be dragged down by chains attached to a tractor. At least it was one of the best recorded houses, not only through our architectural survey, but in the many photographs taken by Fuad Bukhash

Above:
A bulldozer demolishing the south wing of the house in February 1985. A fine building and family home was reduced to a heap of rubble in just a few hours.

Right:
Members of the family at Muhammed's house in Jumeira in 2006. From left to right: Rashad's nephew Ahmad, his brother Fuad, uncle Abdulrahman, father Mohammed, uncle Dr Aqeel Fikree and Rashad. Fuad, Rashad, Aqeel and Ahmad are all qualified architects.

Survey Drawings 1974-75

The original measured survey of the house of the Bukhash family was carried out over three weeks in February and March 1974, and drawn up in London over the following twelve months. This is the first publication of the complete set of drawings. The house is remembered today as having been one of the most attractive in the Bastakiya. Its plan exhibits all the typical features of the windtower houses, and of those described in this book, it provides the best example of duplication of rooms on two floors for summer and winter living.

Local names are in Khudmooni, the language of Bastak, as given to the authors in 1974. Arabic translations are provided in the glossary.

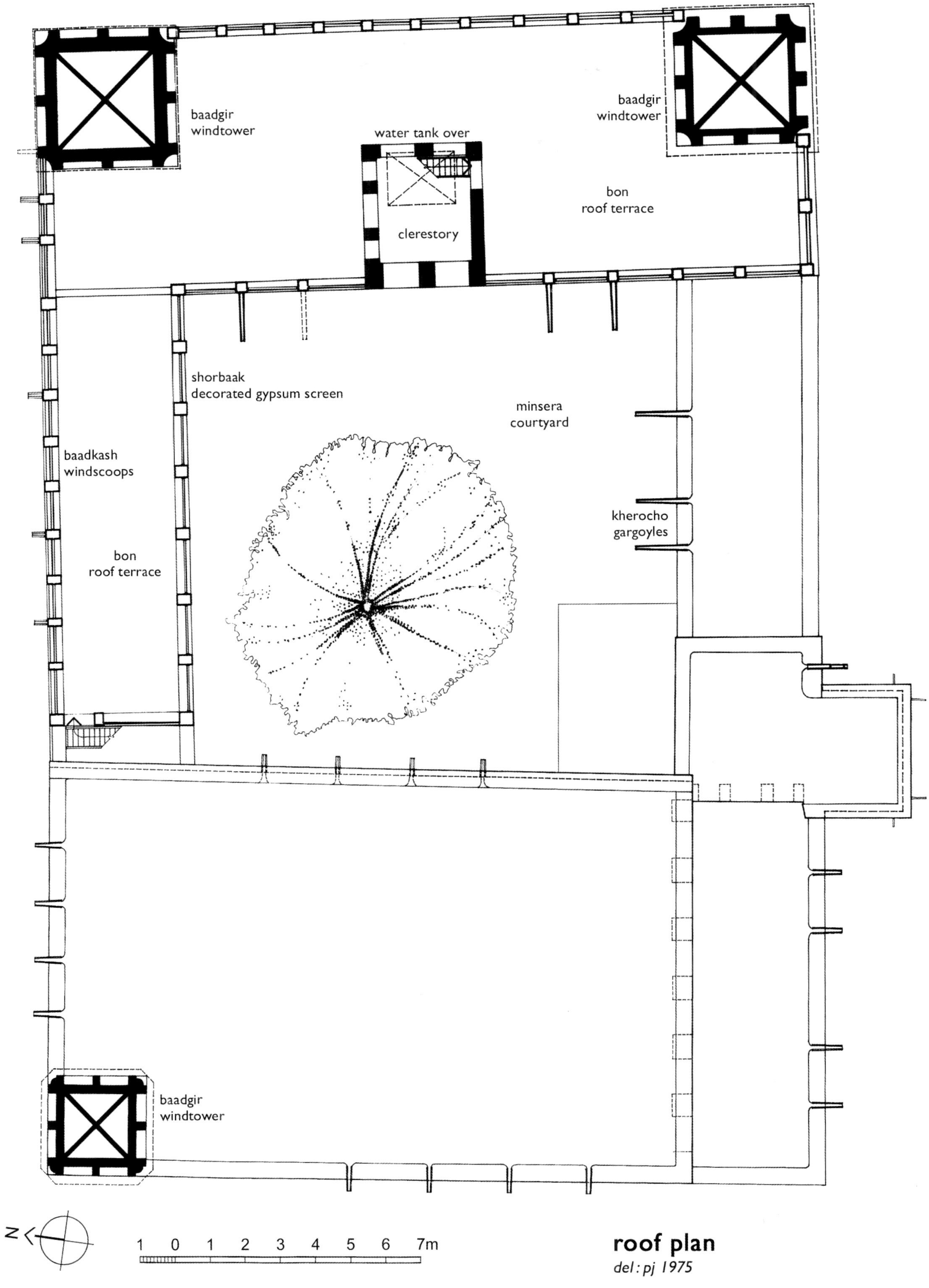

roof plan
del : pj 1975

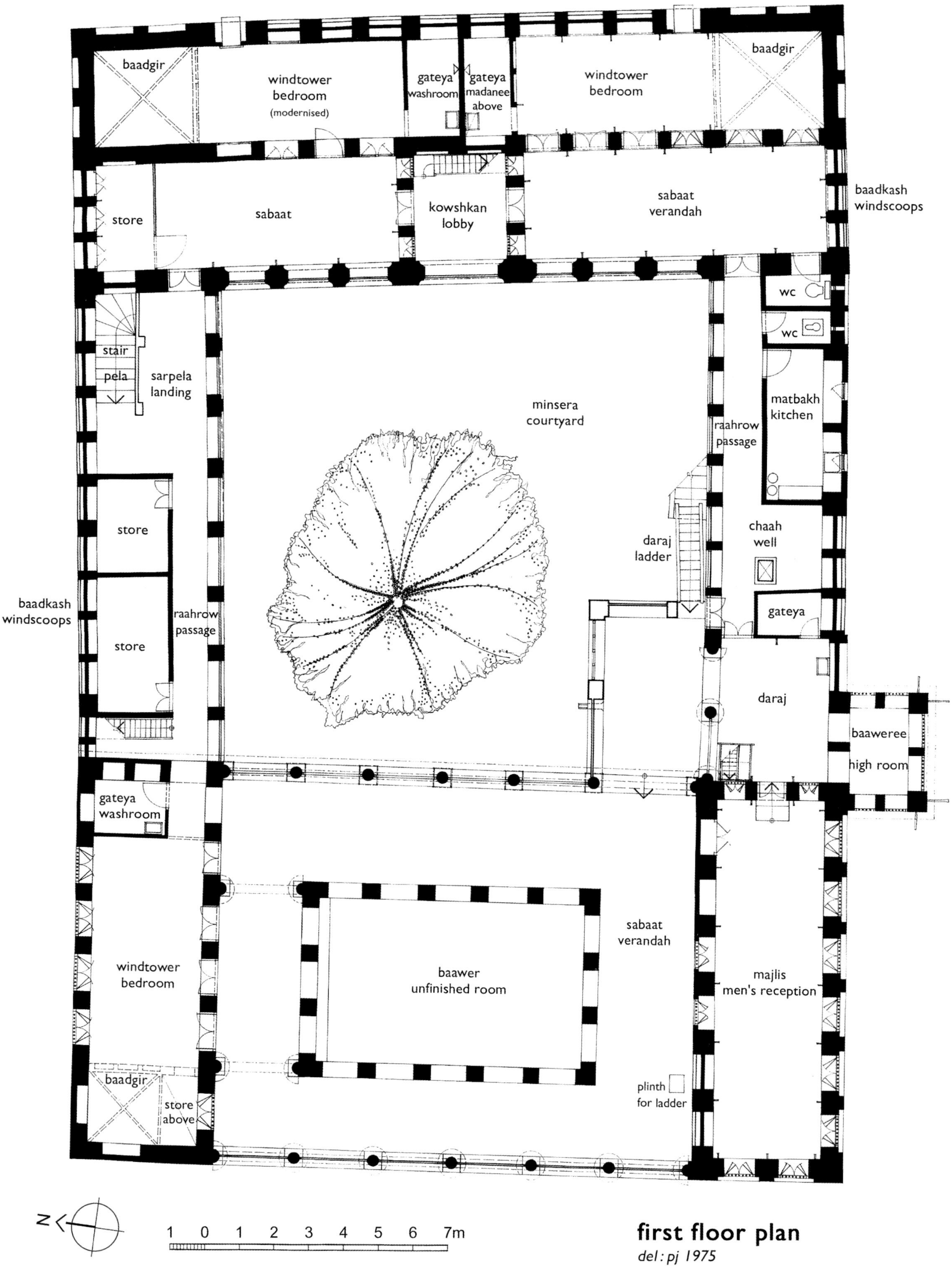

first floor plan

del: pj 1975

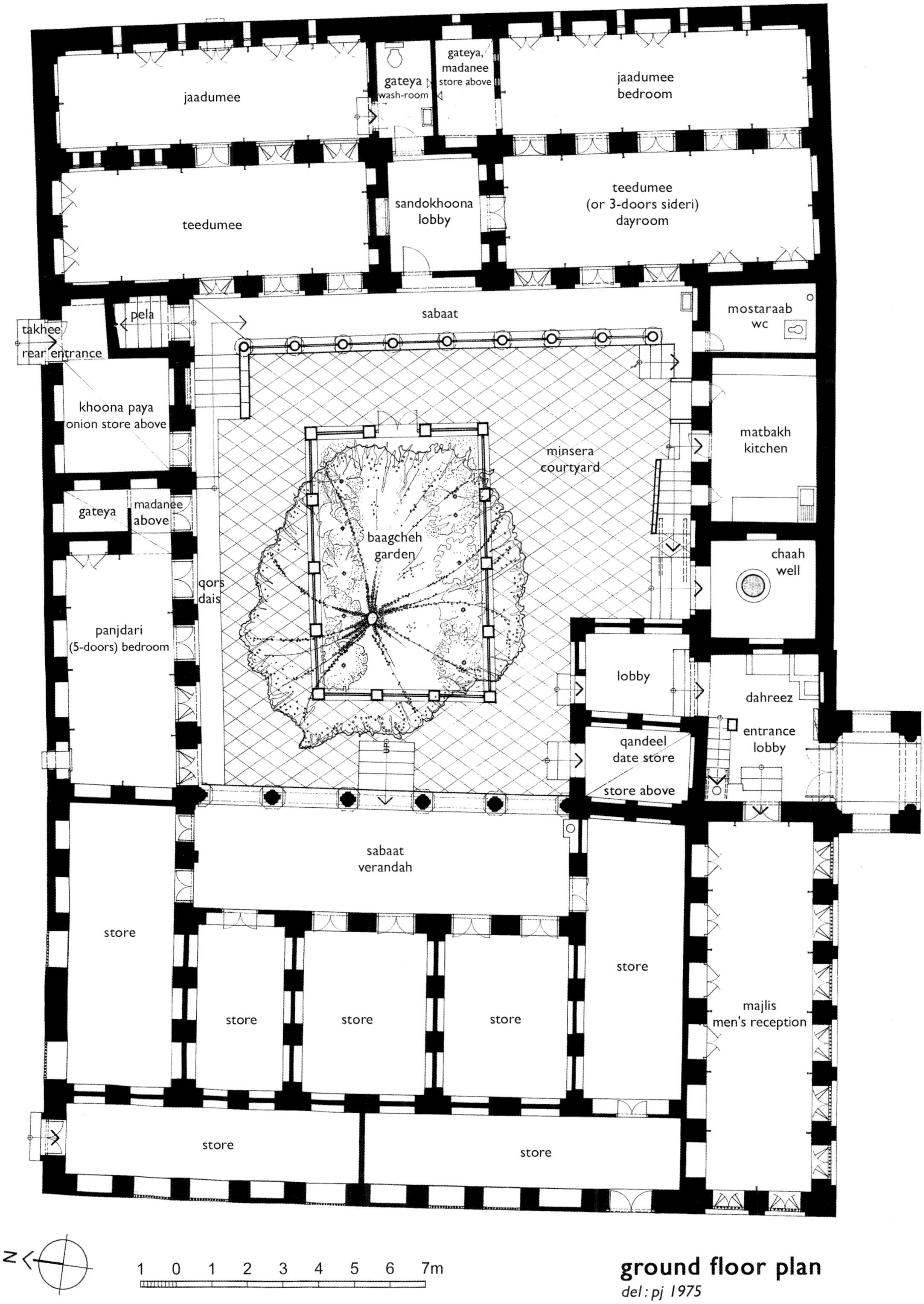

ground floor plan
del: pj 1975

1 0 1 2 3 4 5 6 7m

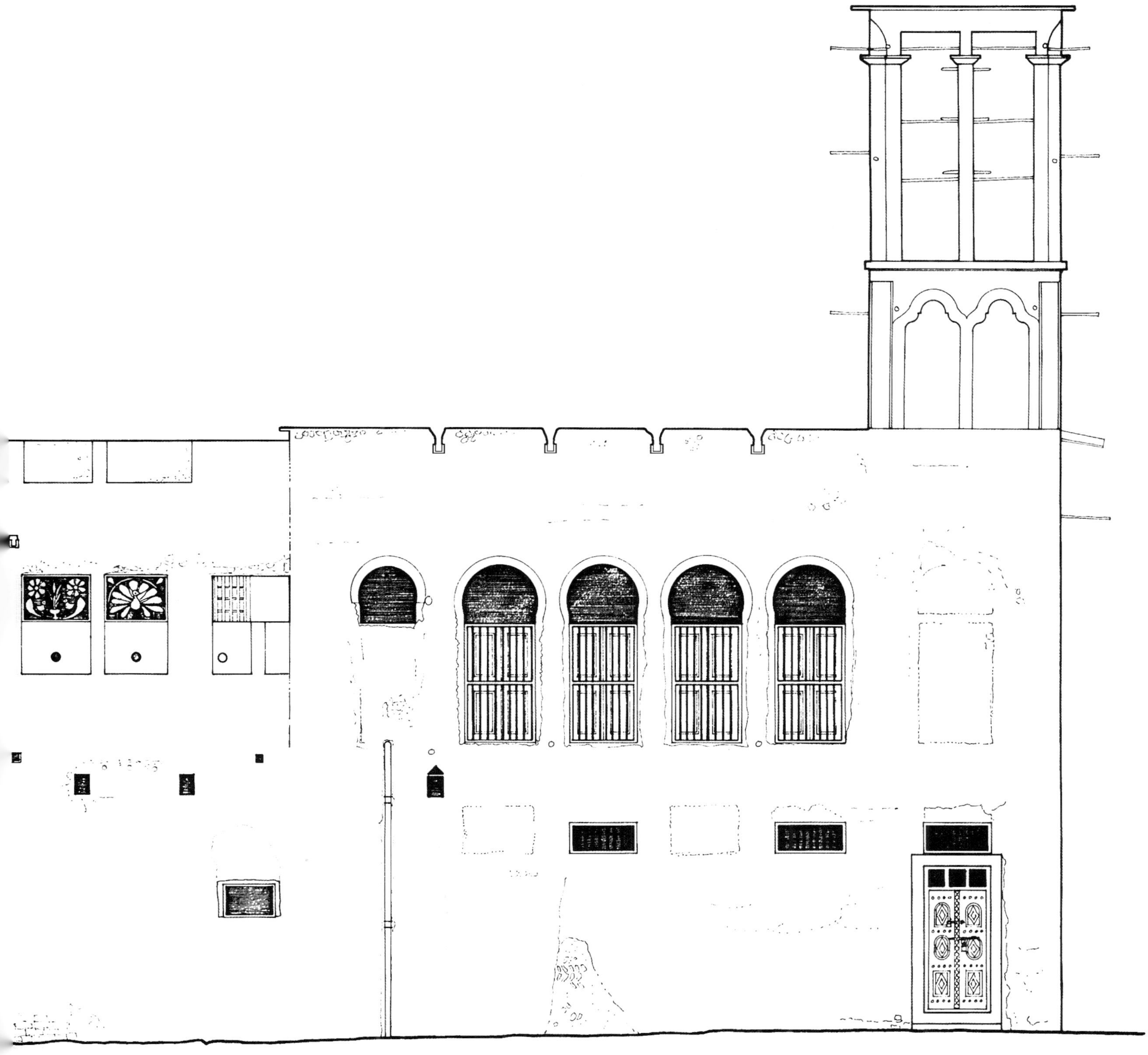

north elevation
del: pj 1975

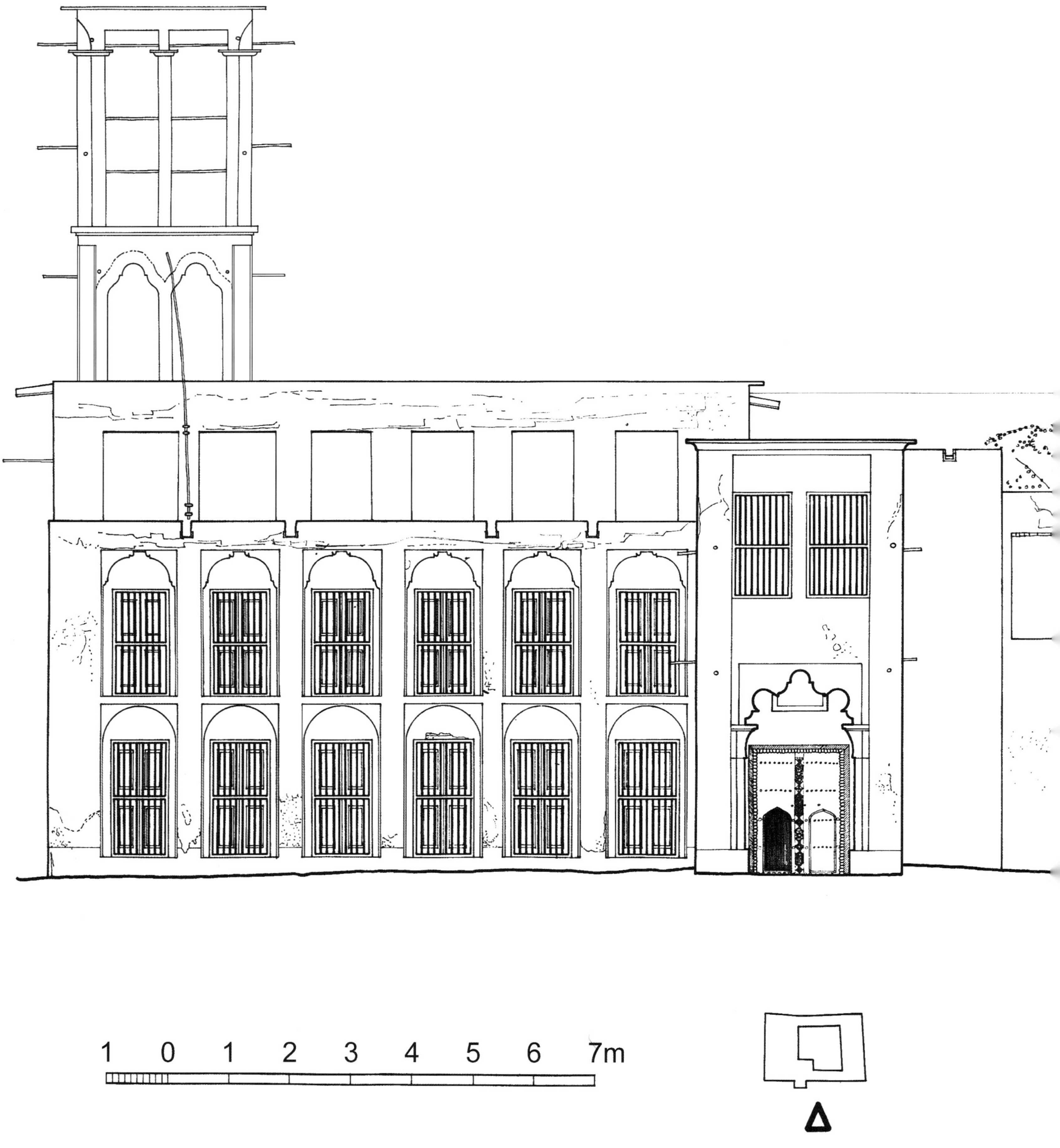
1 0 1 2 3 4 5 6 7m

south elevation
del: pj 1975

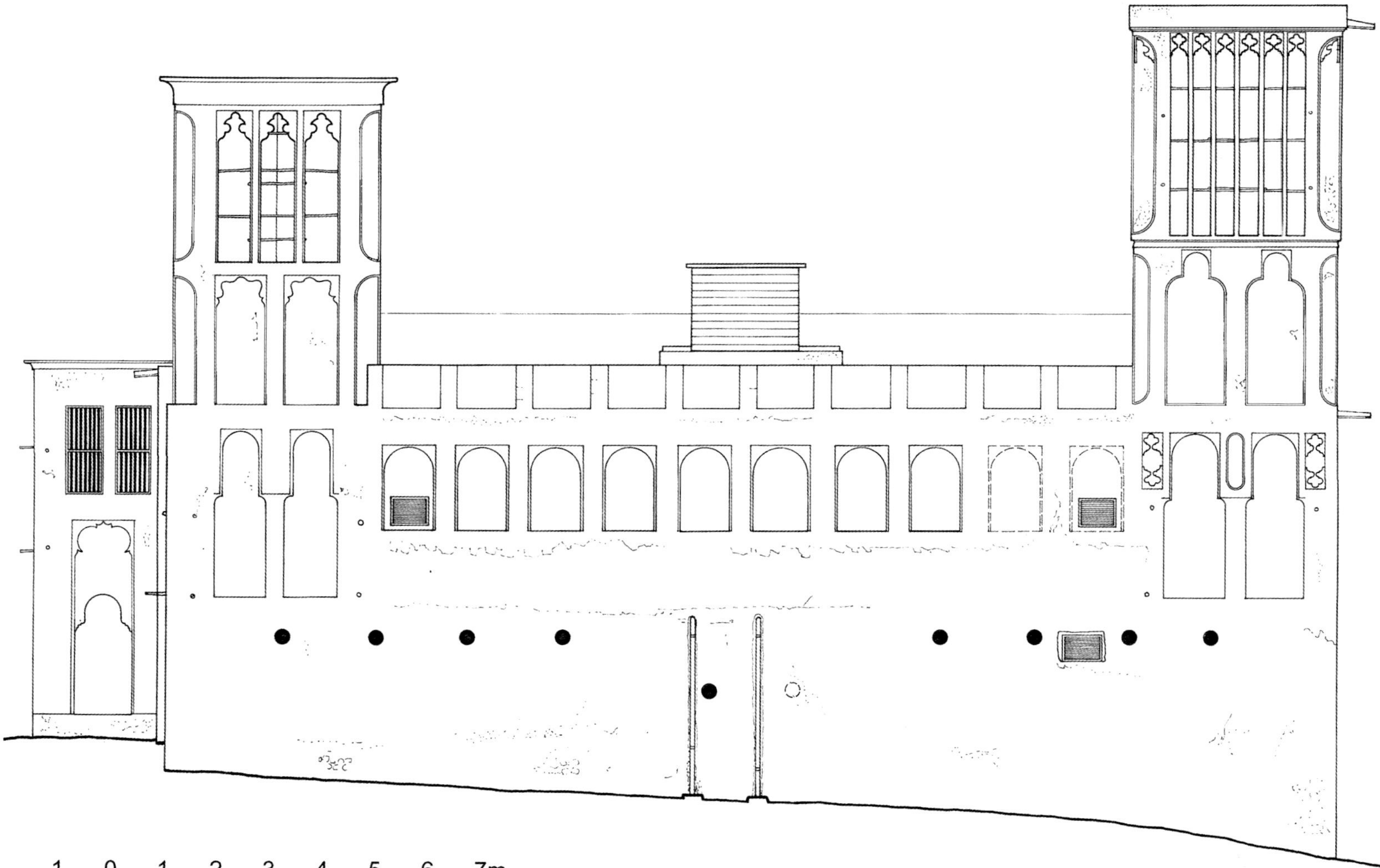

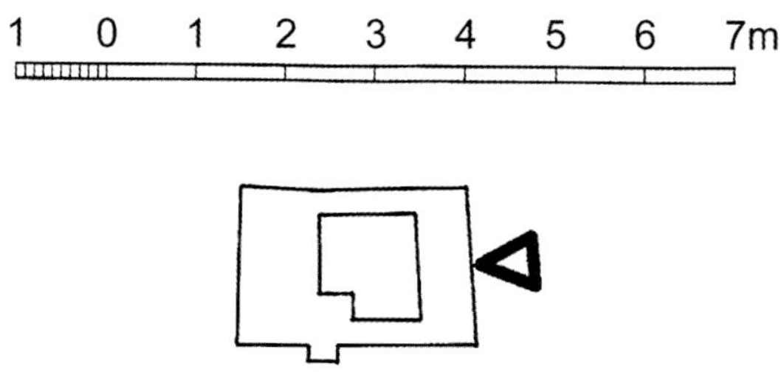

east elevation

del: pj 1975

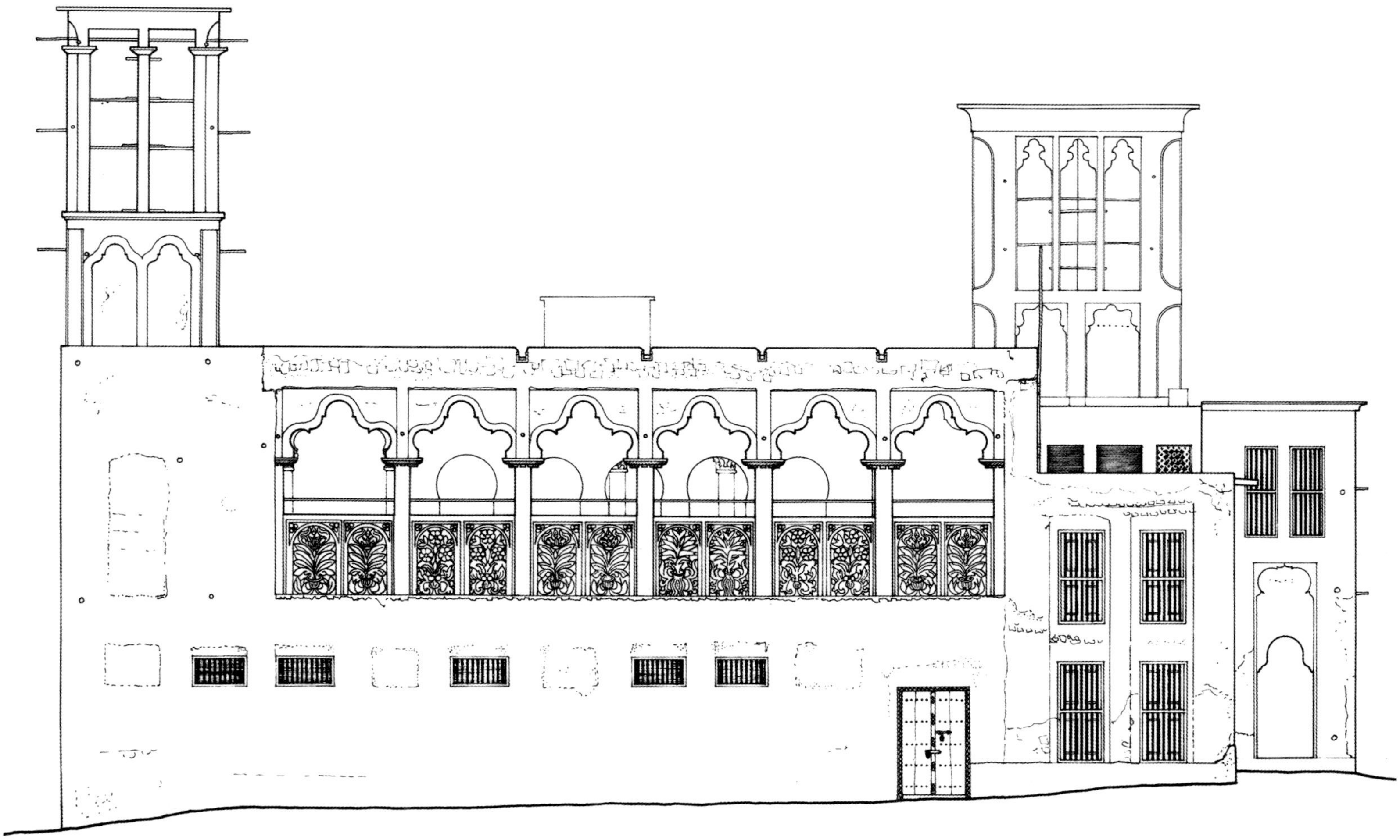

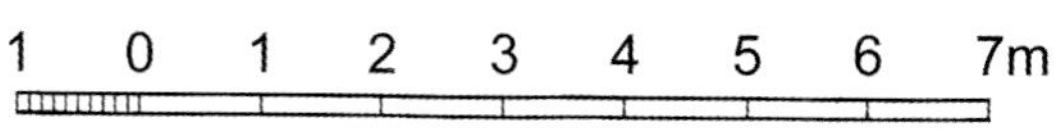

west elevation
del: pj 1975

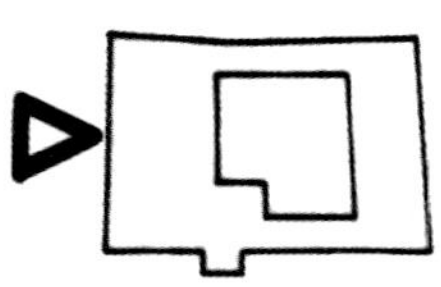

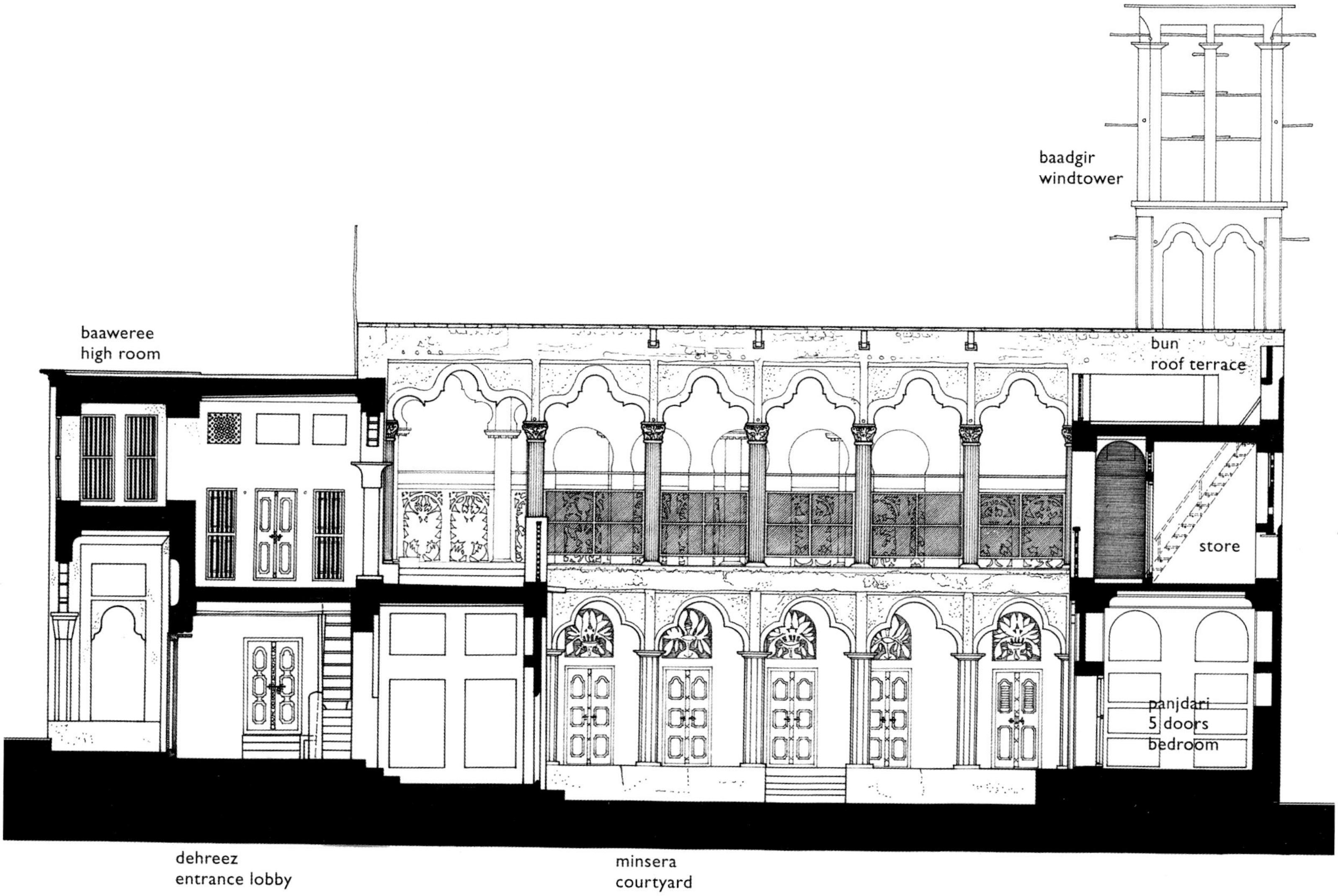

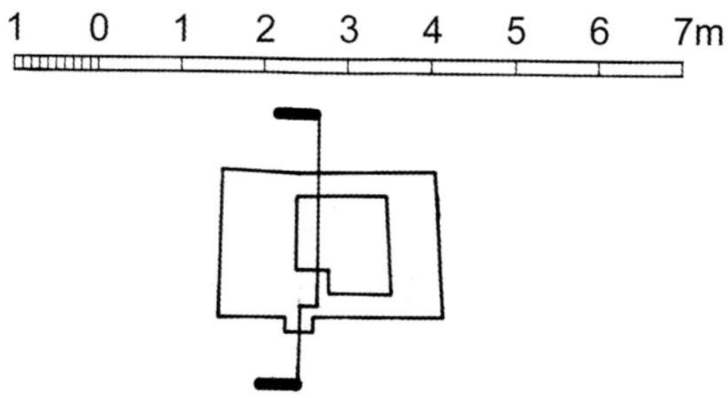

section looking west
del: pj 1975

section looking south
del: pj 1975

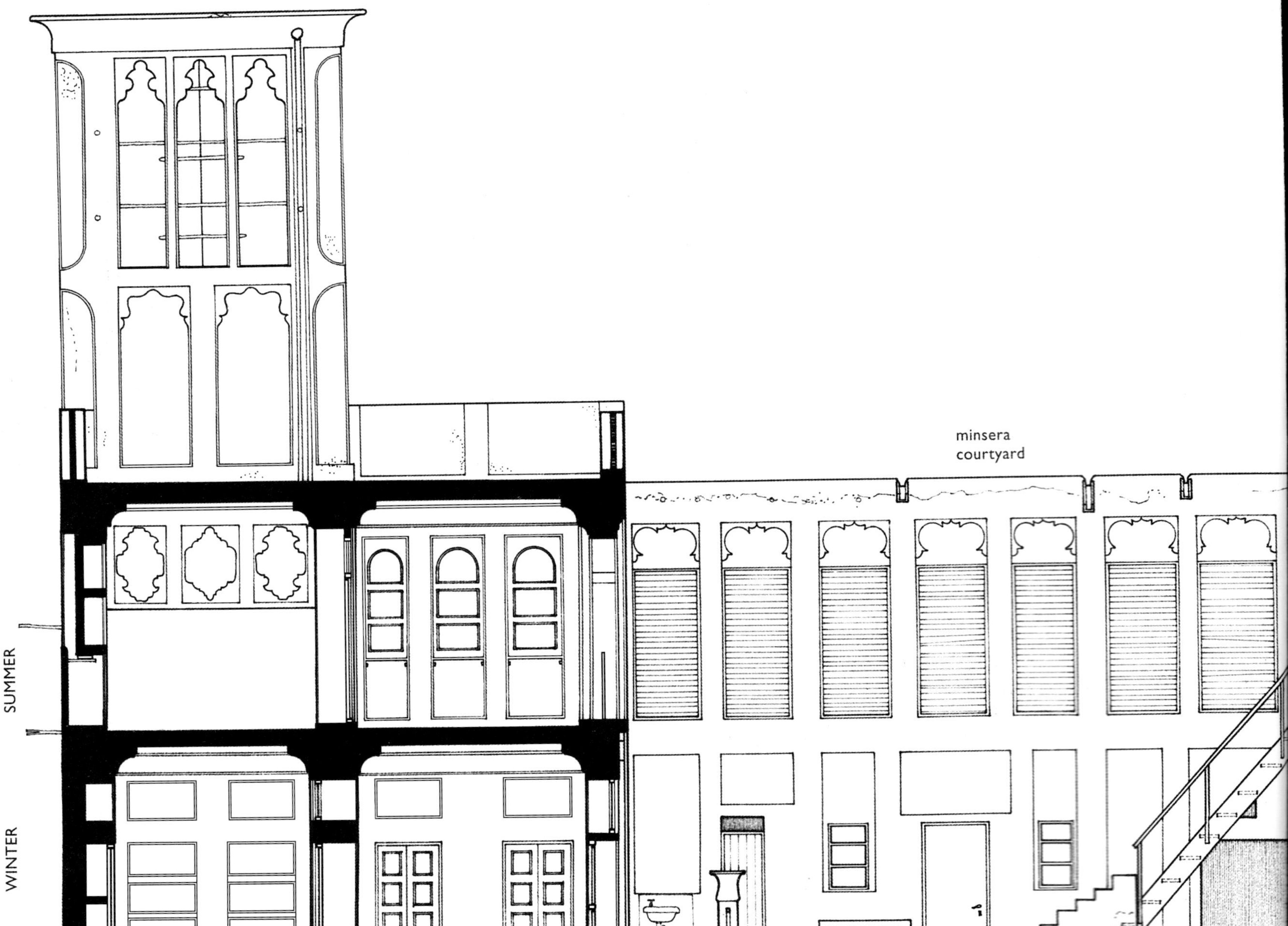
minsera
courtyard
SUMMER
WINTER
jaadumee
bedroom
teedumee
dayroom
1 0 1 2 3 4 5 6 7m

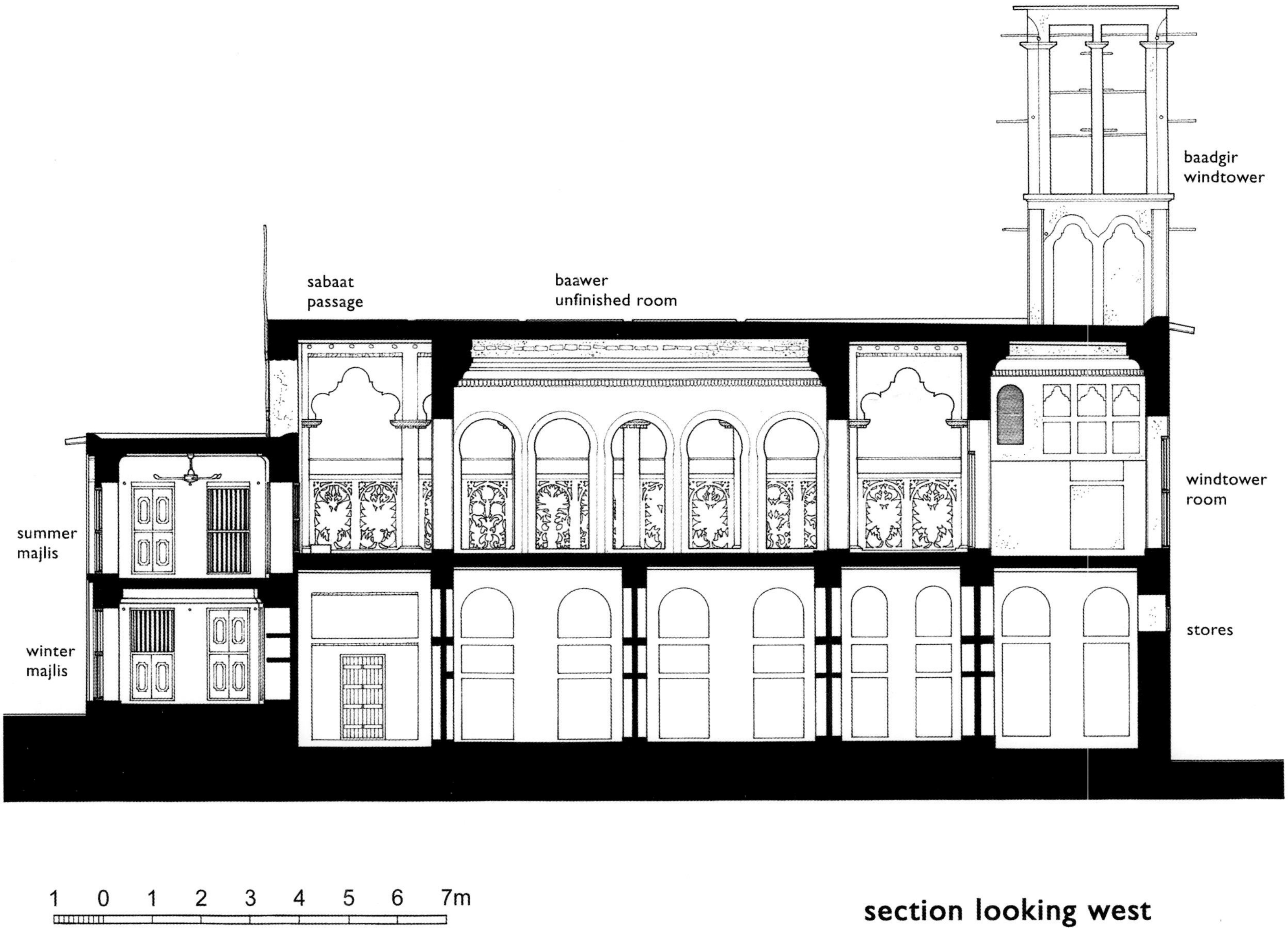

section looking west

del: pj 1975

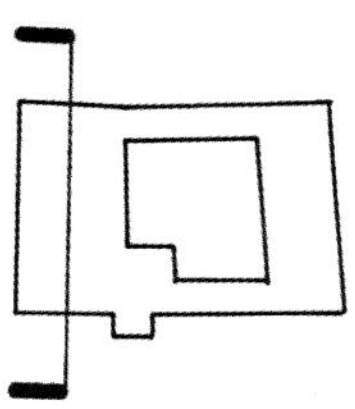

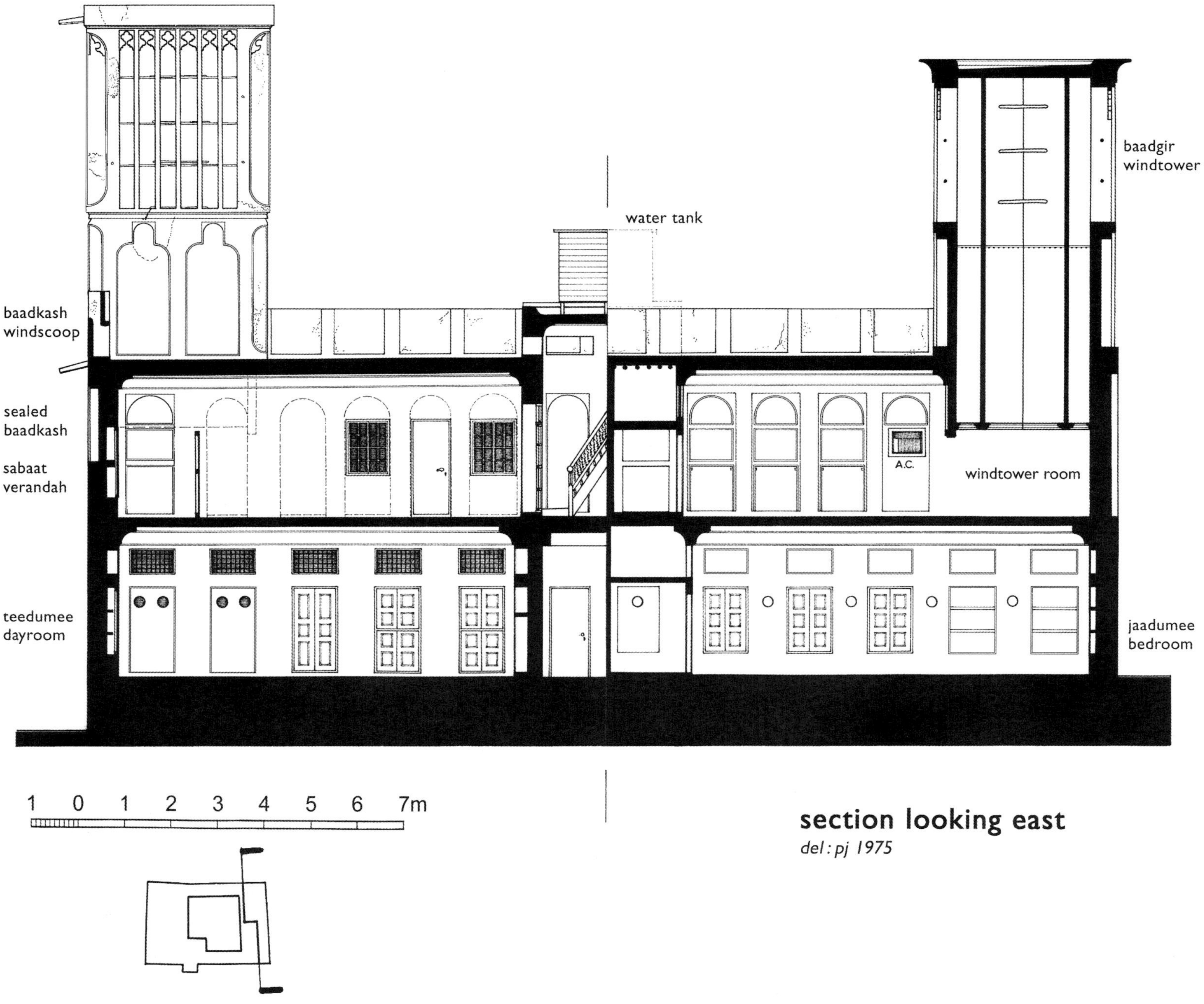

section looking east
del: pj 1975

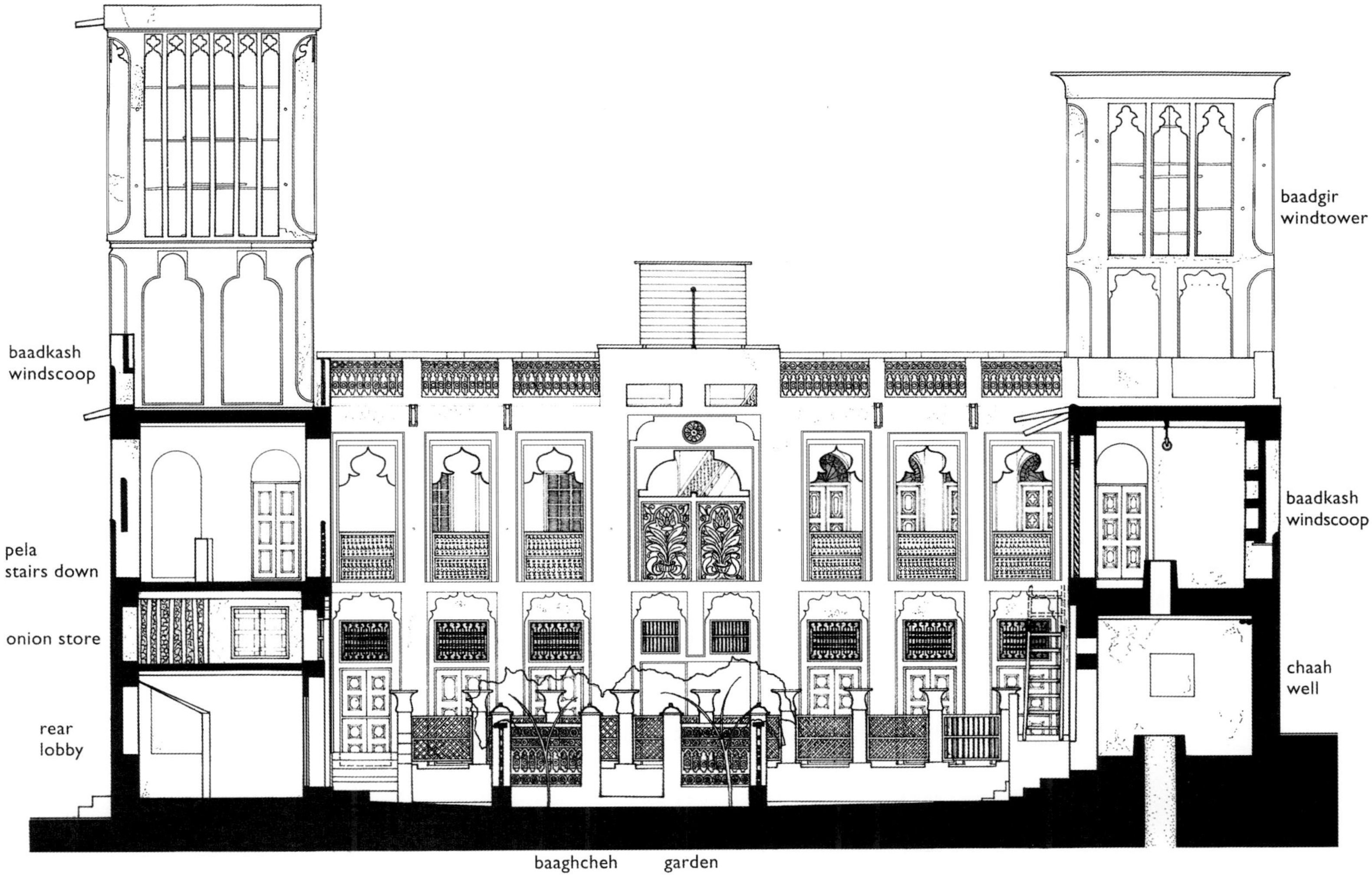

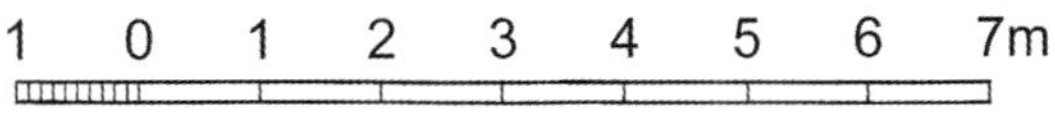

section looking east

del: pj 1975

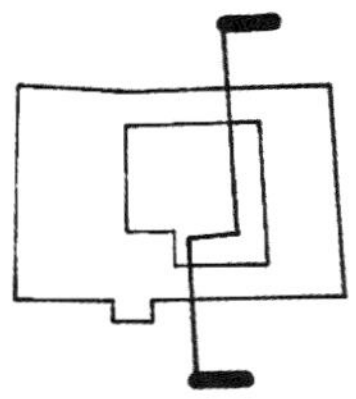

6

House of Mir Ahmed Mir Abdulwahid Amiri

This small windtower house provides a good example of seasonal migration. The family made considerable use of the roof and first floor in summer, returning to the ground floor in winter. The description of how the house was used and the evolving nature of family life within it is particularly vivid. Handsome carved gypsum screens contribute to its architectural quality.

Left:
A contemporary view of the courtyard, looking north towards the Creek.

Left:
Mir Ahmed Mir Abdulwahid Amiri photographed in 1934.

Below:
The textile shop with Mir Ahmed's name in the nearby Souq al Kabeer in Dubai, close to the *abra* landing, is still owned by the family, who continue to sell the same goods.

Recently restored as a philately museum, this house was originally constructed by Mir Abdulwahid Mir Ali Amiri (1890-1974). The family was descended from the Amiris of Faryab, one of the village oases of Bastak. Mir Ali, father of Abdulwahid, was the headman of Faryab and owned gardens there. Mir Abdulwahid first came to Dubai to visit his uncle, Abdulrazaq Abdulrahim Al Bastaki in 1900 (see Chapter 4). After a trip to Bombay to visit Abdulrazaq's brother, Mir Abdulwahid, returned to Dubai, decided to stay and began a business, trading in fabrics and textiles, as well as dates and other foodstuffs, with Iran.

The plot on which the house stands is irregular, 13.8m wide by 23.5m on

Right:
The shape of this otherwise compact plan arises from an irregular plot fitted between neighbouring houses. A double storey block constructed in 1961 is shown dotted.

1. Entrance lobby
2. Ladies' entrance
3. *Majlis*
   a) winter
   b) summer
4. Courtyard
5. Verandah *(sabaat)*
6. Sleeping rooms
   a) Mir Ahmed
   b) Mir Abdulwahid
   c) windtower room
   d) Mir Abdullah
   e) Mohammad Hadi
7. Wash rooms
8. Latrine
9. Kitchen
10. Storeroom
11. Stair
12. Sleeping roof
13. Mir Abdullah's summer room

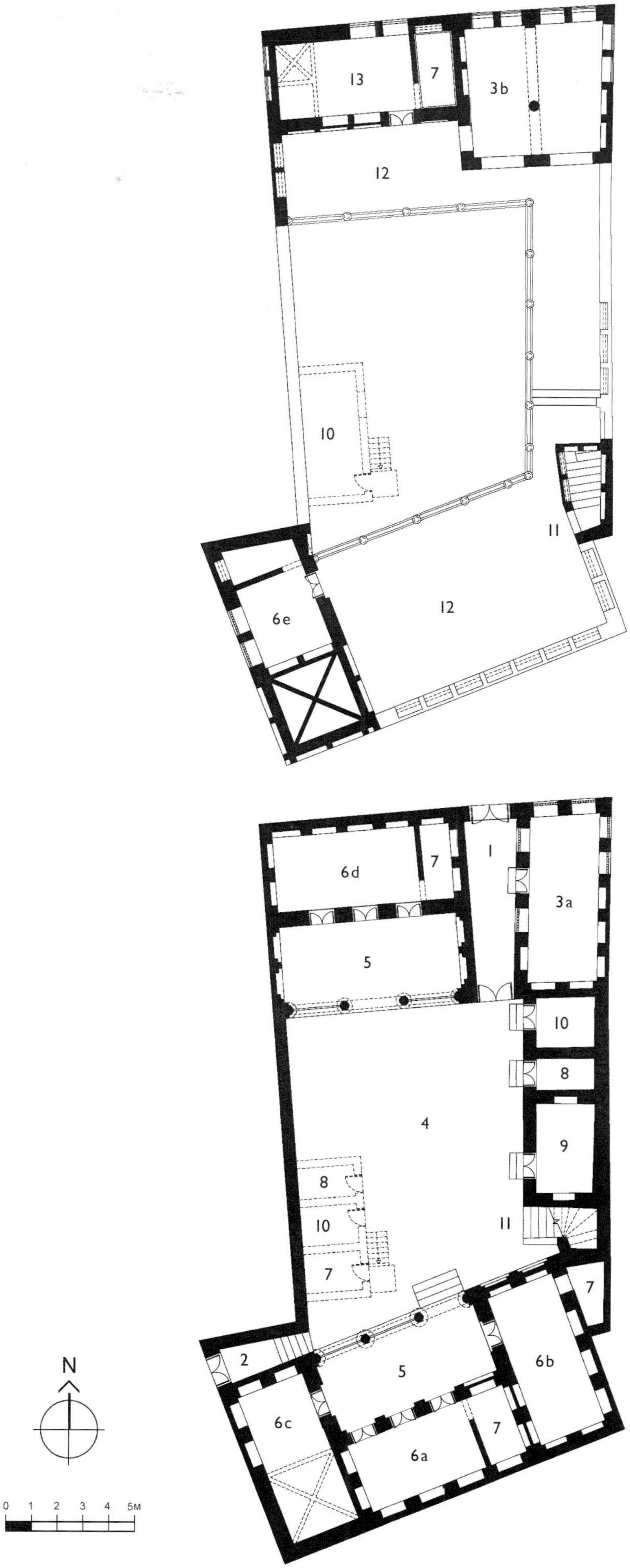

Left:
Ventilation screens are punctuated by clerestory arched openings in the first floor summer *majlis*, in a photograph from the 1980s.

Below:
The evening view of the windtower on the north-east corner of the house, revealing the rich textures of the hand-rendered finish.

its east boundary and 27m long on its west boundary, projecting forward, proud of its two neighbouring buildings. Granted a plot in the Bastakiya, the first house was made of *areesh*. In preparation for the marriage of his son, Mir Ahmed Mir Abdulwahid Amiri (1917-95), to Khadija, daughter of his uncle Abudulrazak, Mir Abdulwahid replaced the *areesh* with a masonry house. The new house was completed in 1940, in time for the wedding celebrations.

Initially Mir Abdulwahid and his family together with his younger brother, Mir Abdullah Mir Ali, and his family were all living in the house. Then in the late 1940s Mir Abdulwahid Mir Ali, with his youngest son, Mir Abdulrahman, moved to Kuwait to expand the family's business. Mir Abdullah stayed in the house until 1957, when he bought the house that would become the Majlis Gallery (see Chapter 9).

The story of the house was told to us by one of Mir Ahmed Mir Abdulwahid's four surviving sons, Dr Mohammed Hadi Amiri, the second of seven children. Born in Bombay in 1947, Dr Amiri first went to Al Saeedi School, in the former house of Sheikh Rashid by the Creek, before he attended Al Shaab School and later Dubai Secondary School. With a PhD in biological sciences from University College London, he now teaches at UAE University in Al Ain, and is one of the Bastakiya's many professionals.

The house has no projecting porch. Owing to the narrowness of the plot, the *majlis* runs parallel to a long entrance lobby. Doors at the inner end close access into the corner of the family courtyard beyond. Dr Amiri's father being a prominent merchant, there were often guests staying in what is remembered as a very lively *majlis*.

On entering the courtyard, there was a pair of rooms immediately to the left (east), which in restoration have been combined as one. The first was a store. The next was the latrine, directly accessible from the courtyard. Adjacent to it was the kitchen, which lacked an oven. Unusually, there was never a tree or garden of any sort in the courtyard. It was always just sand, there being no well and the ground being too saline for anything to grow.

As well as the ladies' entrance door at the north-west corner of the courtyard, there was a second small door on its south-west corner. This led onto a narrow *sikka* between the next house (since demolished), where they kept goats and chickens. The west boundary wall to the courtyard was much higher than it is now, giving more seclusion to the upper floor.

The house has two living wings, on the north and south sides of the courtyard. On the north side, a handsome three-bay verandah (*sabaat*) fronts a three-door inner room (*sideri*), occupied by Mir Abdullah and his family, until they moved away. They also used the first floor summer room immediately above it. Over each pair of doors is a series of fine arched perforated gypsum screens, *panjara*, in beautiful geometric designs. These *panjara*, together with those on the first floor external elevations give this house a very special architectural identity. In reconstruction two shuttered windows on the north elevation have been added at first floor level, replacing two formerly screened openings.

Right:
Dr Amiri emphasized to us that academic achievement would not have been possible for his generation without the generous support and encouragement received from the late ruler of Dubai, Sheikh Maktoum bin Rashid Al-Maktoum.

When Mohammed was young, the east 'corner room' was home to Mohammed's grandparents. Mir Abdulwahid was a very charismatic man, and entertained many visitors in the first floor summer *majlis.*

The central room was another 'three-doors room', the parents' bedroom. On the left side of the bedroom was the washroom, and Mohammed remembered the room appearing very much larger than it actually is. The south-west corner room (known as the Badgir Room), with a windtower, was used by the whole family to rest during summer after the midday meal. It worked very well between 1pm and 3pm. But at night it was quite 'silent', with no breeze at all. The room came to be furnished with sofas brought from India, and the *sideri* fitted with a bedroom suite. These furnishings became the talk of the town, with the sofas being lent out for many weddings.

Dr Amiri remembers food from his childhood. 'Meals consisted of a substantial breakfast. In winter this would be bread (*waggafi*) with honey and fried eggs. In summer, broad beans with fresh dates, yoghurt and bread. Grandmother made the bread early in the morning after her dawn prayers, and when she didn't a servant would buy Iranian bread from the baker. He would take a stripped palm stem with him, and the baker would cut a notch for each piece purchased. At the end of the month Father would pay based on cuts in the stick. Lunch would be rice and fish, with meat (goat) on Fridays. Fresh fruit was rare. In summer there would be lemons, mangos and oranges, brought from Bombay by a friend of my father. We would share 3-6 pieces of fruit with our neighbours. In winter there were dried dates and dried fruit, such as apricots. We had fresh vegetables, onions, radishes, tomatoes and herbs. In earlier days the evening meal was very simple, bread with oil, or fish paste, yoghurt and tea. If there were guests then we would have kebabs. As life styles began to change, the main meal moved to late afternoon and the range of foodstuffs increased with the availability of canned items.'

A small separate two-storey wing against the west wall of the courtyard was added in about 1961, constructed in concrete. It consisted of a ground floor bathroom, flushing lavatory and small store, and an additional bedroom with its own stair, which was only ever used for storage.

A winding staircase leads up between the kitchen and the grandparents' room to the roof terrace. Today the stair is covered, but it was open in the past. Next to it, and above the ground floor *majlis* is the 'square room', Grandfather's summer *majlis.* This room was never completed, and was open on the courtyard side. It is a cool and airy place with a series of rectangular perforated screens, decorated with a mixture of floral vase and geometric designs, each with a semi-circular arched opening above. The summer room thus caught the breezes from the creek on two sides. In the reconstruction, glazed doors have been added, a central circular column has been omitted and the screens and arched openings above have been glazed, as elsewhere, so that the room can be air-conditioned.

In summer the family slept on the roof, outside the south room used by Dr Amiri as a bedroom when he was a student. Because of the heavy morning dew, the youngsters would squeeze with their mattresses into his tiny room. His bed was at the south end and the alcoves were lined with his books. There

Above:
A reconstructed window in Mir Abdullah's first floor summer room, looking towards the Creek.

Below:
The summer *majlis* is still a meeting room – but one that has been modernised. Generous openings picked up afternoon breezes from the Creek.

Right:
This 1976 photograph taken from the east shortly before the house was deserted shows grandfather's summer *majlis* without a roof. The main *majlis* is on the ground floor below.

Below:
A photograph from 1970 of the front (north) elevation provides a glimpse of the courtyard through the open entrance door.

were two containers of water: sweet water for drinking; brackish for bathing. The original ceiling had mangrove *chandals* as opposed to sawn beams today. There was one opening with a *panjara* (not the windscoops as reconstructed).

The family had permanent piped water towards the end of the 1950s, and soon afterwards sufficient electricity for lights and fans. That was a real luxury. By the end of the 1960s they had a proper electrical supply, and were able to run air conditioning. The first air conditioning unit was put into the corner room for the grandparents. In due course the windtower was sealed. The family vacated the house, moving to a villa in Jumeirah in 1977.

7

House of Sheikh Mohammed Shareef Abdulrahman Al Ulama

Surely the grandest of the surviving houses, this impressive building shows Bastaki architecture at its apogee. Sheikh Mohammed Shareef was a religious teacher and the ruler's legal advisor. His daughter-in-law arrived in Dubai in 1952 and vividly describes family life within its walls.

Above:
As water became available for irrigation in the 1970s, doves proliferated, sharing with gargoyles the roof edge of the first floor verandah.

Opposite:
The rich textures of old timber against gypsum plastered Persian arches and palm-headed columns frame a skyline of windtowers. This winter scene from 1976 contains surely some of the finest architecture in the Bastakiya.

Bibiya was born in Lingeh. Her grandfather was a pearl merchant and had a house with four windtowers. Her grandmother's three brothers were pearl divers, and would throw the oyster shells onto the roof of the house where she would extract the pearls.

The house was one of their five family homes in Lingeh, and is still standing. From the age of 2½, Bibiya was brought up in Karachi by her grandmother, speaking Hindi and Khudmooni (Bastaki), and learning English. She went to a mixed secondary school, playing cricket and football with the boys, until her sister told on her. She passed her matriculation despite hating maths. She and her cousin Abdullah married in 1952. Her father-in-law, Sheikh Mohammed Shareef, was legal advisor to the ruler of Dubai, Sheikh Rashid. While pregnant, Bibiya insisted on going to her future home in Dubai; she was so excited to see it, even though she knew she would have to return to Karachi in time for the birth.

Daily life in the new home had its own particular rhythm. Abdullah worked in the office with his father; she only saw him at night. Their family business was trading in textiles and foodstuffs. At midday Abdullah ate with

Above:
Sheikh Mohammed Shareef Al Ulama was an *ulama*, a religious teacher and the legal advisor to Sheikh Rashid, the ruler of Dubai.

Left:
This 1976 view of the south-east corner of the house shows the introduction of steel framed and glazed windows and overhead power cables, combined with the first signs of neglect to the original fabric.

Right:
Diagonal timber fencing screens and a masonry partition at door height enclose the western verandah. A slender concrete blockwork pier supports a precarious balcony above.

Below:
Abdullah Mohammed Al Ulama, Bibiya's husband, photographed at the time they were married in Karachi.

his father and men from the office. Then they returned to the office; in the evening they were again in the *majlis*.

As well as parents-in-law there were three other brothers, Ahmed, Abdulrahman and Abdulraheem, two of whom were married, and sisters Fatima, Miryam and Asma, all living in the house, together with a good number of children – maybe thirty or more people in all, but the house was big enough so that it never felt crowded.

Men and women took their meals separately. The men ate first, and the women and children would eat what was left. There were about ten women who would eat together. It was always fish curry with onions, poured over a

mound of rice. On Fridays, Bibiya's father-in-law would slaughter a goat.

Before electricity, paraffin lamps were used at night. In the mid-1950s an electric line was strung over from Sheikh Rashid's house (where the Ruler's office would later be built). Each nearby house was allowed one hundred-watt light bulb. Bibiya suggested they put it in the middle of the house so that everyone benefited. This house had neither mains water nor electricity. In the 1950s the family bought their first paraffin fridge from Aden, and they regularly provided their neighbours with ice. The black and white television that they had in the late 1960s was battery powered.

Bibiya learnt to drive. Her husband was initially against it and shocked that she would have to sit next to a strange man. She wore her *abaya*, but removed her veil. She encouraged other women to get their licences, thereby attaining greater freedom.

She had her first two babies in Karachi and then had the third in Al Maktoum hospital with an Indian lady doctor. Hers was the first delivery in the hospital. In the early days they were rowed across the Creek in an *abra* and then walked for half an hour over the soft sand. Later she used to drive patients and accompany pregnant women to the Rashid Hospital.

Mrs Tripp, wife of the British Political Agent, invited Bibiya to discuss founding a society. Bibiya invited her back to meet a group of women, and thus the Women's Society was born. Until they had their own building, they

Above:
The sculptured form of the traditional Bastaki kitchen chimney, as well as television aerials, contribute to a skyline of windtowers in this 1976 photograph.

Right:
The formal plan of this house is made complex by its many small mezzanine rooms, particularly in the north wing, requiring a number of staircases.

1. Entrance lobby
2. Doorkeeper
3. Ladies' entrance
4. Courtyard
5. Verandah
6. Sleeping rooms
   a) Sheikh Mohammad Shareef
   b) Mir Mohammad Salah
   c) Unmarried sisters
   d) Unmarried son
   e) Ahmed and Fatima
   f) Abdullah and Bibiya
7. Wash rooms
8. Latrine
9. Ladies' sitting room
10. Well
11. Kitchen
12. Storerooms
13. Stairs
14. *Majlis*
15. Sleeping roof
16. Enclosed balcony
17. Open balcony

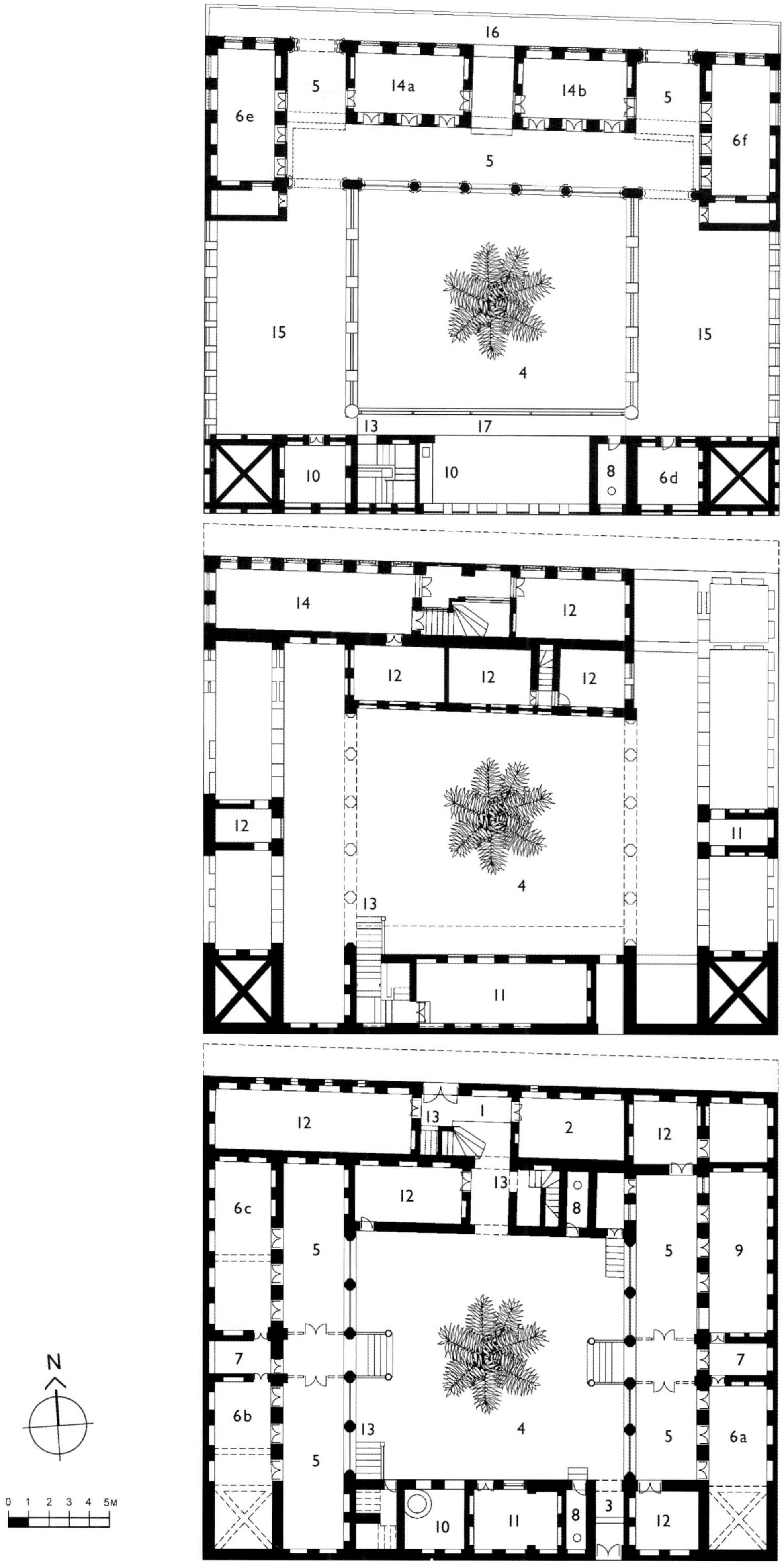

Above:
A view of the windtowers on the south-east and south-west corners of the house in 1972. The south-east windtower is massive with the openings on each face divided into narrow slots. The south-west tower (in the foreground) is simpler, each side with three openings. Here the head of each slot is finished with a stylised pair of prancing peacocks facing each other.

met weekly in each other's houses. Bibiya voluntarily taught knitting, embroidery, sewing, cooking and English every day in her house to thirty or forty women. She continued as an active member of the UAE Women's Society, serving as President for thirty years, and made a lasting contribution to improving the role of women within the community.

Through the 1970s, the house gradually emptied. Her eldest brother-in-law moved out with his family, leaving the family business to set up on his own. Then another brother left to engage in the gold trade. Finally Bibiya's own family left in 1974, taking their elderly mother and an unmarried brother, moving to three new villas that they had built on a large plot near the textile souq. The house stood empty, the family living in these villas until they moved to the future suburb of Al Barsha in 1985.

The land on which the house stood was in the area that had been reclaimed from the Creek, the work being undertaken by families of the Bastakiya. The house was built on a plot 28.8m by 23.5m in around 1940. Ostad Mohammed Ahmed Al Banna was the mason with the decorative work being carried out by Ostad Ghulum Ali.

There are a number of special architectural features. The colonnaded verandah in front of the first floor rooms which overlooks the courtyard has a row of handsome palm-headed columns supporting the rectangular frame above, with elegant Persian brackets arching between. The colonnade is separated from the open lobbies between the northern rooms, by lintels supported on brackets shaped as lion's feet, a similar detail to one that was used in the Farouk house (Dar al Nadwa). The many ventilation screens above the doors and windows on both floors provide beauty and delight in their variations of flower-in-vase motifs. Similarly the decorated screens around the courtyard edges of the roof terraces contribute to one of the most architecturally mature houses within the Bastakiya.

Renovated between 1996 and 2000, the house now provides office accommodation for the Historic Buildings Section of the Dubai Municipality. We had the privilege of sharing Bibiya's first return to the house, 32 years after leaving it.

We first walked to the front – the Creek facing side – of the house. The Creek originally came within a few metres of the house. The ground has been raised around the house so that the front door is now below the present ground level, with a ramped access. The large doors were used daily by the

Right:
The finely modelled south-east windtower that cooled the sleeping room of Sheikh Mohammed Shareef, viewed from the verandah on the north wing.

men, who would knock to gain entry, otherwise they were always shut. There was a second door into the courtyard – now only a timber frame.

Bibiya recalled that the *abras* used to beach immediately outside the house. She pointed out the windows to the majlis on a mezzanine floor which Sheikh Mohammed Shareef used. However Abdulrazak Abdulrahim's *majlis* was the main meeting place in this part of the Bastakiya, and her father-in-law was more often there than in his own. A timbered louvred balcony runs the full length of the building above the level of the *majlis* windows.

We returned to the former ladies' door. Its lobby used to be closed from the courtyard by a second door. As Bibiya was about to enter, she looked around her, remembering that all of her neighbours had been relatives. All her own children attended the Qur'an school. Although an *ulama* (a learned man), her father-in-law never taught, though he performed wedding ceremonies.

In the courtyard Bibiya remembered that there had been a large palm tree in the middle. Goats kept in a wired pen around the palm were milked by her mother-in-law. They had no chickens; eggs and cows milk were purchased from one of the neighbours.

The steps to the east led up to the suite occupied by Sheikh Mohammed Shareef. There were two inner rooms originally lined with doors. The room to the north was a *panjdari* and that with the windtower a *sideri*. He had his bed immediately below the windtower, even at nights. There was no other

Above:
A view of the courtyard, looking north-east. Summer rooms sit within a wide verandah above screens ventilating mezzanine stores.

furniture in the house, except rugs and cushions. The windtower was closed off in winter with timber boards placed over the top. The verandah in front used to be divided by pairs of doors in walls at either side at the top of the central steps which were always horribly broken. On the adjoining verandah the women all met with Fatima, wife of Abdullah's eldest brother, who would tie her three year-old daughter's leg to the timber balustrade, to keep her from wandering.

In the west wing opposite, the same plan was repeated. Abdullah's sister Fatima and husband Mir Mohammed Saleh occupied the *sideri* windtower room, and two unmarried sisters Miryam and Asma lived in the *panjdari*.

In the north wing, a ground floor storeroom below the majlis was lit and

Right:
A view of the east wing, with its verandahs and bedrooms behind. The small stair on the left leads to the first floor and roof. Because the house was set so close to the Creek, the ground floor rooms were raised well above the level of the courtyard.

vented by small openings (now glazed in), used to store rice and flour. The doorkeeper's room was opposite. A steep, dark stairway led up to the low-ceilinged mezzanine stores, and two store rooms. A second winding stair led up to two further mezzanine stores for trunks and cases. It was dark and eerie, and was known as the 'jinn's house'.

In 1970, Bibiya had described family migration upstairs during the early 1950s. In its later years the house was always too crowded for any summer migration to take place between ground floor and first floor rooms. In summer though they all slept on the roof.

At the top of the stairs on the south side of the courtyard the cantilever verandah link collapsed a couple of years before they left the house, and was never repaired. It is now roofed over. A square room abutting the windtower on the south-east was the bedroom of a brother-in-law, with an enclosed latrine next to it. That on the south-west was Fatima's (Ahmed's wife's) kitchen.

The well on the ground floor was accessed through a hole in the roof, with a *chandal* above for the pulley. The room facing the courtyard is a product of the conversion to offices. On the roof there used to be a tall rectangular chimney with pointed conical finials, serving the oven in the kitchen below.

The principal first floor living rooms were along the northern side of the courtyard, facing the Creek, and concealed from view behind the screened balcony. The rooms were in two L-shaped pairs, separated by a central passage to the balcony, and with open areas between the two rooms of each pair. The north-west rooms were Ahmed and Fatima's suite. The space between the corner rooms was enclosed with plywood to create an area for the children to sleep and play. The north-east pair of rooms was Abdullah and Bibiya's suite. The central rooms served as a dayroom, and the corner rooms were for sleeping, each with an adjoining wash room.

Above:
The north Creek-facing frontage of the house with its distinctive timber balcony, and mezzanine windows below.

Below left:
Part of the first floor summer living rooms, which are divided by a clear view of the Creek. Beyond the summer rooms a balcony runs the entire length of the Creek-side of the building.

Right:
Today the building provides an approriate home to the Historic Buildings Section, ran by Ahmed Mahmoud Ahmed.

Below:
Bibiya describes her former home to the Prince of Wales and the Duchess of Cornwall during their visit to the Bastakiya in February 2007.

The Creek-facing balcony verandah was a great favourite with the women, who sat on rugs watching the water without being observed. They would wait here for the men to come home from the souq. Bibiya taught groups of local women to do *talli* embroidery in the evenings. They sat on the verandahs next to the bedrooms, unless meeting in a large group on the ground floor. Later Bibiya had carpets to cover the balcony floor. Bibiya turned her end of it into a kitchen for a while – until the wind gusted and it caught fire from the flames of her gas burner! The balcony was badly damaged and had to be repaired. After that she had her own kitchen built of plywood onto the end of her bathroom.

Abdullah and Bibiya's bed was screened by a curtain from the six children she brought up in this room. Infants slept in a wooden rocking cradle. The sitting room was very breezy, overlooking the Creek, with shutters and doors on both sides.

Back in the courtyard, Bibiya spoke of her father-in-law who died aged 59 of a heart attack, in 1954. She told us how he had filled in the well because fish appeared in it. He and Bibiya became very close; she would cook and knit for him and his wife Amina, as well as for Abdullah and her own children. At first the women sewed by hand until Bibiya asked her father-in-law if he could get them a sewing machine. Within half an hour, a Singer machine arrived from the souq on the head of one of his staff.

On Sheikh Mohammed's sudden death, Dr McCauley was brought over from the Maktoum Hospital to sit with the body for 24 hours, in case he might revive. The body was buried in the nearby Sheikhs' graveyard. The house remained in mourning for a full year, with black everywhere.

When it looked likely that the house would be demolished, two of Sheikh Mohammed Shareefs' sons made a plan to open the house as a restaurant, but nothing came of it. Today, visitors can still view this fine example of a large Bastakiya house, in its new role as the offices of the Historic Buildings Section.

8

House of Abdullah Mohammed Al Bastaki

The windtower of this house was used in research for this book, continuous recordings of air temperature and movement being taken inside the tower, and in the room below. The house possesses fine examples of traditional decoration. The family left the Bastakiya in 1982, and restoration was completed in 2005.

Above:
A fine *panjara* screen with an unusual peacock carving, instead of the more common flowers-in-vase motif.

Opposite:
The courtyard in 2005 showing the windtower, the decorative gypsum screens surrounding the roof on the inner side and the fine pillars of the verandah.

Ahmed Abdullah Al Bastaki was born in Dubai in 1928. His wife Haleema is the daughter of Sheikh Abdulraheem Mohammed Al Janahi (See Chapter 10). Haleema and Ahmed were neighbours but they never met or saw each other before marriage. She was 17 and he about 36. He had remained single, as a dutiful son, helping his father, although his brothers had both married around the age of 21-22. His father eventually put pressure on him to marry. Today Ahmed and Haleema live in Al Jafeleya district of Dubai with their son Mahmoud. Born in 1970, Mahmoud is an executive with the Ports, Customs and Free Zone Authority.

The date carved into the main door shows that the house was completed in 1947. It was built by Ahmed's father, Abdullah Mohammed Al Bastaki, who was born in Bastak in 1899. Abdullah was a merchant in the family

Above:
Ahmed Abdullah Mohammed Al Bastaki was born in Dubai in 1928.

Left:
Abdullah Mohammed Al Bastaki (born in Bastak in 1899), for whom the house was built, joined the family business, trading in textiles in Dubai.

Right:
The plans show the house's formal planning around a central courtyard. The kitchen and sleeping rooms occupy much of the ground floor. The verandah runs along the length of the courtyard. The sleeping roof, wash rooms and the summer room are located on the first floor, the mezzanine floor being used for stores.

1 a) Entrance lobby
  b) Entrance lobby
2. Ladies' entrance
3. *Majlis*
4. Courtyard
5. Verandah
6. Sleeping rooms
  a) Ahmed Abdullah
  b) Abdulrahman Abdullah
  c) Abdullah Mohammed
  d) Windtower room
7. Wash rooms
8. Well
9. Kitchen
10. Incomplete room
11. Stair
12. Storerooms
13. Summer room (Amin Abdullah)
14. Sleeping roof
15. Latrine

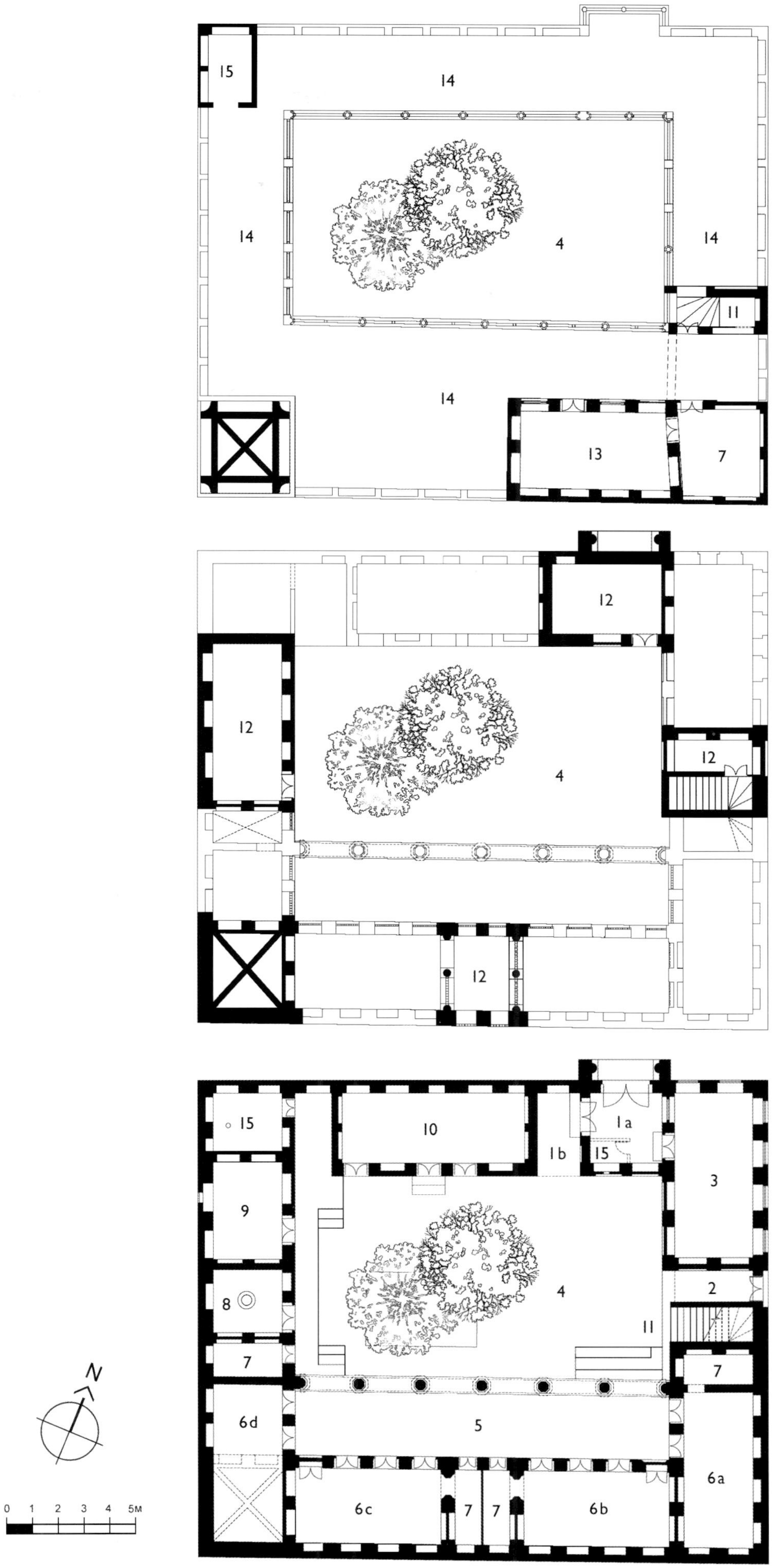

Left:
The handsome teak door with its wicket is the original.

Above:
The porch faces into a narrow alley so that its grandeur can only be appreciated obliquely.

business, importing and selling blankets and bed-linen. His first shop was in Bur Dubai. Later he rented one in Deira, in a busy part of the souq, where he was very successful. When his sons were young, he used to take them to help him and to be trained. There was no-one else working in the shop, so the boys needed to be there if he was called away. His business was entirely in Dubai, not requiring him to travel. Abdullah died in 1967, and his four sons moved into separate occupations. The oldest, Abdul-Rahman, became the family representative. Amin had his own shoe shop in Deira and Ibrahim joined the British Bank of the Middle East (BBME) for 25 years. At the age of 52, Ahmed joined the national telephone company, working as a security guard in a maintenance depot, until he retired in 1994.

Right:
The edges of the windtower are highlighted in blue and its crenellated top is painted with doves in black outline, sitting behind a pattern imitating a wrought iron balustrade.

Below:
The original deed from the Ruler, which reads:

'In the name of the one God, from Saeed bin Maktoum Al Hasher to everyone who sees this document. Regarding the areesh house related to Abdullah bin Mohammed Al Bastaki who is in Dubai, which is next to the new Farouk areesh house to the south, which land east to west is 50 dheraa, and its width is south to north 50 dheraa. We permit him to build his boundary wall with gypsum and stone as he wishes, and no-one is to object, except if the above mentioned person wishes to leave Dubai forever to wherever he wants, then he has no authority to dispose of this house, to sell or rent or mortgage or grant it to anyone else, but this house will revert to ourself, and this must to be clear to everyone.'

This was written by Salim bin Abdullah, 21 Ramadan 1364 (30 August 1945).

Signed and sealed:
Saeed bin Maktoum Al Hasher

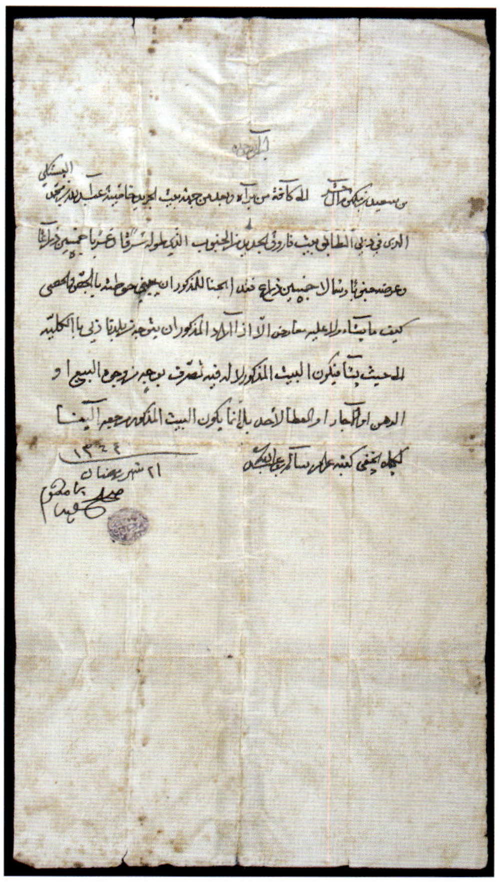

Constructed on a plot about 22.3m long by 18.6m deep, the masonry house replaced a larger *areesh* house, the walls of which had extended right up to the adjoining buildings. The new house was built in sections over the period of a year.

An earlier *areesh* house had been destroyed in the fire of 1940. The fire in 1955 burnt fiercely in this area too, damaging the masonry house quite badly, burning the exposed *chandals* of the windtower and those of some ceilings. Abdulrahman tried to put out the flames above him by spraying them with water, using the pipe from a *qalyoon*. None of the roofs collapsed, but damage was extensive and cost 10,000 rupees to repair.

Six masons were involved in the building of this house: Mohammed al Banna, his brother Abdullah, and his sons Aqeel and Abdulkarim, assisted by Ostad Abdulkarim Parawi and Ostad Hassan Janahi. The decoration was all carved and painted by Abdulkarim al Banna. The row of birds at the top of the windtower was Abdulkarim's choice of decoration. Ahmed does not know any other windtowers that were painted with birds or other animals. The house was finished just before Sheikh Saeed's new Customs Building; Abdullah Mohammed knew Sheikh Saeed very well, but it was then a small community.

The house is entered from its north side, where there is a projecting porch framed with traditional pilasters and crowned with a pair of perforated gypsum screens, with flower-in-vase motifs.

Apart from the row of shuttered windows of the *majlis* wrapping the north-east corner, and the discreet ladies' entrance next to it, the high walls enclosing the house are blank and austere, giving no hint of what lies within. In contrast, at the south-west corner, a single windtower with painted decoration rises elegantly 14 metres above the ground, marking the house as unusual. The simple lively drawings of doves contrast with the stylised forms of peacocks on one of the Saheefi house windtowers. While not as grand as the windtowers found on the former Bukhash house or on the Sheikh Mohammed Shareef houses, this is unquestionably the most delightful surviving windtower in the Bastakiya. Possessing delicacy and elegance, with a combination of sculptural and two dimensional decoration, it shows the artistic skills of the masons at their very best.

From the main entrance, an enclosed lobby gives indirect access to the family courtyard on the right, or on the left into an elegantly proportioned *majlis*. Its shuttered windows face east and north, to receive Creek breezes funnelled through the lanes.

In the now paved courtyard, there were once three trees, now all dead: an Indian almond (*loz*), a fig and a pomegranate. The last survivor struggled on uncared for until it failed to come into leaf in 2006. (A shoot from the *loz* was planted at their present villa.) The trees were enclosed within a rough fence. There was an *areesh* goat shelter next to it.

Below:
The arcade of the *sabaat*, which being north facing is permanently shaded. Behind are the panelled timber doors to two bedrooms, with a wash room in between. The decorative screens above provided ventilation.

Above:
Details of the magnificent *panjara* screens, with flowers-in-vases and, most unusually, a parrot. Before restoration, traces of blue pigment were still visible, as in this picture.

As part of the reconstruction, the north side of the courtyard has been completed with a tall room *sideri* (a three-doors room) something that Ahmad had always intended to finish for himself. When the house was visited in 1970, this was incomplete and was divided into a row of five animal pens, using concrete blocks. Goats, chickens and pigeons were housed there. (Haleema still keeps livestock at Al Jafeleya, including 4 or 5 goats for milk. She thinks that goat's milk is healthy, especially for children, regretting that the present generation do not drink it.)

The north-east corner room was a traditional latrine with its floor raised over the pit below. On the west side of the courtyard the kitchen was situated next to the well room. In 1970 the well was still in use although there was a piped water supply. In the kitchen there was a primus stove, and a wood fired grill set into the floor. There was no chimney and the walls and ceiling were typically smoke blackened. The rear wall comprised regularly spaced built-in masonry shelves. Cooking pots were stacked on the floor. Over the well and above the entrance lobby were mezzanine storerooms. These were reached by wooden ladders from the courtyard, and were used to store household things not presently required, such as the cradle, or extra pillows and mattresses for guests. A third store over the ladies entrance was reached from the masonry stair up to the roof. This was used for everyday necessities such as rice, sugar, dates and onions, and salted fish.

Across the full length of the south side of the courtyard is a fine verandah, behind a columned arcade of six bays. Being north-facing this benefits from being permanently shaded. There were rooms off each end, that in the south-west having the windtower. In summer the windtower was used by Abdullah for an afternoon nap when he came back from his shop. The two pairs of doors would be kept open. The windtower might also be used to cool someone who was sick.

In winter Abdullah slept in the next room, which was his main bedroom. He had a large Indian four-poster bed. Two *sideri* run parallel to the length of the *sabaat*, separated by a washing room. When two families were using these rooms, (the families of Abdullah Mohammed and his eldest son

Abdulrahman), the washroom was partitioned, to provide one for each family. A beautiful feature of the house is the mezzanine storage area over the washing room. On each side carved gypsum screens with flower-in-vase motif are framed between traditional short Persian columns highlighted with blue paint against the white gypsum. These screen the low mezzanine area, and with a pair of barred windows onto the lane, this upper area glows with daylight that filters into the rooms on each side. These two rooms were originally designed as a suite, there being no barrier for sound between them.

Abdulrahman's room was shared with his wife and their three daughters. After the death of his father, Abdulrahman occupied both rooms. In his original room can still be seen traces of flowers-in-vase wall paintings, which originally adorned both rooms. The same stencils that were used for the carved gypsum screens were probably applied to these walls, and then painted over (see Chapter 11).

Over each of the doors and recesses between the *sabaat* and the inner rooms are a series of decorative *panjara*, further displaying the talent of Ostad Abdulkarim. Again there are bird motifs, in the form of peacocks displaying their tail feathers, and parrots perched in foliage. These alternate with differing flower-in-vase patterns. Before restoration, traces of blue pigment were still visible on these.

Above:
Abdulrahman's former bedroom shows all the typical features of a Bastakiya room, including two surviving murals. The AC unit and electric sockets were added during restoration.

Opposite:
View through the main bedroom wing with the wash room and mezzanine store above it between the two rooms.

Above:
The summer room on the roof in around 1970, showing the rich range of textures on the original building as it weathered.

Left:
The summer room following its renovation in 2005.

Above:
The *majlis*, set in the north-east corner, receives breeze from the lanes outside. Its two sets of large windows have wooden shutters and are barred for security. Before Amin Abdullah was married, the *majlis* was also his bedroom.

The south-east corner room and an adjoining washroom were occupied by Ahmed, his wife, four sons and two daughters. Ahmed also had an Indian four-poster bed – these two beds were the only pieces of modern furniture in the house, apart from the babies' cradle.

Next to the ladies' entrance is a staircase to the roof. The roof is enclosed by solid screens for privacy. In earlier days these used to be windscoops, with the courtyard parapet formed by decorative gypsum screens. A summer suite was built on the southeast corner, with perforated screens and arched openings to maximise through-ventilation. When Abdullah's youngest son Amin married, he and his wife permanently occupied this, with their six sons and two daughters. In the 1960s a plywood extension was added to serve as a kitchen.

Although electricity was connected, they did not have air conditioning in the house until 1976, when a hole was broken through the wall for an air conditioning unit in Ahmed Abdullah's and Haleema's room.

When the house was most densely occupied it provided a home for 23, together with any visitors. When the family left the Bastakiya in 1982 they first moved to Al Qoz, where the Sheikh had compensated them with a new plot. They later moved to Al Jafeleya to be more centrally located.

9

House of Mir Abdullah Amiri

Known today as the 'Majlis Gallery', this house has an unusually well-recorded family history – one that includes both that of early owners and of the expatriates who later made it their home. Now successfully converted for commercial use, it demonstrates the potential vitality of the Bastakiya as a conservation area.

Above:
This photograph taken in the 1980s shows the entrance porch to a European home, with a temporary roof shading the balcony.

Opposite:
The elegant though sturdy tusk-like leaf motif of the entrance archway decoration contrasts with the roughly trimmed chandal poles supporting the ceiling. Plastered benches on either side of the entrance provide a place for social interaction without intruding into the privacy of the house.

Entering the courtyard of the Majlis Gallery on a Thursday morning in winter to find it buzzing with a class of painters, their easels set up around its walled garden of bougainvillea and shady henna tree, is to appreciate the benefit that careful conservation can bring to the urban fabric of a city. It is not enough only to restore old buildings, a massive task in itself. The key is to create meaningful uses for the buildings, to bring community and life back into the restored environment. The Majlis Gallery achieves just that.

The gallery is the oldest established art gallery in Dubai, in what has always been one of the more visible houses in the area, facing the road on the southern edge of the Bastakiya. It was one of the first houses to be lived in by Europeans, and the first to be converted for commercial use.

Above:
This 1970 photograph shows the distinctive frontage of the house. The *majlis* with large barred windows and arched recesses is on the left, with the roof enclosed by windscoops.

Below left:
The house was one of the first houses to be occupied by Europeans. The distinctive interiors adapted attractively to western usage.

Right:
The unadorned windtower viewed across the courtyard. The interior parapet of the roof is perforated to encourage air flow across the surface of the roof. Projecting gargoyles drain the flat roof after occasional rain, throwing water well away from the walls.

Below:
The open entrance doors offer a glimpse of the interior beyond. Although the lobby openings are offset, it is possible to see into the courtyard. A curtain was therefore used over the inner opening to provide privacy.

The masonry house was built by Abdullah Hassan Awadhi in 1945. He sold it in 1957 to Mir Abdullah Amiri (1912-78) a wholesale merchant, trading mainly in textiles and tea. The Amiri family originates from the Bastak area, and before moving to this house lived closer to the Creek.

Ali Amiri, who is a partner with Alison Collins in the Majlis Gallery, remembers his childhood growing up in this house and in the Bastakiya with pleasure; the feeling of community, and the convenience of living so close to the creek and to the souq. In the house, children played ball together in the courtyard. Outside, with the neighbourhood's youngsters, marbles and football were popular.

Above:
The imposing frontage of the restored building on the street edge of the Bastakiya.

There used to be no hotels in Dubai, and the house was always full of guests and visitors. People passing by the *majlis* might have thought it was a hotel. They always had guests staying, from Oman, Bahrain, Lingeh and Qatar. On one occasion the Sheikh of Dibba (on the Batinah coast) came to stay for a few days with his entourage, guns and all. When the house became the Majlis Gallery, Ali Amiri gave the enterprise his full support and encouragement. He clearly enjoys the vitality that the Gallery has brought to his old family home, to which he is still strongly attached.

The house is single storey, with a narrow street frontage, and arranged around a long courtyard on a nearly rectangular plot approximately 15 metres wide by 26 metres deep.

The principal room in the house is that with the windtower, which is fronted by a formal verandah across the width of the courtyard. The favourite place to sleep after lunch, all through the hot afternoon until *Asr* prayers, was below the windtower. The door would be shut but all the window shutters kept open. Omani mangoes purchased in the souq, fresh dates and local fruit, such as small bananas, sweet lemon and loz, were put in a bowl of water, with purchased ice and lemon juice, and placed below the windtower to keep them as cool as possible, ready for when everyone awoke.

An interesting feature of the windtower, which can be seen in a number of houses, is where the plan of the tower is smaller than the width of the room it serves. Then the space between the side-wall and the windtower provides a useful high level store.

Right:
The plan of this 1945 Bastakiya house continues to follow the same principles found in older houses. The rooms along the west side of the courtyard were added during the 1960s. Its north-south orientation exposed east and west facing rooms to the morning and afternoon sun.

1. Entrance lobby
2. *Majlis*
a) Seasonal majlis or store
3. Courtyard
4. Kitchen
5. Well
6. Sleeping rooms
7. Wash rooms
8. Family living room
9. Latrine
10. Verandah
11. Stair
12. Sleeping roof

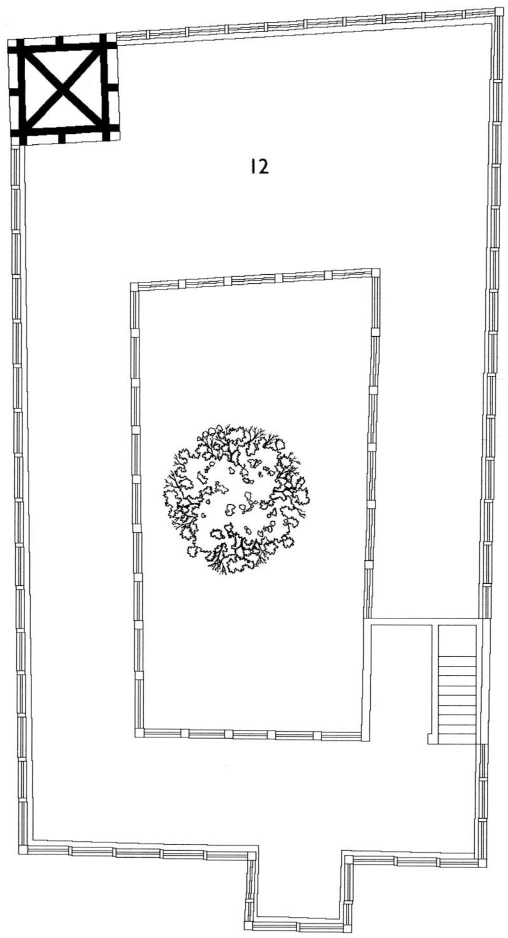

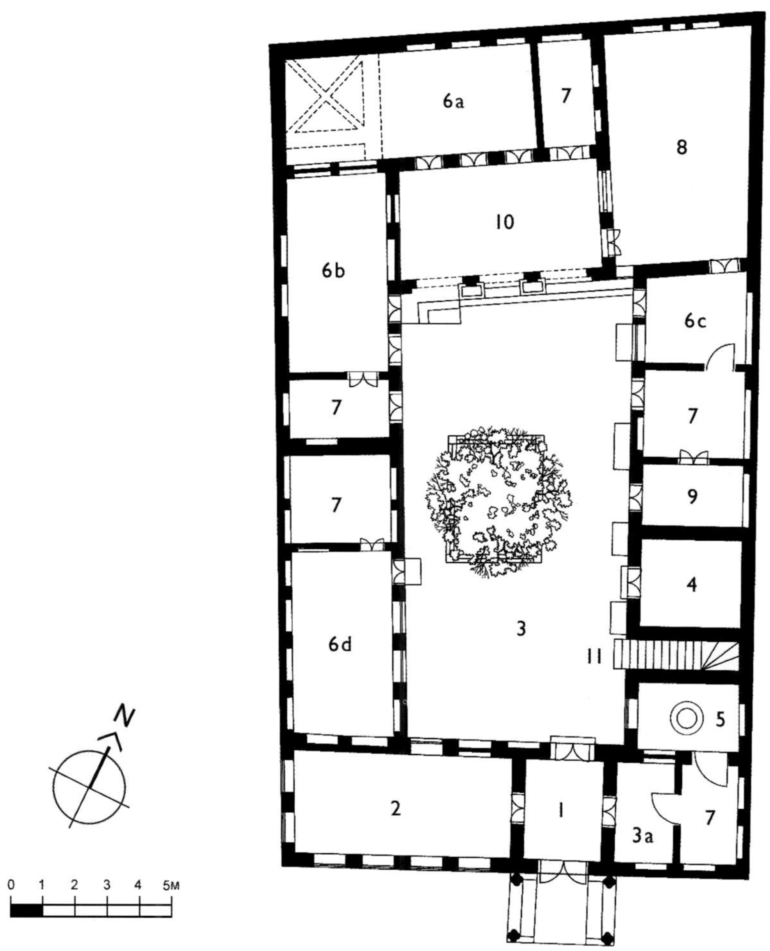

Left:
Below the balustrade and cornice, shallow recessed panels with incised flower-in-vase designs above each opening enliven an otherwise plain wall.

Below left:
The courtyard of the Majlis Gallery, furnished with old furniture and pots.

In summer everyone would sleep on the roof, the perimeter of which was lined with the split wall windscoops. The Amiris used air conditioning only towards the end of their stay in the house. There was a generator close by with a line to the house, enough for light bulbs and ceiling fans until a permanent connection was provided.

There was always only one entrance to the house, with no separate women's entrance. Facing the majlis on the other side of the entrance was a square room that was used during Ramadan for readings from the Qur'an. Sometimes it provided overflow accommodation for the many guests; at other times it served as a store or godown. Later it was converted into a bathroom. Until then, only visitors close to the family could use the latrine accessed from within the family courtyard.

Above:
The south-east corner of the courtyard showing the staircase to the roof, flanked by the former kitchen on the left, and well-room on the right.

On rare occasions, when there were no visitors, the family ate together, with no separation of women and men. They would gather around the *soufra* (a circular mat woven from palm fronds) laid out in one of the larger rooms. When there were visitors the women ate separately in the windtower room.

On the west side of the courtyard were two bedrooms, both with wash rooms. The one next to the *majlis* was added sometime in the later 1960s and served as a bedroom for Mir Abdullah Amiri. The room in the north-east corner was used as a family sitting room. Ali's room was to the south of this, with a washroom and a store between it and the kitchen. This wing has a projecting cantilevered timber verandah roof which provided a little shade over the openings below. The kitchen was next to the stairs up to the roof, with the well room by the entrance on their other side.

In the south-west corner of the courtyard was a raised stone platform, *dechaa*, for sitting on during summer evenings. There were several trees, not just the single henna tree which has survived, enclosed within a low plastered decorated screen wall, framed between distinctive square corner pillars.

Visiting merchants from Iran sometimes brought a young deer as a gift, which would be kept in the courtyard by the children. These would sometimes sleep in the store next to Ali's bedroom. Unfortunately, they never lived very long as pets. Other families also mention having pet deer, but as the animals grew they became ill-suited to life in a courtyard.

The Amiri family all moved out of the house during 1973, after which it was rented to an English couple, Dudley and Lesley Heathcote. In 1978 Alison Collins and her veterinary surgeon husband Dick moved into the house with their first baby, adding two more children in the ten years that followed. Exhibitions were mounted in the windtower room, and during them the Collins would move all their furniture out.

Above:
Detail of a perforated screen. The geometric design is in perfect keeping with the 'chunky' character of this single storey house.

Left:
A corner of the old majlis is now used as one of the display galleries. Fine glassware is well displayed within the shuttered and barred windows.

Right:
Below the windtower: The gallery began as a hobby, with occasional informal exhibitions to show the work of local and visiting artists.

Below:
A carved recessed gypsum panel sits above a barred gallery window, now glazed.

In August 1988, eviction orders were issued by the Municipality. By this time the house was becoming rather dilapidated. There were major structural problems, with part of the roof, which could no longer bear any weight, leaking so badly that rainwater dripped into the rooms below. The Collins moved out of the house, but within four months were advised that they could return. Unfortunately, in the meantime it had been let to a gang of labourers and was now in a terrible state. At this stage they had not envisaged restoring the house, but their four year old son William said, 'Mummy, you mustn't let the house die.' Thankfully, they did not.

In the spring of 1989, a company was formed, and a plan for restoration embarked upon. Architect Dariush Zandi assisted with technical advice. The Majlis Gallery opened with its first exhibition in November 1989.

By 1998 the building was again falling apart. This time, the repairs and restoration were undertaken by the Historic Buildings Section. It was one of the earliest houses in the Bastakiya to be restored by the Municipality. Its restoration took a year during which time the gallery temporarily occupied the adjoining Al Awadi house. The Gallery re-opened in time to celebrate its tenth anniversary, in November 1999. Now, as the municipality owns and maintains all the buildings in the area, there is much greater security of tenure.

Today, the architectural qualities of the house can be appreciated by the many visitors to the Gallery. Rectangular recessed panels over the doors and windows lining the west side of the courtyard frame a variety of flower-in-vase gypsum reliefs, some still highlighted in black charcoal. A dentelle cornice below the parapet screens provides a formality not present in the simpler older east wing, where over each door and window there is simply a small square opening for ventilation.

If the new galleries, boutiques and museums in the recently restored buildings of the Bastakiya, can provide as lively and stimulating an environment as that offered by the Majlis Gallery, the popularity and success of the district will be assured. Sadly, however, there is no longer the sound of the neighbourhood's children at play.

10

House of Sheikh Abdulraheem Mohammed Janahi Al Abbassi

The youngest of the windtower houses in this study, this traditionally planned house was constructed in sand-lime blocks. Integral to the story of the house is its rich social history, which records the life of a revered Imam and his renowned Qur'an school.

Above:
The courtyard can be glimpsed from the entrance of Sheikh Abdulraheem's house. This was formerly the ladies' entrance before the house was divided.

Opposite:
A view of the north side of the courtyard with a palm shading the windtower during the hot midday sun.

The father of Sheikh Abdulraheem Mohammed Janahi was from Janah, one of the villages of Bastak. His mother lived in Shindagha, where he grew up and he may have been born there. When he died in 1996 he was believed to be over 100 years old. At about the age of 15, he went to Lingeh to study the Qur'an and Sharia law with Sheikh Mohammed Ali Sultan Al Ulama, brother of Mohammed Shareef Abdulrahman Al Ulama. He married Fatima, a cousin, in Bastak.

During his early teens he became a pearl diver, based out of Lingeh, and this was to provide his livelihood for twenty years (see box, Chapter 4). He would dive during the summer months, and pursue his Qur'anic studies during the winter.

Mohammed Noor described his grandfather's philosophy: a man should always prove himself; always extend help to others and never be lazy; do anything for anyone but expect nothing in return. Sheikh Abdulraheem was not prepared to live on the support of others, unlike many religious men. He never wanted to be wealthy; rather he became rich from the respect he gained. 'Rarely do you see someone who sacrifices himself entirely for others. He was someone who never complained or said he couldn't do something'. He was devout, straightforward, and never did anything that was *haram*.

Above:
View of the house from the west. The building is undergoing restoration. Constructed of sand-lime blocks, cement has been used in its reconstruction.

Above:
In his younger days, Sheikh Abdulraheem would go pearling for up to four months at a time during the summer. When at sea, the men would look to him to lead prayers, and to offer advice He became a noted navigator of the Gulf, following routes by the stars.

Below:
Mohammed Noor Janahi standing below the windtower in his grandfather's house.

Sheikh Abdulraheem moved back to Dubai, where his mother was already living, probably around 1918. His home, until he ceased diving in the 1930s, remained in Shindagha near the Bin Zayed Mosque, facing the creek. There he would occasionally stand in for the Imam when he was absent. He was close to both Sheikh Juma and to the Ruler, Sheikh Saeed. Sheikh Abdulraheem had a large number of children, but he lost five young sons. Another son had given him a grandchild but died in early manhood. The child, Mohammed Noor, was then raised as a son by Sheikh Abdulraheem and Fatima. He was the only male descendant, whose duty it would be to look after and protect the family. Of the Sheikh's four daughters, two died as children. Maimoona and Haleema both survived to marry, raise families, and teach in his Qur'an school. Haleema's later home is described in Chapter 8.

Fatima had a blind sister, Khair Al Nissa (meaning 'best of women'), who lived with them. She was very active, and ground flour by hand. She never married, but was much respected in the neighbourhood. If children, while playing, saw her come out of the house, they would immediately run to offer her help. She died in 2003, aged 90.

Mohammed Noor recounted one of his grandfather's stories of a trading dhow from Mahara in Yemen that anchored in the creek close to the *areesh* homestead. Sheikh Abdulraheem was away at the time that the *nokhada* and his crew came ashore to erect a shelter, tying their ropes to the poles supporting the house, despite complaints from Fatima that they could see through the *areesh* walls into their house. When the Sheikh returned he found the crew encamped and fearlessly accosted them. They ignored him; he tried to strike the *nokhada*, who was very much taller. The crew took hold of him and the *nokhada* struck him in the chest with his knobkerrie. Abdulraheem left at once to explain the problem to Sheikh Saeed. The next morning the Ruler sent one of his bodyguards, Rashid Al Nazar, to bring the *nokhada* before Judge Sheikh Ali Janahi. The *nokhada* was fined five rupees and told to move his camp further along the Creek. Sheikh Abdulraheem gave two rupees of the fine to Rashid Al Nazar for his assistance. Many years later Mohammed Noor would marry Rashid's granddaughter.

In summer the family used to move to an *areesh* house among a group of palm trees in the dunes beyond the British Political Agency, less than two kilometres away, where it was less humid. People in the Bastakiya considered this was far out in the desert and very dangerous. Asked whether Sheikh Abdulraheem was not afraid that the children would be taken by bedouin to be sold as slaves, he replied, 'No. I am not afraid – I depend on God'.

As the Imam of the Bastakiya, Sheikh Abdulraheem was authorized to issue marriage licences and divorce papers. He established a *maktab*, a Qur'an school, on the plot of which this house is now part. He was especially concerned at the widespread illiteracy, and sought to reduce it. He taught for many years, finally stopping in his early 60s. (See box, Chapter 3.)

He was not only a religious man; he had a great knowledge of traditional herbal remedies. He could treat illnesses and skin diseases, and cared for the dying. Several merchants helped him financially in this work. Abdulraheem would go to the Deira side, collect sick men from the streets and bring them back to an area to the south of the Sheikh's Graveyard. There he had two *areesh* houses, where he treated his patients with herbal infusions. To clean wounds, he used chicken feathers and warm water, covering them with strips of cotton until they were healed. He would then advise the person what to do next or help them to find a job.

The house and school were *areesh* buildings. At the time of the 1955 fire Abdulraheem and Haleema were staying with his son, Khalil, in Kuwait. Both their house and school were completely destroyed, as they had been in the fire of 1940. Afterwards, a sand-lime block house was erected, 24.1m long by 13.9m wide. A schoolroom with a windtower was added later. A second classroom in *areesh*, with a gunny-sack windtower, was put up on the northern half of the plot.

The plot was divided into four during the 1960s: the north-west portion was sold to Abdulraheem Darweesh, the builder of the windtower room; the north-east part was given to a cousin, Sheikh Abdullah Shareef. This house occupied the south of the plot; the south-east part was given to Mohammed Noor and the south-west portion was retained by Sheikh Abdulraheem.

Before the house itself was divided, its main entrance was into the *sikka* at its east end. The bedouin used to bring wood from the desert near the Omani border, in caravans of between five and ten camels. The camels would be set down outside the door and the firewood would be piled inside the courtyard.

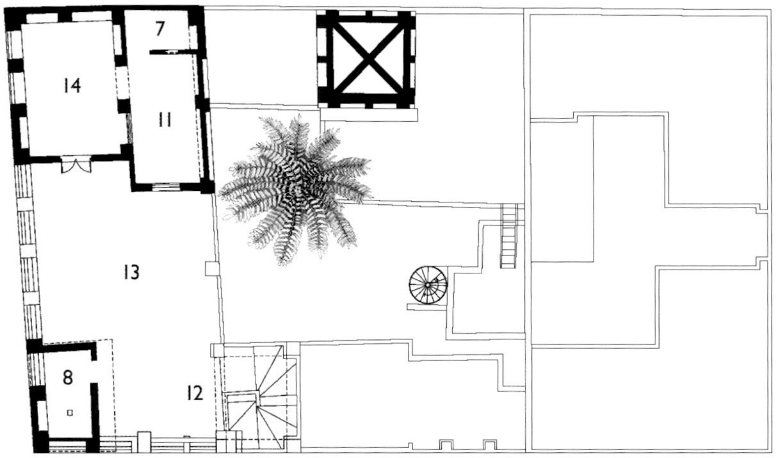

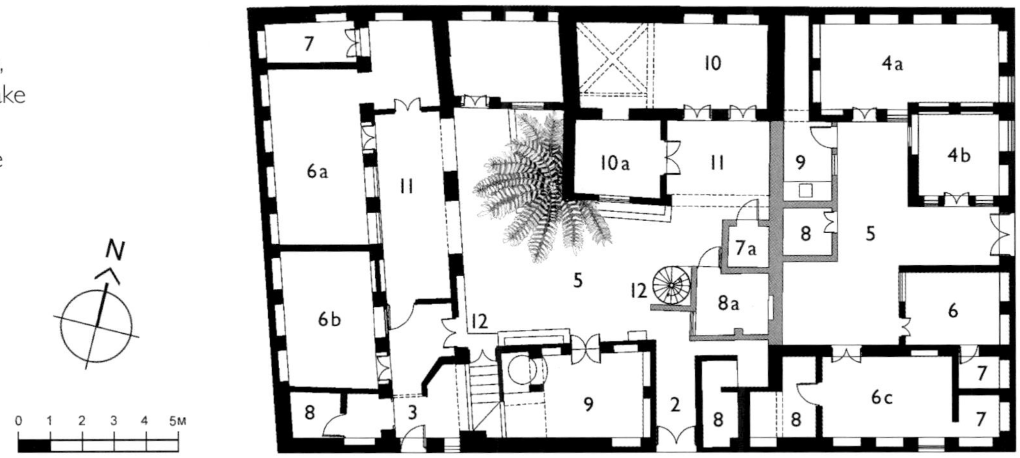

Opposite above:
View from the classroom verandah showing the vivid Mediterranean colours, timber pergola and cast iron spiral staircase added by European tenants, which change the character of the house but have added to its charm. These features were removed during restoration work.

Opposite below:
A small room that was knocked through to provide an extension to the classroom, with the small covered verandah to the right. Sheikh Abdulraheem's office is to the left. An areesh screen heightens the sub-dividing wall.

Right:
These plans reflect the condition of the original building immediately before its restoration in 2005. The long central rectangular courtyard had been split in two, with rooms built off the dividing wall, to make two independent smaller houses. Rooms shown in grey were added when the house was subdivided in the 1960s.

1. Main entrance
2. Ladies' entrance
3. Entrance added in the 1980s
4. *Majlis*
   a) large
   b) small
5. Courtyard
6. Sleeping rooms
   a) Sheikh Abdulraheem
   b) Aunt
   c) Mohammed Noor
7. Wash room
   a) for school
8. Latrine
   a) for school
9. Kitchen
10. Classroom
    a) extension
11. Verandah
12. Stair
13. Sleeping roof
14. Summer room

On a Friday morning between breakfast and Dhur prayers, Sheikh Abdulraheem would take an axe and cut all the wood needed for the next week's cooking.

The main house today is entered from the narrow *sikka* running along its south side, through a pair of carved timber doors, formerly the women's entrance to the larger house. (The steel door was added in the 1980s by a tenant.) A small lobby between the kitchen on the left and the original pit latrine on the right leads into an irregular central court, dominated by a magnificent palm tree. One of originally two, these were a gift brought from Oman by a close friend, Ibrahim Jengaan, following his Hajj pilgrimage.

The kitchen, between the entrance and the masonry stair up to the roof, contained the well, now sealed over. The windtower room and its verandah on the north side of the courtyard would be full of children. Sheikh Abdulraheem would teach below it. An opening was made through the wall, to join the adjacent small room and enlarge the class. The room to the west of the windtower was where the Imam did his legal work, including the preparation of marriage certificates.

The west wing comprises a pair of bedrooms with an open *sabaat* in front. The north-west room was occupied by Sheikh Abdulraheem and his wife, Fatima. The south-west room was for two of their daughters, Maimoona and

Haleema. The rectangular beams in the rooms are mango wood, imported from India.

The house was divided by a high wall, built in the 1960s, and the opportunity was taken to add two additional bathrooms in the courtyard for use by the schoolchildren. On the roof, the covered enclosure in the south-west corner was another long-drop. The corner room was a summer room, with a verandah on its east side, which was later enclosed. The families used to talk across the rooftops with their neighbours on the south side, across the narrow *sikka*. They slept on the roof in summer; the windscoops were very effective in picking up the slightest air movement and directing it across the roof at low level, even when no breeze could be felt above the parapet.

In the late 1980s, a British architect and his wife lived in the house for two years. This was the house visited by Prince Charles in March 1989. There were a number of other expatriate occupants in the years that followed, until the house was acquired by the Dubai Municipality in 1998. Both buildings were being restored at the time of writing in 2006.

Born in 1954, Mohammed Noor Janahi studied in England. When he married, he and his wife, Habiba Al Kazim, lived in the small eastern subdivision of the house with their eldest son until he was two. Mohammed worked as an administrator with the state telephone company for sixteen years, until he retired to run a property business, close to the Bastakiya.

Double entrance doors opened onto the *sikka* to the east. On the right of the entrance are two *majlises*; one long and one small square room. Men and women would use either according to the size of the group. The kitchen is in

Right:
View into the courtyard of Mohammed Noor's house, while under restoration.

Opposite:
The summer sleeping room on the roof; the extension on the right was originally an open verandah. The windscoops in the wall are now obstructed by a built-in bench.

Opposite below:
View up one of the vents of the windtower. The modern timber frame for glazing to seal the room for air-conditioning is where the windtower used be sealed in winter.

Below:
The larger of the two *majlises* that fell within Mohammed Noor's portion of the house. A Restoration Unit plasterer works on the walls.

the north-west corner of the yard; until the house was divided this was part of a single verandah in front of the windtower room and *majlis*. The main bedroom is on the south side of the courtyard, with a smaller bedroom immediately to the left of the entrance.

Sheikh Abdulraheem and his family vacated both houses early in 1982. On moving to Al Mankhool, he became Imam for the Al Mankhool Mosque. He was also appointed Friday preacher (*juma khatib*) at Al Zabeel Mosque. Sadly, in 1985, he was paralysed by a stroke. Nominated by his grandson Mahmoud for the Sheikh Khalifa bin Zayed Al Nahyan Award for Teachers, this award was presented postumously in 1996, a few months after his death.

11

Construction

Over time, a variety of materials were employed in the building of Bastakiya windtower houses, extensive use being made of a limited range of locally available resources. Most early houses were constructed of palm fronds (*areesh*). Over time, the houses of wealthier families were replaced by more permanent masonry buildings constructed of sea-stone, gypsum, and mangrove poles, and later of moulded sand-lime blocks and sawn hardwood beams. No drawings were prepared; masons designing and building within a centuries-old tradition.

Left:
In the past Dubai was a mix of *areesh* and masonry buildings, as shown in this 1948 photograph by Wilfred Thesiger. Both house types were defined by compound walls enclosing the courtyards. The nearest *areesh* house contains both a pitch-roofed winter building and a flat-roofed summer room with a windtower. In the foreground are piles of sea-stone awaiting purchase by the owners.

Areesh houses

When the first Bastaki families moved to Dubai, almost the entire population was living in houses made from palm fronds (*areesh*), with linings of matting and timber uprights. Though made of temporary materials, these houses were remarkably well designed and versatile in use. The buildings' construction, style and functions varied across the region depending on the climate and their occupants' needs. Such buildings were found not only along both sides of the Gulf but also on the Batinah coast facing the Indian Ocean.

In rural areas *areesh* houses were often built entirely from local materials. In Dubai *areesh* panels and woven matting were commonly imported from Oman or Iran, the former being more expensive but of better quality and having a life expectancy of 5-10 years. The supporting poles usually came from India. The palm frond panels would be made up in different ways, the leaves being either trimmed or stripped according to whether insulation or ventilation was required. The panels were rolled up, and transported by dhow. Before their use in a building the panels would be made more rigid by the additional of cross pieces to give added strength. No nails were used, the frame and *areesh* panels were tied together to provide strong but flexible joints able to cope with the wind. The craftsmen involved were highly skilled, employing a variety of techniques appropriate to summer or winter forms of construction.

Aerial photographs of the Bastakiya show that there were always *areesh* houses both within and adjacent to the quarter. Certainly some of the

Above:
A view of a new suburb of *areesh* buildings on the sandy edge of Dubai in 1970.The areesh compound walls and the windtowers are clearly visible.

Opposite below:
Areesh buildings were ideally suited to the hot humid climate of Dubai since the walls could be constructed either to achieve a dense effect that protected and insulated the owners from the cool of winter, or to achieve an open, screen-like effect. This reconstructed room shows both techniques.

Below right:
Many *areesh* houses would have 'seasonal' windtowers, which were constructed to provide relief from the summer heat.

Below:
In 1970 between late April and the end of June, some 1,500 windtowers were erected on *areesh* buildings in four of Dubai's new suburbs. This graph, with its slightly S-shaped curve shows the speed with which windtowers went up as the heat of summer set in. Daily maximum temperatures rose from an average of 29.3°C for the week beginning April 7, to an average of 38.3°C for the week beginning July 7th. (Windtower data based on regular counts, temperature data from Sharjah airport.) A similar survey made in 1971 confirmed the 1970 figures, with only slight variation due to the different onset of summer weather.

incoming families made use of *areesh* housing when they first arrived. Photographs from 1912 onwards show that *areesh* houses, too, often had windtowers. They were made by erecting a square frame of tall poles, with the diagonal partitions and lower walls of the tower typically made from gunny sacks or canvas. The roof was of palm fronds. These windtowers, with their vents bending and billowing sail-like in the wind were remarkably effective.

Areesh houses had their particular disadvantages. The materials of which they were constructed were not long-lasting, they were susceptible to fire, and not especially secure. There were two spectacular fires which are vividly remembered by the people of the Bastakiya. After both occasions steps were taken to forbid areesh construction in the area, but the *areesh* buildings crept back, continuing to be built between masonry dwellings. Given their relative cheapness they were a practical way for incomers and the less wealthy to attain a reasonable home in the city. In 1970, the municipality moved the remaining *areesh* dwellers (most of whom were squatters), to rent-free plots in newly laid out suburbs a few miles out of town. The *areesh* houses were readily dismantled and transported on lorries to their new sites, where their owners were able to re-erect their homes, often beside former neighbours.

A typical house in one of these areas consisted of an *areesh* wall, encompassing the owner's plot. There was a winter room (*khaimah*), with a pitched roof, the *areesh* materials of which might be covered with a tarpaulin to make it watertight. The walls were made of closely spaced palm fronds and probably lined with a basket-work layer, to which plain or decorative woven matting could be attached. In front of the winter house there would be a reception room, with a flat roof, and walls through which the breeze could blow. Often walls consisted of partially shaved palm fronds, providing ample ventilation. Across the courtyard there was a kitchen shelter open on one or more sides, a secluded wash room, a separate toilet and possibly an enclosure or shelter for domestic animals.

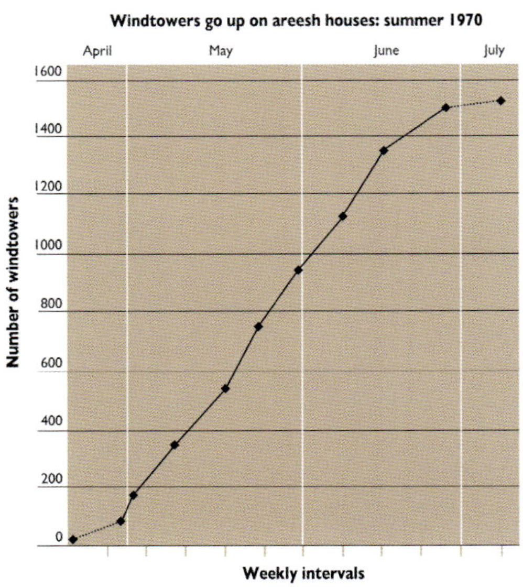

Left:
Areesh windtowers were built around a square frame of poles. The diagonal partitions and lower walls were made from gunny sacks, canvas or occasionally more palm fronds. (Later, boards or packing cases might be used.) The windtower here has just been completed. The ladder for reaching the roof is still in place.

Below:
This shows an earlier stage in the erection of a windtower; only the wooden frame and areesh roof are in place; the lower walls and diagonals need to be added. Note the wooden external wall and the pile of palm fronds in the foreground ready for use. (*Photographs from 1970.*)

The use of the house changed in summer. The winter room essentially became little more than a store, used also when privacy was desired. Importantly, a windtower was erected over the reception room, which now was used both for daily living and sometimes for sleeping or receiving guests. But there was also a large raised *areesh* platform in the middle of the courtyard where the family slept and guests could be entertained after sunset.

One of the most vivid examples of how people responded to Dubai's harsh summer climate was the way in which these windtowers were erected every summer. Since seasonal migration had declined, families needed to construct a home that was suitable for year-round use on a single plot, within an increasingly urban environment. As the weather warmed, men could be seen on the roofs of their houses, grappling to fasten billowing sacking around the projecting poles. When the cool weather came towards the end of September, all would be swiftly dismantled and stored.

Above:
Ostad Mohammed Ahmed Al Banna (*top*) pictured in 1974, built in Dubai, Abu Dhabi and Bahrain, and was the tenth in a line of architect-builders. This family of masons included his three brothers Abdullah, Mohammed Saleh and Abdulrahim, with his sons Aqeel (*bottom*) and Abdulkarim (who undertook the decorations). There were three to four families of masons in Dubai including Ostad Ghuloom and Ostad Al Banna in the Bastakiya, and Ostad Ahmed Kookherdi in Deira. Most of the builders were from the Bastak area, the windtowers in Lingeh having been built by Bastakis.

Masonry houses

The materials used in the construction of masonry buildings are described below.

Sea-stone

Two types of calcareous marine stone were used for building. The first was coral blocks, *fesht*, sourced from coastal reefs and left in stacks to weather in the sun for a year, to lose salt and traces of organic material. Coral is characterised by being light and easy to shape. When dry it floats. Its lightness provided walls with good insulating properties.

Another type, shell-stone, *farush*, was collected from the creek at low tide. A sea sand and shell conglomerate bound together by salts over a long period, it was generally found in shallow water lagoons where the water was calm and very warm. Being stronger, it was used in foundations, and for the walls of wells and towers. Some sea-stone is recorded as sourced from Umm Al Qawain; that from Ras Al Khor on the Creek being of poorer quality.

Salafa

Calcareous sediments were found at the end of the creek. *Salafa* was formed in layers about 15 cm thick. The top surface, worn flat by the action of the sea, offered a ready made finish. These would be chiselled into slabs 5-7cm thick, which, being light, were ideal for the construction of fine masonry.

Tabuk

Sand-lime blocks were made in hand presses from the late 1940s onwards. Unsieved sea sand, including small stones and shells was mixed with lime and sweet water and pressed, sun-cured and built-in, all within 24 hours. Much cheaper than coral, the blocks had a high salt content, and were very vulnerable if exposed to rising damp or the rain. From 1956 on they were replaced by stronger and more durable cement blocks, using imported Indian cement and finer pit sand as an aggregate.

Jus

Gypsum used to be extracted by digging in the Al Qusais and Jebel Ali areas of Dubai, but the best quality came from Mount Poloorghar near Lingeh. It was imported in large blocks. The stone was broken into pieces (*kura*) and stacked to form a kiln with openings at each end, before being burnt for three days and nights to make it soft. The burnt stones and ash were then hammered with sticks (*kapoor*) to a powder, and filled into 75-80kg gunny sacks. Firing was done by the supplier in Al Qusais. On site the powder was sieved and slaked, mixed with water before mixing into three parts to one part sand as a bond for the building stones. For plastering and interior work it was powdered and sieved to a finer constituency and mixed with lime (*nurah*). Gypsum is hydroscopic, readily absorbing water from the ground and moisture from the atmosphere; damp walls were a common problem after rains.

Nurah

Lime provided an alternative material for plastering. It was sourced by burning coral and seashells, but was also mined in the mountains of Ras al Khaimah. The resulting quicklime was crushed to a powder to be slaked with water. It was a more costly alternative to gypsum, but when mixed one part lime to three parts gypsum, provided a durable plaster. Lime plaster was naturally water resistant.

It possessed good insulation properties, reducing thermal conductivity through the masonry, and provided an attractive white finish. Additionally, if lime was mixed for two days in a barrel with salt, it made a waterproof lime-wash, which was used as an external paint.

Sarooj

Red silt clay was imported from Iran, and was known as 'Lingeh cement'. It was first mixed with hay and cow or donkey manure, and mixed with water for two to three days. The paste was spread on the ground about five

Above:
Coral building blocks *(left)* are light and easy to shape. When dry coral floats. Shell-stone *(centre and right)* was cheaper and more readily available, and the compacted shells from which it is formed make it significantly more durable.

Below left:
A traditional hand-press for sand-lime blocks photographed in Ajman in 1972.

Right:
Slabs of *sarooj* piled to form a kiln. A wood fire would be lit inside and burnt for ten days.

Below:
Mangrove poles determined the width of rooms. Typical spans vary between 2.7m to a maximum 3.5m. Woven mats of palm leaves would be laid directly over the *chandals*, or across an open diamond pattern fretwork of stiffening palm stems or bamboo laid across chandals at intervals of about 20-25cm. The bamboo was imported from Basra in Iraq, Kerala in India, or from Iran.

Sawn hardwood provided squared rafters with a ceiling of regular planks above them *(bottom)*. So rigid and regular a material could not be laid over uneven *chandals*. Rooms continued to follow the traditional dimensions established by mangrove *chandals*.

centimetres deep and dried in the sun, before being cut into slabs. These were burnt in a kiln for ten days. When they had cooled, a heavy circular grinding stone some 90cm wide and supported by an iron rod, was rotated by ox-power to crush the burnt stone to a powder. The product was then mixed with water to provide a strong and waterproof bonding agent.

Being resistant to rising damp, *sarooj* was used in the building of foundations, but being much more expensive than gypsum, the use of *sarooj* in the superstructure was limited to the plastering of walls in bathrooms and latrines to provide a durable finish. Masons considered *sarooj* to be better than the cheaper imported cement from Bombay, which came to replace it during the 1950s.

Timber

Several types of timber were used: *yadhaw* – halved and quartered palm trunks – provided rough and irregular 10cm wide beams and lintels which were not very strong. In the Bastakiya they are sometimes found as lintels to openings, or supporting the panels of windscoops. More commonly used, mangrove poles or *chandals* are circular in section, much stronger and more durable than palm trunks. Mainly imported from Zanzibar and the East African coast they, too, were used for rafters and lintels. The island of Lamu had the reputation for the longest poles with the fewest knots.

Sawn hardwood planks, *murabah*, imported from India from the 1930s onwards, provided an alternative to *chandals*. The main types of sawn timber were teak (*saaj*), the most expensive, and meranti (*sinawa*), the cheapest, with various other redwoods mid-range in price. Teak was preferred for doors, window frames, shutters and screens. It was durable and strong, resistant to weather and termites, particularly when treated with preservatives.

Construction methods

The owner of the house would describe to the mason how many rooms he required, and the mason then planned this out on the ground. There were no formal drawings. The arrangement of rooms was generally dictated by tradition, with the particulars being determined between the mason and the owner.

A new building would be planned and built by about three masons, each leading a team of about four men. Smaller houses might only require two teams, and larger houses as many as six. Traditionally only one house was being built at any one time. The mason laid the stones, assisted by a labourer who laid the gypsum bedding; another who shaped the stones; one who carried; and a fourth who mixed the gypsum. Carpenters would be hired later, coming mainly from Lingeh and other towns in the south of Iran.

There was no written contract, and builders were paid daily for their labour. The mason and his artist would each be paid 3 rupees per day. The assistant would receive 1½ rupees, and the other men 1 rupee each. Construction would continue as long as the owner had sufficient money. Wages for building were similar in Dubai, Iran and India. All building materials were purchased directly by the owner.

A mason usually commenced by enclosing the plot with stone walls about 12 feet high. The compound walls were built sufficiently strong to be able to be incorporated within future rooms. After excavating shallow trenches along the line of the walls, the mason would lay the foundations of shell-stone bedded in *sarooj*. These were small foundations considering their base on sand, only some 60 cm deep by 50 cm wide. Walls were built over these with the same thickness, in regular horizontal courses of stone laid in a mortar of gypsum. Gaps were left in the walls for doors, windows, windscoops and decorative gypsum panels. Openings for doors and window were approximate, and would require to be adjusted to fit the final size of the prefabricated carpentry work.

Above:
The baskets for carrying stone and gypsum were made of tightly woven palm leaves *(top)*. Sea-stone walls were characteristically laid in herrring-bone patterned courses. Each stone was placed on end, at a slight angle, with stones laid square at the ends or corners of a wall. As the height of the wall increases, the stones settle under their own weight, and lock themselves in place.

Left:
A Baluchi mason shaping sea-stones for use in restoration work in the Bastakiya.

Opposite:
Thin limestone slabs *(salafa)* form infil panels and high diagonal cross-walls within the north-west windtower of the now demolished Bukhash house.

Tools & Measurement

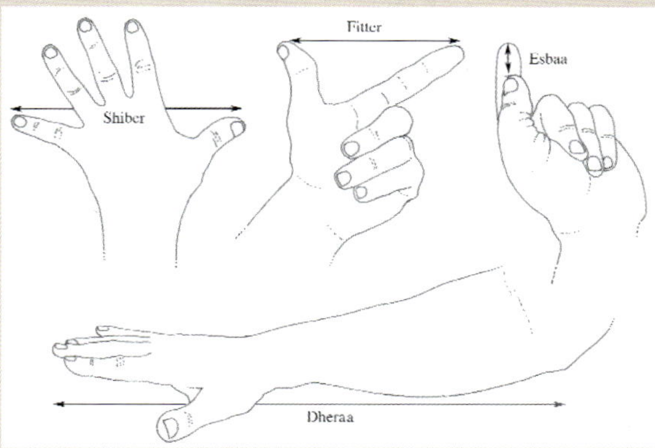

The simple tools used in the past were to assist the mixing, transferring, alignment and levelling of materials to suit the requirements of the building. Masons also adapted some carpentry tools to their needs. They used the trowel, chisel, hammer, adze and axe, together with measuring tools such as the spirit level, plumb-bob and folding rule. Tools for decoration included compasses, a knife, as well as various types of carpenter's saw, drills and a 90 degree square.

A spirit level was used to check horizontal levels during construction; a plumb-bob, *(al bulbul)*, was used to check vertical edges and faces. A square, *(al zawya)*, assisted in establishing right angles. A standard six foot folding carpenter's rule, *(al miqyas)*, was used to determine the sizes of openings.

The migration of many craftsmen to Dubai at the beginning of the twentieth century brought new tools, and this was reflected in the development of a more elaborate architecture.

The period over which the Bastakiya was constructed saw the transition from traditional to imported western tools and measures. Traditionally the human body was the main source of measurement: the *dheraa*, measured from elbow to the tip of the middle finger, *shibher,* spanned from thumb to the little finger, *fitter* spanned from thumb to tip of the index finger, and *esbaa*, the length of the top of the index finger. There was no local measurement for area, only for length, an area being defined by the length of two of its sides, described in *dheraa*. The British presence in the region resulted in the introduction of a more accurate system of measurement: feet and inches.

Internal partitions and the first floor walls were of lighter, thinner masonry built between columns, in order to reduce the weight of the structure. It would appear that the first floor of these houses was usually built when the ground floor structure was complete, as the alignments of columns and walls only approximately matches between floors. Thin walls were formed of *salafa*, 30-40 cm across, supported on *chandals* and laid on edge in a diagonal pattern. *Salafa* slabs were used for the panels in wind scoops and the cross-walls within windtowers.

A finishing plaster of gypsum and lime was applied to the masonry. Where decorative pilasters or columns were incorporated within porches or verandahs, they were cylindrically cast in timber shuttering. Their decorative arches were not structural, but were built within the main framed openings, the weight of masonry above being supported on beams formed of *chandal* corded together with jute, and plastered to form a rectangular shape. A paste of gypsum and lime was cast in timber moulds to provide permanent formers for the elaborate shaped arches.

Stairs were either simply steep hardwood ladders with narrow treads and a handrail or integrally formed with the masonry. A single flight was laid on a sloping base of tightly spaced *chandals* supported on beams at top and bottom. Steps were built over this in coral stone, and then rendered smooth with gypsum.

Floor and roof finishes were applied either on top of timber boards, or over

Left:
Palm mats are laid over *chandals* and then protected by unstripped palm stems (shown here) loosely laid across, before a clay floor is laid on top in reconstruction work in Shindagah.

Below:
Chandals (and palm logs) were used extensively in building. They were randomly laid between stone courses, to reinforce against cracking of the brittle gypsum bonding over minimal foundations. Stairs were constructed over sloping *chandals* supported on beams at the top and bottom, seen here in the onion store of the Bukhash house.

woven palm frond mats. When board ceilings later became more common, these would span rectangular hardwood rafters laid at intervals of 40-50cm. Floors were made with clay from Iran, mixed with straw or maize husks to prevent cracking, and compacted to about 10cm thick over the mats or boards below. Because clay had to be imported it was expensive, and local gypsum was often used instead.

Roof finishes were laid over sloping *chandals* towards long timber gargoyles (*mirzab*), projected through the up-stands of screen walls or from beneath a capping of thin stone slabs, throwing water into the courtyard or *sikka* well clear of the porous walls. Roofs were made watertight each year by additional renderings of mud and straw, or plaster to fill the cracks which had opened up through the summer. As buildings aged they become less and less watertight, and winter rain would find its way into the living spaces.

Despite protection, the biggest problem was insect attack, and the average life of the *chandals* was expected to be 20 years. For protection against bees and termites, various natural preservatives were used. *Sol* was a substance made from fish left to rot in a covered pit. Mixed with oil from the surface of the decomposed mass, the resulting red sticky paste was applied to the *chandals*. In addition to the threat of insects, timber built into gypsum and coral walls was very prone to rot, as gypsum retained moisture from any winter rain and from the high summer humidity.

Joinery

Finally, there followed the fixing of timberwork, such as doors, windows, and verandah and parapet screens. Where occasionally ceilings were provided in living or reception rooms, timber boarding would be pinned to the underside of the rafters, sometimes with decorative plaster cornices or scalloped, painted timber edging.

Right:
Infested or rotted *chandals* were individually removed and replaced as required. The roof was maintained every year at the end of summer, before the winter rains.

Below:
An intricately carved stair up to the roof of the east wing of the Bukhash house.

Traditional boat-building skills were readily adapted to the requirements of building joinery, with similar styles of traditional decoration being applied to doors, frames, and window shutters as were found on dhows. Using a hammer and chisel, geometric, sometimes floral, decoration was incised into the frames and meeting styles of doors, as well as the panel frames of door panels and window shutters. Joinery work took place on the building site rather than in separate workshops, items generally being made to standard sizes. Alternatively, an owner might import sets of doors and windows from India.

Heavy hardwood doors were hung and pivoted on projecting lugs supported in sockets in the bottom and top rails of the frame. Hinges were not used. Vertical boards were secured to horizontal rails behind with iron nails with large round heads, exposed in horizontal rows externally. Larger and grander main doors (*dahreez*) would contain a wicket (*farkha*) in one of the leaves of the main entrance door. The main doors were locked with one or two large rectangular timber sliding bolts, which sometimes incorporated a hidden peg to prevent children or strangers sliding it open. Other doors were secured by brass or steel bolts and hasps, able to be secured with a padlock. Alternatively a chain at the top of the door could be slipped over a hasp in the top frame, again to take a padlock. This was commonly used for doors opening from the courtyard.

Windows were not glazed except from the 1960s onwards when individual rooms might be modernised and air-conditioned. Traditional window frames were barred for security, with two pairs of upper and lower shutters often carved with framed panels, opening inwards and held closed by a simple rotating knob of wood.

Sanitation

A deep hole would be made through the building down to within a foot or so of the water level. Latrines were often constructed at the first floor as well as at ground floor level, connected by a masonry duct to the same pit. A rectangular hole in the floor opened over it, with two stone blocks on which to place the feet while squatting. The pit had to be as dry as possible. Dirty water from associated ablutions was poured away, led through a channel in the wall to the outside so as not to enter the latrine pit. It might be 20 years before such a latrine needed emptying and then this could be done from the outside. They were not too smelly because the latrine room was always ventilated. Contamination of wells, which were often located close to latrines did not matter so much because their brackish water was not used for cooking or drinking.

In a few larger houses in the town there was a second external soakaway pit in the *sikka*. The fouled water from ablutions was discharged into the pit through a pipe passing through the wall. In the Bastakiya this system was seen only at the Bukhash House. Rashad Bukhash recalls that two men would come to empty this occasionally. It was a foul job; they had to climb right in and throw the black and evil smelling liquid into the *sikka*, where it soaked into the sand.

Decoration

Decoration was normally carried out by the mason. Sometimes a specialist painter assisted with the decoration of rooms, colonnades and windtowers. In the case of Ostad Mohammed, Aqeel's older brother Abdulkarim al Banna did this work. Another artist who worked in the Bastakiya was Ghulum Ali. To achieve the pigments, charcoal was crushed into a fine powder and then applied by wrapping it in a thin cloth and dabbing it onto the surface to be coloured. Reckitts Blue, normally sold for laundry purposes, was also used.

Above:
Roof finishes *(top)* were sloped to falls towards long timber gargoyles *(mirzab)*, projected through the up-stands of screen walls.

The carving of doors derives from the same skills and traditions as dhow building *(centre)*.

The scalloped cornice to a timber ceiling in the first floor *majlis* of the Bukhash house *(bottom)*.

Left:
A chain at the top of the door could be slipped over a hasp in the top frame to take a padlock, as on this door to the Heritage House in Deira.

Above:
A canvas pattern was prepared for the outline of repeated painted patterns. The painted canvas would be reversed onto a wall while still wet, providing an accurate stencil for reproducing. This rare surviving example of such painting is in the house of Abdullah Mohammed Al Bastaki (see Chapter 8).

Right:
A similar technique was used to lay out the pattern on gypsum screens. The stencil pattern was applied before they were fully set, before being carved away by hand.

Windtowers

One windtower would normally take one to two months to erect, depending on how large and elaborate it was. Windtowers were constructed of a framework of poles, tied together to give rigidity and tensile strength to the thin masonry slabs which it supported. Where the *chandals* were to be built into the diagonal walls they were wrapped in cord and plastered with gypsum to create a strong bond. The ends of the poles were left projecting after the tower was complete to serve as scaffolding when the tower needed to be closed, or for maintenance. Ostad Aqeel Al Banna suggested that they also were left projecting for their appearance. One of his windtowers (see Chapter 8) had been built on a framework of ninety *chandals*. Over time the ends would rot away. Windtowers sometimes became structurally unsafe and would have to be carefully demolished before they fell.

To close a windtower for the winter, sloping triangular boards were fitted over the top of the enclosed portion, behind the external fins. The boards were then plastered to seal them against rain. In other cases, eight timber triangles fitted into the base of the tower. The task of opening the towers again was messy because of the accumulated bird droppings, sand and dust.

12

Windtowers

The elegant windtowers of the Bastakiya were highly effective at funnelling air into the rooms below. The earliest uni-directional wind-catchers and wind scoops, dating from around 2,000 BC, had evolved into complex multi-directional structures by the eighteenth century. Advances in climatic recording techniques have cast light on the diverse factors that affect the functioning of a windtower. The results of this research, which builds on that undertaken by the authors in the 1970s, are published here for the first time.

Above:
The tallest known windtower is the magnificent 33 metre high octagonal structure serving the garden pavilion at Bag-e Dawlatabad near Yazd in Persia.

Opposite:
The open vents on this classic Bastakiya windtower show the diagonal vanes which direct air into the tower, and thence through the rooms below (see Chapter 8 for restoration).

Left:
The tall windtowers on this building in Kashan, in the Isfahan province of Iran, contribute to a complex ventilation system, typical of central Iran but not found in the Gulf. It illustrates the extent to which wind-catchers (and windtowers) varied in their design and use according to the climate, traditions, economy and materials found in different regions.

Below:
The delightful circular and tiled windtower, serving the Majlis of Ibrahim Al Midfaa in Sharjah is unique in the UAE. Behind, imitation windtowers reach new heights on a modern office building.

Windtowers are an elegant and striking form of wind-catcher, from which they evolved as a result of particular social, technical and climatic conditions. In looking at the history of wind-catchers in the Middle East, we define the term broadly to include any vent rising above the level of the roof, designed to funnel air into the rooms below in order to improve the internal climatic conditions. There is some uncertainty about when the use of wind-catchers first became common in this region. One difficulty is that, as can be seen in the case of the Bastakiya, wind-catchers, as structures rising above buildings, were often the first parts to deteriorate and fall into ruin.

There are depictions of what appear to be wind-catchers in Egyptian tomb paintings going back as far as the second millennium BC. Large houses in Cairo in the fourteenth century certainly had 'malqaf', unidirectional wind-catchers which descended into summer quarters. Unidirectional windscoops occurred on houses in the continuously occupied ancient city of Bam in Persia, but there is uncertainty as to their date of construction. There have been wind-catchers in the Gulf at least since the thirteenth century when Marco Polo commented on those in Hormuz and there are several confirmed examples of wind-catchers on the Persian plateau, dating from the fourteenth century. Seventeenth-century European travellers recorded them in Isfahan, Shiraz, Lar, Kashan, and Tabriz, as well as Bandar Abbas.

Early wind-catchers seem to have consisted of a single ventilation shaft, with the opening usually oriented towards the prevailing summer wind. The more complex multidirectional windtowers of Persia and the Gulf were considerably more advanced and, while their origins remain obscure, they were probably to find their finest expression in the classic windtowers of Yazd. The magnificent octagonal windtower serving the garden pavilion at Bag-e Dawlatabad was built for a Shah who made Yazd his summer residence in the second half of the eighteenth century. Given the elaborate conception of this windtower, both in terms of its architecture and its use of pools of

Above:
Wind-catchers in the desert town of Maybod are predominantly unidirectional, and oriented to face the prevailing summer breeze.

water for cooling, it is likely that multidirectional windtowers originally developed much earlier.

During the Qajar era (1781-1925), windtowers were used to cool water cisterns in central Persia, both in towns and along caravan routes. They were used in markets in Teheran and Kerman to ventilate the covered passageways, and even adorned a few mosques. Their use in houses seems closely related to particular trade routes and to the commercial prosperity that gradually increased through the eighteenth and nineteenth centuries. Many of the grand houses of Yazd, which have tall brick windtowers, were built in the late nineteenth century, by merchants who had benefited both from Yazd's key position in the Indian trade and the emerging market in opium, which had replaced silk as the main commodity of value. As the trade routes between the interior of Persia and the Gulf coast became well established coastal settlements, such as Bandar Abbas, Lingeh and Bushire, and in the early twentieth century, Bahrain, Dubai and Hyderabad developed their own, distinctive style of uni- or multi-directional wind-catcher appropriate to their climate.

Wind-catchers were remarkably practical responses to particular physical conditions. The main clusters of wind-catchers in the Middle East were discontinuous and those that were unidirectional ranged from the distinctive

large windscoops of Hyderabad to the low vents entering the domes of houses on the border of Iran and Afghanistan. In Iran, in places where the desert winds are particularly harsh, smaller vents might be orientated towards the softer breeze from a village's irrigated farmland. There were no wind-catchers along the cooler, humid climate of the Caspian. Depending on the terrain and regional building styles, the catchers might deliver breeze to basements, ground or first floor rooms.

Above:
These buildings demonstrate the variety of form and materials of the windtowers of Lingeh. The oldest ones in the town are the immediate forebears to those that were to be built in Dubai.

Below left:
This dramatic and finely built brick storage cistern on Kish Island has four windtowers to cool the water.

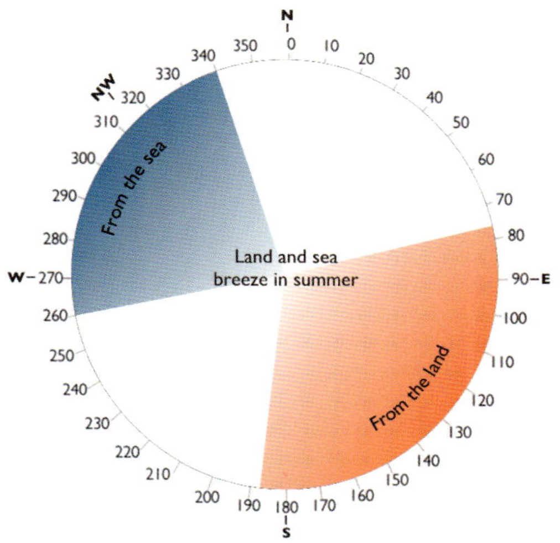

Above:
This wind rose shows the predominant direction of the hot desert morning breeze and the afternoon sea breeze during the summer months in Dubai. Typically the land breeze increases from an average of about 6 to over 8 knots during the morning. The sea breeze averages just over 12 knots. There are often periods in the evening or night without any discernible breeze.

Windtowers, which probably originated as a response to the very dry and hot climate of the southern desert margins of the Iranian plateau, spread more widely following commercial development in the early twentieth century, eventually reaching the shores of the Gulf, where the climate was different, being both hot and humid. To be effective in a relatively humid environment it is desirable for a windtower to provide a large volume of strongly flowing air down into the building it serves. Gulf windtowers were designed to achieve just this. To increase the cooling effect of the breeze within the house, windtowers were ideally combined with additional shaded openings.

Windtowers became an important feature of the building style of Qeshm, Bastak and Lingeh, and, indeed, can still be seen on the beautiful old merchant houses that edge the waterfront at Lingeh. Meanwhile, on the Arab side of the Gulf, comparable wealthy courtyard houses found in Bahrain, Kuwait and Qatar typically had massive walls with an open upstairs reception room for summer. The development of this Iranian architectural style on the Arab side was associated with the immigration of merchants, craftsmen and masons from the Bastak region. The distribution of windtower houses was not uniform along this coast. The greatest concentrations were to be found in Dubai and Bahrain, which had the largest immigrant communities (see Chapter 1). Elsewhere there were some windtower buildings, usually associated with a particular Iranian merchant, local ruler, or commercial quarter such as those found in the Sharjah souq, the forts at Ajman and Ras al Khaimah, and on the leading businessman's house at Jazirat Al Hamra. There were comparatively few higher up the Gulf, and an examination of their distribution on both coasts has led to the suggestion that they were the creation of wealth, not only obtained from maritime trading, but more specifically from pearling. The larger houses, which make most use of imported materials and often have decorative features that apparently derive from India as well as Persia, reflect a cosmopolitan grandeur.

The windtowers of Dubai and how they work

People in Dubai were highly sensitive to variations in summer heat. They bore with fortitude – and some frustration – the high humidity marking the end of summer, and relished the very slightly cooler temperatures that seemed to occur every week or so. Diurnal fluctuations, too, were remarked: people were irritable if the dry, hot desert air persisted an hour or so later than normal, delaying the onset of the fresher afternoon sea breeze.

With the arrival of electricity, a few homes installed fans and some rooms were adapted to receive individual air conditioning units, but these were noisy, expensive and relatively ineffective in high rooms originally designed to facilitate external airflow. The first air conditioning units were usually installed in the rooms of the household head, and were invaluable when the wind dropped, especially at night. However, during the day, many elderly people preferred the less chilly, gentler, fluctuating windtower air.

Windtowers brought many benefits to a household. In summer, the family would take their afternoon rest there. Babies might sleep beneath them during the day, homework might be done (though the breeze was apt to blow the pages about), the elderly sometimes prayed beneath them, and the frail, unable to climb onto the roof, might sleep beneath them. Importantly, although the breeze beneath the tower was strongest, the airflow extended into the room as a whole (and even into the verandah and courtyard beyond), providing choice as to where people sat. The vents of the windtower were blocked off in October at the end of summer, so that the rooms could be used throughout the cool season.

Windtowers in the Bastakiya

The existing windtowers of the Bastakiya are invariably almost square in cross-section, with four vents, separated by diagonal vanes. They rise well above roof level and typically descend a metre or so into a ground floor living room, although where there is a first floor they may open onto an upstairs room. Most of the remaining windtowers are around 12 metres above ground level, though two of those in the Bukhash house were over 15 metres. This compares with roof heights that range from a little over 8 metres for a two-storey house with a mezzanine floor and high parapet, to about 5.5 metres for a one-storey building with a low parapet.

The higher the windtower, the more effective it is likely to be in contributing to the comfort of the occupants in the house it serves. Generally air is cooler and less dusty, and wind velocity greater as height increases. This is particularly so in urban areas where at low levels the built environment, with its traffic and human activity, generates and retains heat. Buildings

Below left:
This sectional sketch through a windtower room in the Bukhash house shows the thin diagonal cross walls supported in a frame of timber poles for the full height of the tower. The poles often project beyond the face of the windtower to provide a support for maintenance. The vertical openings occupy approximately half the height of the tower above the roof. The scoop of the cornice profile is valuable in directing wind, which would otherwise blow over the top, into these openings. The base of the tower descends to just above head height in the room below. This increases its effective height and also concentrates air flow in the occupied lower part of the room.

Below:
The windtower descends into one end of the room, with wind scoops *(baadkash)* within the thickness of the external wall, as well as in the roof parapet above. The vertical openings are usually divided by narrow fins, with decoration at the top. Closely spaced fins provide security, as well as effectively shading east and west facing vents from the sun.

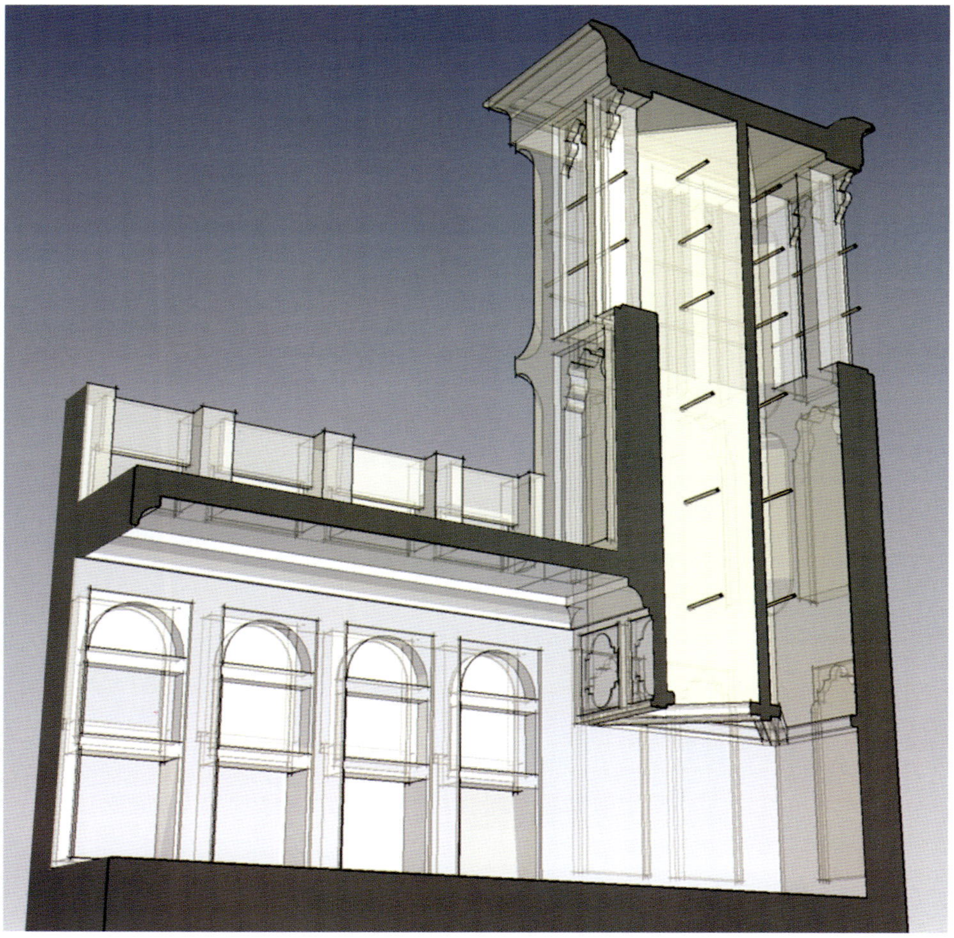

obstruct airflow, creating turbulence. Height raises the windtower into a faster air stream and puts the vent opening further from hot roof surfaces. Air also cools in the process of descending a windtower. Windtowers work best if the open area at the top is about twice the area of the cross-section in the triangular chimney below. The velocity of air entering the windtower increases as it descends, an example of the Bernoulli Principle. Thus, the size of vent openings as well as height is important in determining how windtowers contribute to human comfort. The great merit of multidirectional windtowers is that they can 'capture' the breeze from whichever direction it comes.

The orientation of most of the windtowers in the Bastakiya coincides with the prevailing north-west strong afternoon sea breeze. The towers have vents open, approximately, to the north, south, east and west, optimally exposing their diagonal to this breeze. However, this orientation may have occurred because the houses were generally aligned to the Creek, and while windtowers in the Dubai and Deira souqs are similarly oriented, it does not apply in Shindagha. Ostad Aqeel Al Banna, a retired builder, was adamant that wind direction was not significant in planning a house because multidirectional towers catch wind from any direction.

The research

Preliminary climatic measurements were made in houses with windtowers in 1969-71 but, given the nature of the methods available, the results generated tantalising hypotheses rather than yielding firm conclusions. The results had suggested that the effectiveness of a windtower depended on, among other things, wind speed, the orientation of the tower's vents in relation to the direction of the prevailing winds, the orientation of the room in relation to

Below:
This diagram shows that if the wind's direction is precisely oriented to the vent of a windtower, air will travel down that vent into the room below, with a return flow of air from the room up the other three vents, the greatest flow being up the opposite vent. In this situation there is considerable turbulence, with a bubble effect at the entrance to the vent as the air is compressed on entering.

When the wind direction is diagonal to the sides of the windtower, the breeze enters down two vents, and returns up the other two. The volume of air entering is greater than in the former case and its velocity is greater as the air is able to turn smoothly against the face of the dividing vanes, which are at right angles to it.

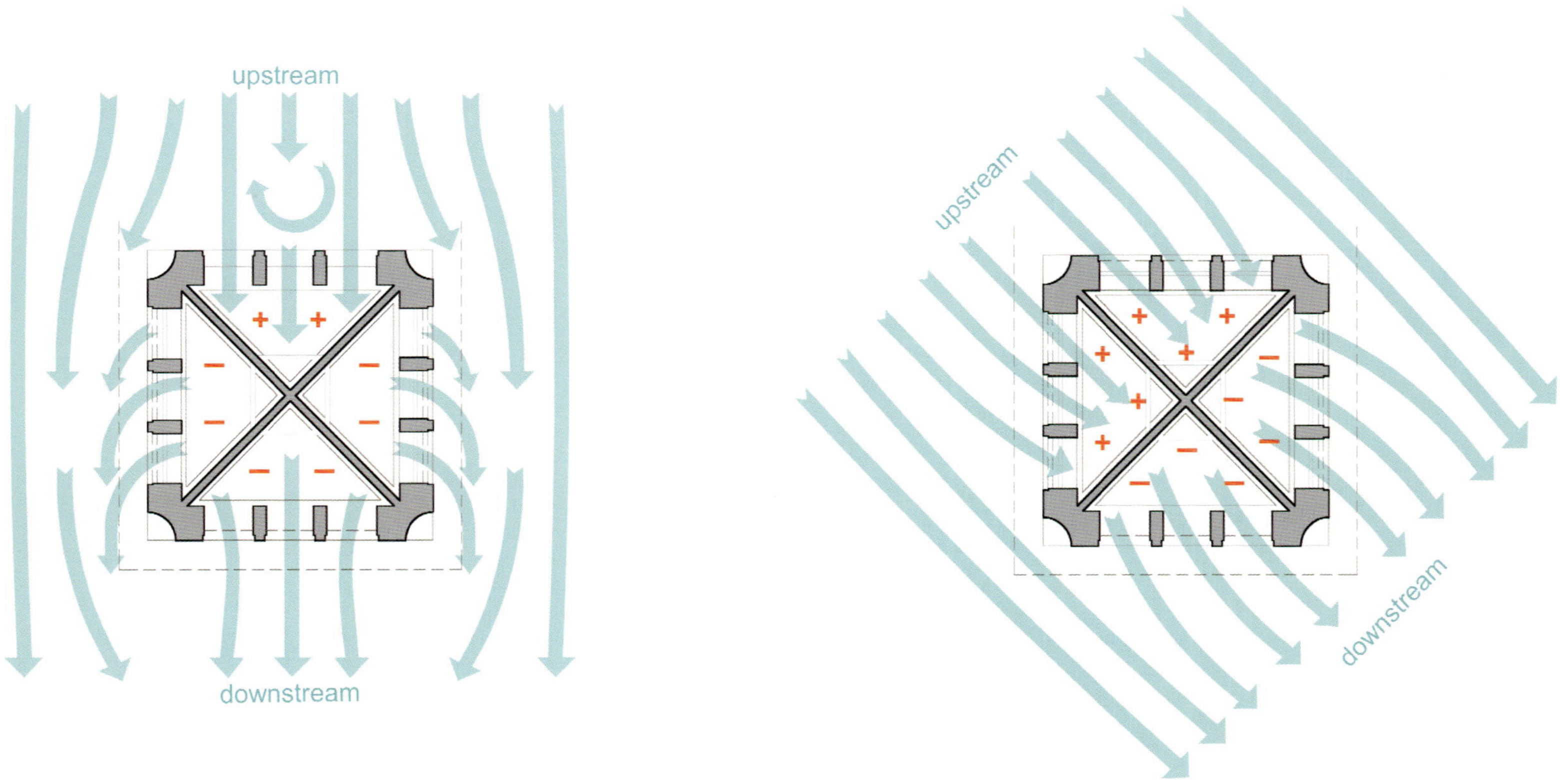

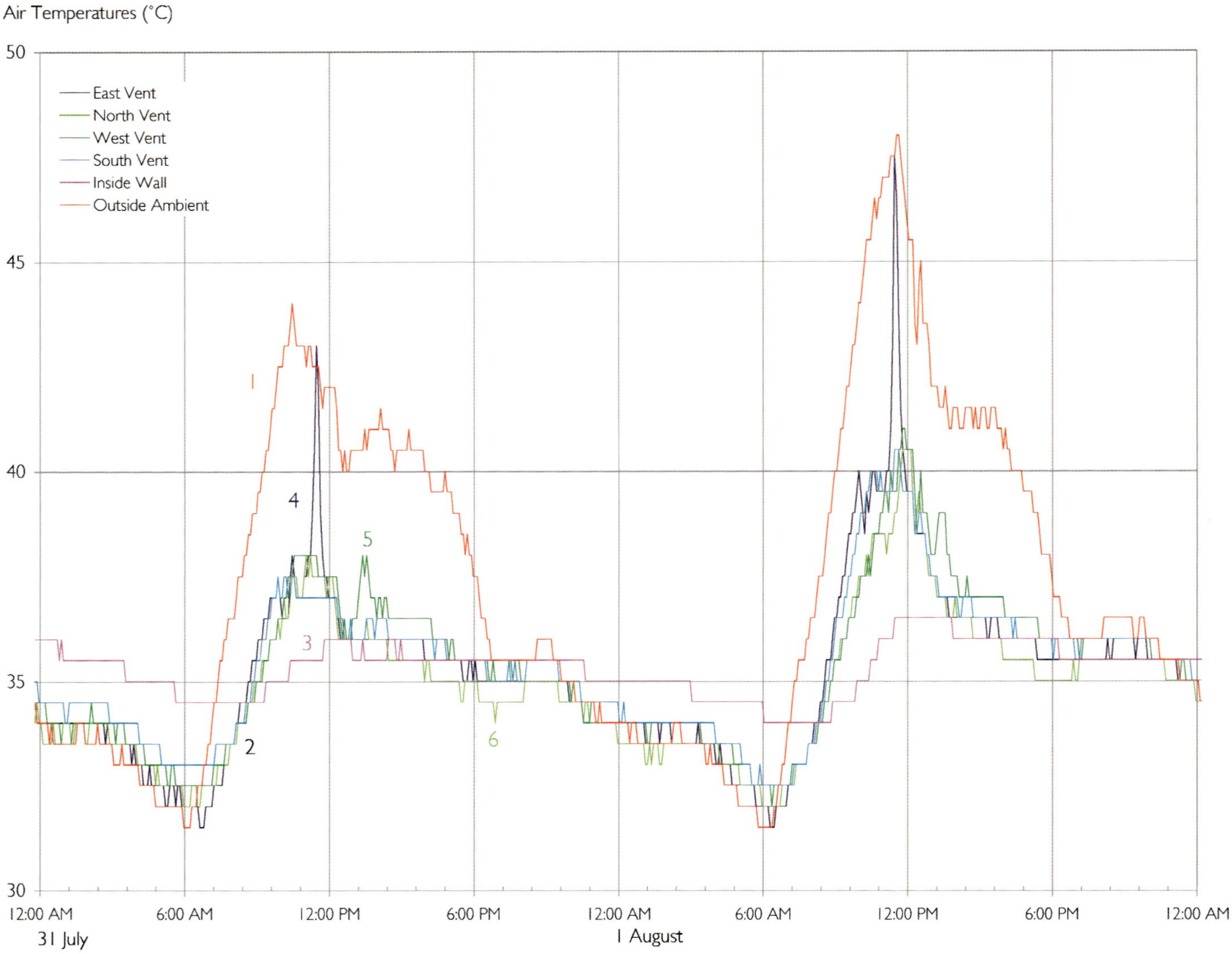

1. The outside air temperatures start to rise at dawn from a night time low of 30-33°C. They increase rapidly until about noon, pause briefly (at 43-45°C in August), then drop until the mid afternoon when they stabilise for several hours at approximately 40°C. They fall again in the evening reaching about 35°C between 5 and 6pm. After sunset they decline slowly throughout the night.
2. The air temperatures in the house (not shown in this graph for the sake of clarity) lag behind the outdoor air temperatures by approximately one to two hours. Room temperatures show a much smaller diurnal range and, in particular, a much lower maximum temperature than outside. The windtower temperatures and the room temperatures rise as a group – considerable air mixing takes place as air enters and leaves the windtower. In the morning winds are from the south-east so that this rise is often led by the east tower vent (the blue line to left of group), closely followed and sometimes led by the south vent. Daytime room temperatures are cooler (by 1-3°C) than the windtower air temperatures.
3. The temperatures in the wall lag behind the air temperatures, and rise or fall only 1-4 hours after the outside air temperatures rise or fall. They are quite stable (at around 35°C for August) with a daily variation of 2-3°C.
4. Almost every day there are spikes of temperature in the windtower vents when temperatures rise sharply and briefly. The east vent (dark blue) shows spikes between 11.18 and 11.53am. A fortnight later these occurred in the south vent.
5. On 31 July there is also a west spike. Typically these are a couple of hours later. These spikes are caused by direct ingress of sunlight into a vent.
6. For most of the afternoon, temperatures are higher in the west vent, down which the outside wind is normally flowing. Later in the afternoons the north vent is cooler than the others, its wall having been protected from the heat of the sun during the day.

Opposite:
Measuring the summer climate.
The graph shows how temperature varied in different parts of a house over a 48-hour period. The outside air temperature, as measured in the shade at roof-level, demonstrates the normal daily cycle for July and August, with highs of 43-45°C and night-time lows of 30-33°C. Because the Bastakiya is within the densely built-up city centre, daytime temperatures are about 2 degrees and night time temperatures 1 degree higher than those at the Dubai airport meteorological office.

Measuring the temperature within the fabric of the wall gives an indication of the rate of heat absorption of the masonry. With only a small daily variation and a time lag of up to 4 hours compared with the outside temperature, wall temperatures remain high all night, warming the room. Hence, it was preferable to sleep on the roof, benefitting from any slight breeze and from heat loss via radiation to the night sky.

One result observed was that during the morning and middle of the day, the temperatures measured in the windtower vents in which outside air is descending, were significantly cooler by 3-5 degrees than the shade temperature just above the roof height. But while the windtower provides a flow of air that is cooler than that at the rooftop, the air descending the windtower is actually hotter than the air in the room below from soon after sunrise until shortly after sunset. Because of the time lag through the masonry, temperatures peak in windtower rooms in the early afternoon, about two hours after the outside maximum. Nonetheless, residents of the Bastakiya regarded the afternoon as the time when windtowers were most useful. The explanation lies in the way in which windtowers contribute to comfort. (Data collection 2005.)

the windtower and the prevailing winds, and opportunities for opening windows and doors.

In 2005, collaboration with Vipac Engineering brought modern techniques to the research and provided a unique opportunity to understand better how windtower houses performed, and to evaluate the additional comfort that the windtowers achieved. A variety of methods were used. Continuous recording of temperatures was made throughout the summer in two existing windtower houses consecutively. A physical model of the Bukhash house was tested in a wind tunnel and exposed to winds typical of those in summer in Dubai, with subsequent modelling of the velocity and turbulence profiles. Computational Fluid Dynamics created a three dimensional virtual model of the Bukhash house to provide more detailed understanding of air flow and its velocity in the building.

Air movement

Windtowers make use of differential air pressure effects to achieve natural ventilation for the rooms below. They greatly increase the air circulation that takes place, without letting in the heat of the sun (sunshine). The increase in airflow increases the convective heat loss from the surface of the human body by means of evaporation.

Given the high summer temperatures and the relatively high humidities in Dubai, which mean that rates of evaporation are low in still conditions, air movement becomes a vitally important component of heat loss. Put simply, if there is no wind, people become sticky, stay damp, feel hot and get hotter, but if there is a good breeze, sweat evaporates from the skin and the body is kept cooler and more comfortable. Thus the cooling effect achieved by windtowers is essentially different from that achieved by air conditioners, where the main means by which comfort is achieved is through the provision of cooled air with low humidity.

The wind tunnel was used first to provide qualitative visual information on air flow in the model of a windtower house, and then to provide detailed quantitative data on air pressure differentials. These were then converted mathematically to provide information on air circulation and air speed. The model's north-west and north-east windtowers, together with their differently oriented rooms, were wired up with over 30 pressure sensors, and were used in the experiments. A range of scenarios was tested, with different arrangements of doors and windows open or closed.

With different wind directions it was noted that whenever any nearby windtowers on adjacent houses were upstream of one of those under study, the neighbouring tower would disrupt the airflow to the study tower in its lee, effectively 'stealing' its wind, and rendering it less effective.

When the wind was from the north-west, two vents of the windtower acted as air intakes with the other two openings serving as exhausts. The effect of this was to increase the volume of air entering the room, and, therefore, the comfort that would be experienced. With all the windows closed, the increased volume of air and the fact that the positive pressure down two vents of the tower was equal to the negative pressure of the opposite two vents ensured very good air movement immediately below the windtower. Indoor

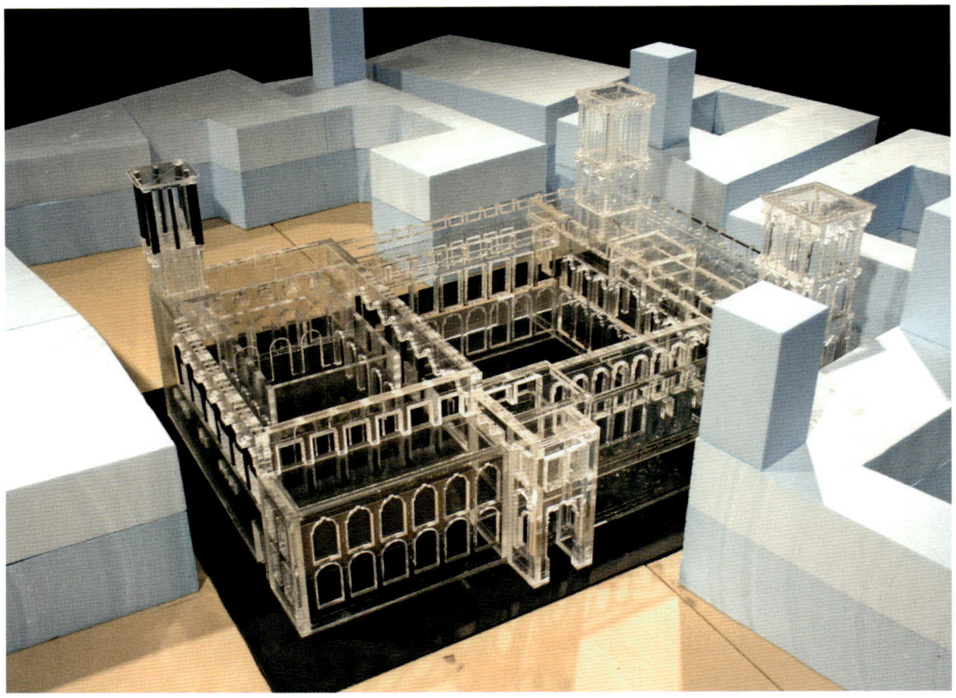

air velocity directly below the tower was measured to be 1.7 times greater than the outside velocity at roof level.

The orientation of the room, in relation to the position of the windtower and the direction of the prevailing wind, was shown to be important. For example, if the wind is from the north and the long axis of the room lies north-south then good ventilation is obtained throughout. But if the room is oriented from east to west then, with a north wind, the ventilation is less effective. This is mainly because the descending air strikes the interior wall before moving out into the room and in so doing its momentum is reduced.

Generally, air circulation immediately below the windtower was strongest when all openings were shut. However, with external openings and courtyard facing doors open, there was better distribution, with around half the air circulating around the room, with some escaping into the courtyard, and the balance being drawn back up the windtower.

Above left:
The Bukhash house was modelled in clear acrylic to a scale of 1:50, and set in the context of the surrounding buildings. The three windtower rooms had door and window openings that could be opened and closed. In order to simulate the urban environment of the Bastakiya, the built environment for 125 metres around the house was modelled, the houses being simple blocks.

Above:
In order to get a first impression of how windtower air circulated, a tube fed smoke into a windtower vent in the model and researchers observed how it circulated around the windtower and billowed into the spaces in the house below. As it left the tower, the smoke was drawn up into the faster air current above.

Left:
Testing the model in Melbourne.
The revolving turntable of the wind tunnel enabled the wind direction to be varied, with fans controlling the windspeed.

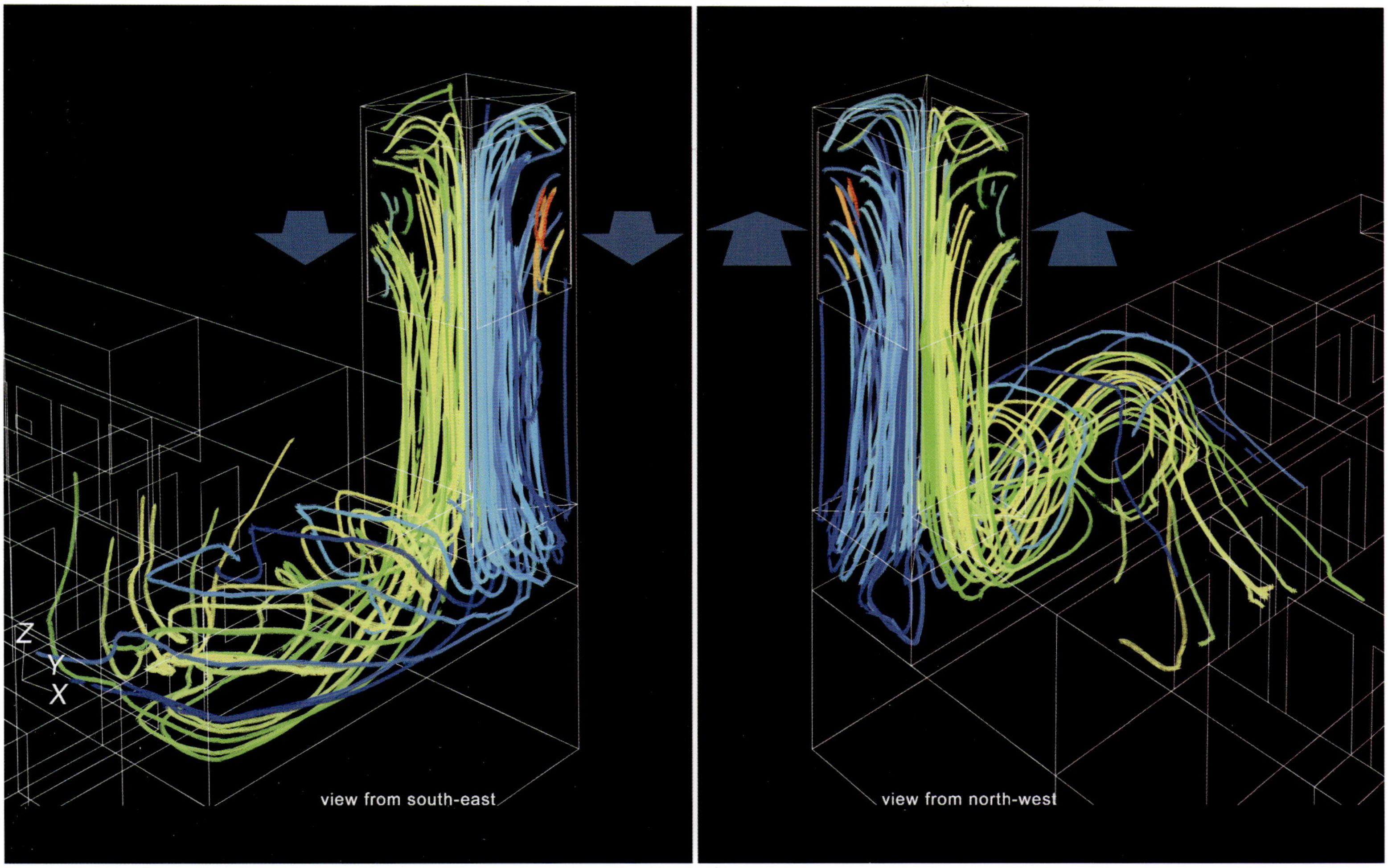

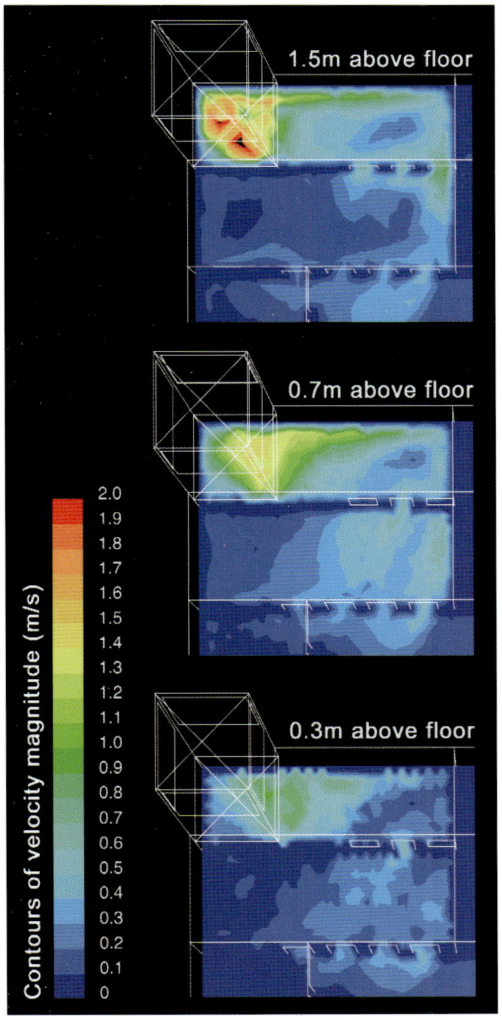

Particle pathways within the north-east windtower of the Bukhash house.
Particle pathways are a means of virtual modelling the movement of individual particles of air over a chosen time period. In these examples the external windscoops of the virtual windtower room are closed but the door and windows on the inside are open.

Above:
Here, the wind is from the north-west. As the air flows in and down, it flows faster at the outer edge of the flow curve, like a river around a bend. The overall quantity of the flow is the result of the total difference between the positive pressure on the upstream face of the tower and the negative pressure at its downstream face. At some times the lowest pressure might be within the courtyard. In this particular instance, some 40 per cent of the particles circulate through the room. The air sweeps around the floor and wall surfaces at twice the velocity of the much calmer air in the middle of the room. Some air flows out into the verandah. About 60 per cent of the air descending the north and west vents of the windtower travels only part-way to the floor before returning back up the opposing pair of vents. The movement of air is complex with turbulence, fluctuating pressures and variability in flow.

Left:
This series of horizontal sections below the north-east windtower shows relative speed in metres per second of air movement at heights where it would be felt sitting on cushions on the floor, lying on a bed, and standing up. Greater air movement is clearly visible below the windtower, with the flow of air along wall surfaces leaving a relatively static centre in the room.

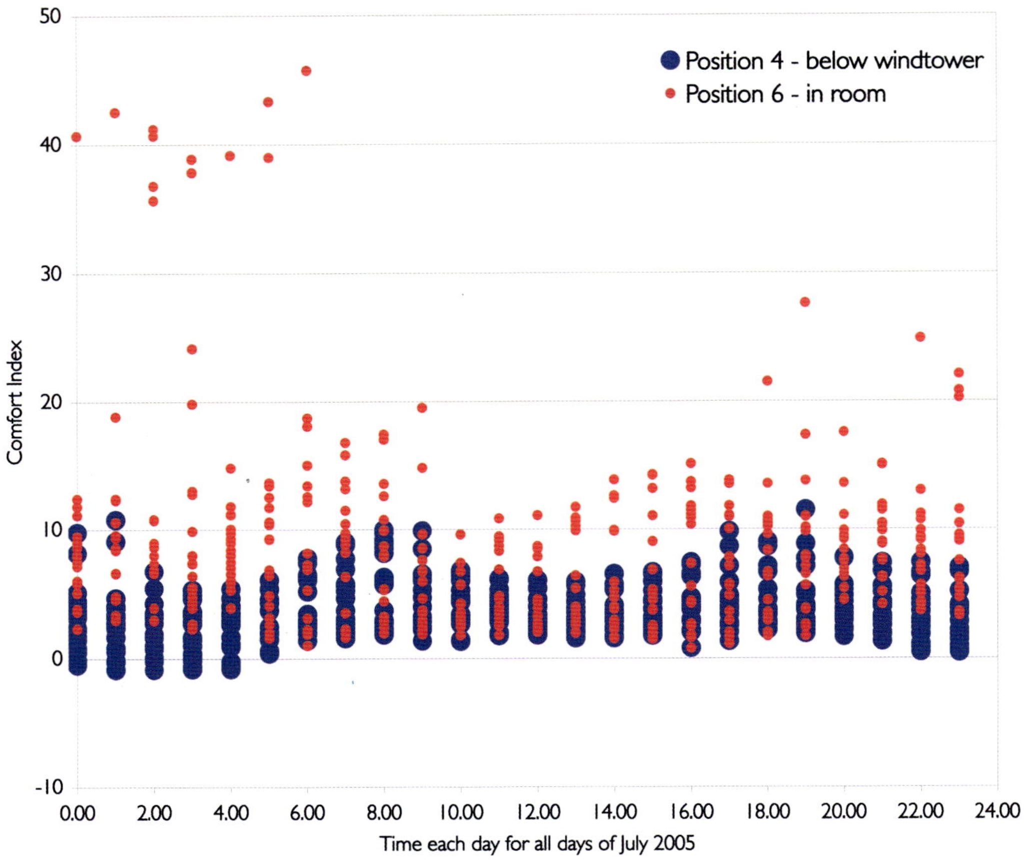

According to Wind Direction

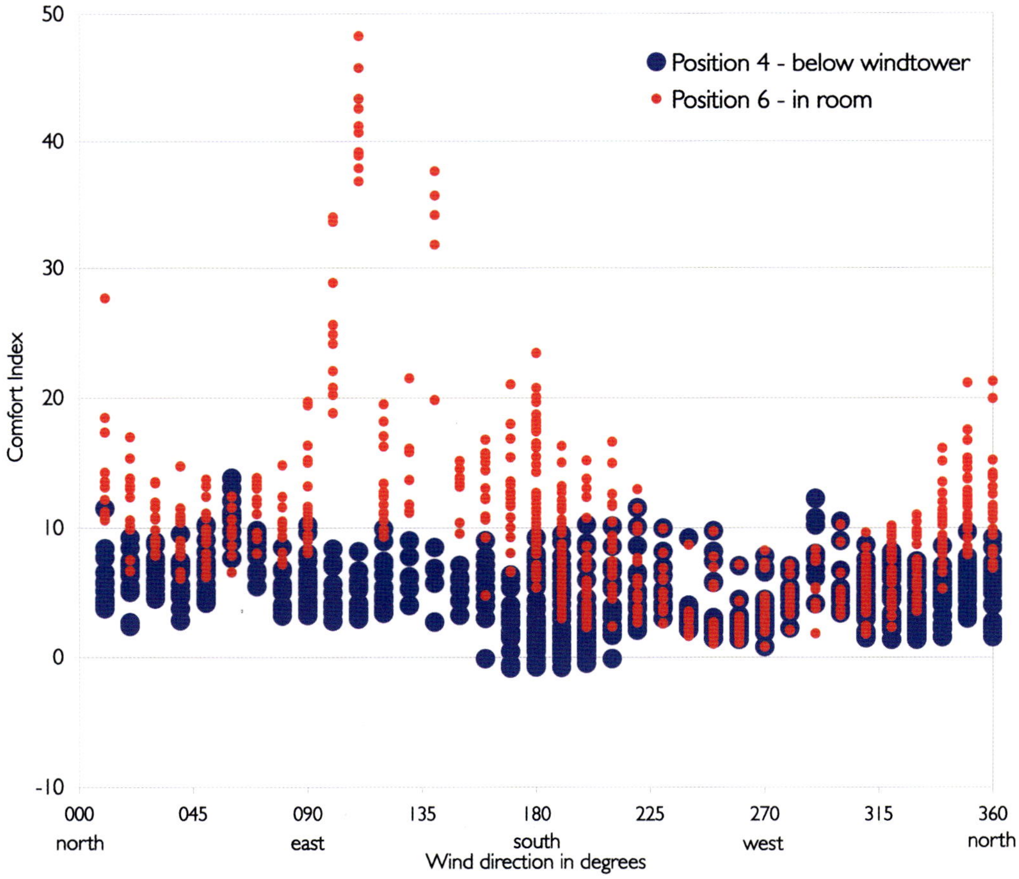

Calculating comfort in the Bukhash House. For these studies, the Heat Stress Index was used to measure levels of comfort. It takes into account air velocity as well as temperature and humidity, and is based on the need to keep skin temperature below 35° to limit rise in body temperature, and to avoid sweating more than 1 litre per hour to limit loss of body fluid. The index ranges from –20 (when mild cold strain is experienced) to +100 (the maximum strain tolerated by fit young men over an 8 hour period). 0 represents an optimum level of comfort, with +30 corresponding to moderate discomfort.

Predicted air velocities were calculated, using the results of the windtunnel studies together with hourly data from Dubai airport for wind speed and direction. Then, by incorporating the comparable temperature and relative humidity data from the airport, it was possible to calculate how comfortable it would have been inside, had the Bukhash house existed today. The comfort index can be calculated for the various combinations of open and closed doors and windows, as well as for any part of a windtower room. As an example, comfort was calculated for each hour during the month of July 2005 in the room below the north-west windtower, with its north facing windows open. The top graph shows that a position under the windtower is comfortable all the time. In contrast, while a position elsewhere in the room is comfortable for much of the time, it is sometimes, apparently randomly, very uncomfortable.

When the same data is plotted again (bottom graph), not by hours of the day but by wind direction in degrees of the compass, it can be seen that at the same position in the room the level of comfort is good with a west or north-westerly breeze but poor when the breeze is from the south-east. So points that appear to be random in the time graph, can be explained by the directional graph. If we were sitting inside the room when the south easterly wind was blowing we would, of course, take some action to become more comfortable, such as moving below the windtower, opening more windows, or going somewhere else for the duration of these adverse conditions.

Right:
This diagram of the Bukhash house shows the velocity of the volumes of air moving around the house. Air speeds are greatest in and beneath the windtowers. Where doors and windows are open, the moving air spreads into the courtyard.

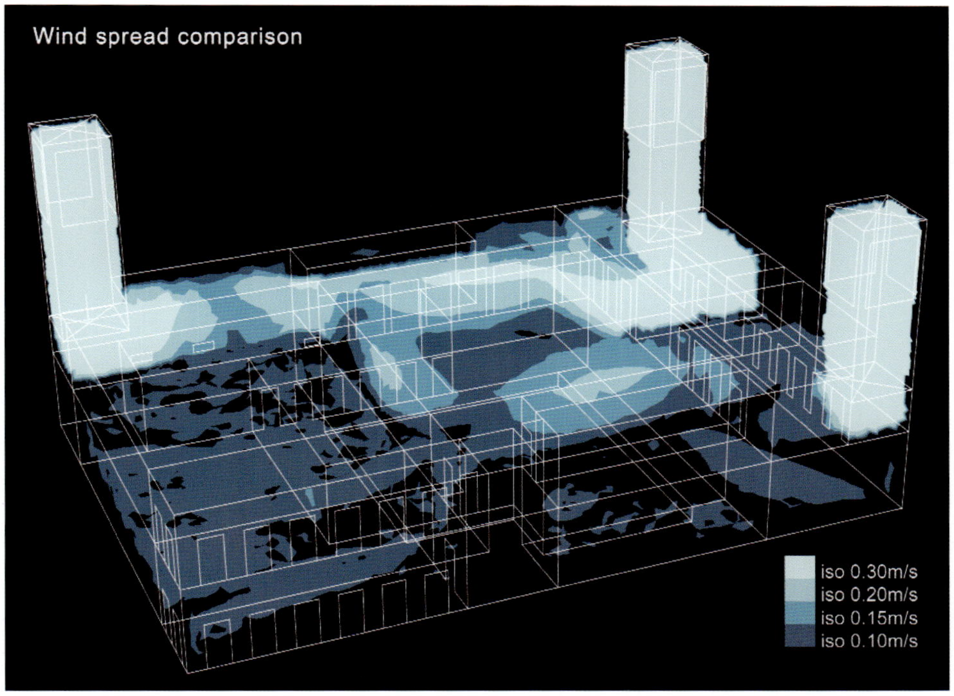

Conclusion

Within physiological limits, people partially adapt to the conditions to which they are accustomed, an adaptation that is at least partly psychological. The calculations show that good thermal comfort would have been maintained beneath a windtower for people who were sitting, rather than physically active. Conditions further into the rooms would have been more variable, less comfortable and sometimes more than moderately stressful. However, there was no doubt that the windtowers were effective in reducing the impact of the summer climate. Superimposing temperature and wind on the comfort graphs shows that comfort was more dependent on wind speed than on temperature. Similarly when more air movement was enabled by opening outside windows or windscoops, the discomfort otherwise experienced in a windtower room after midday was very much reduced.

Windtowers can make an important contribution to improving comfort in relatively humid, as well as dry, hot climates, and can continue to do so. In a world where issues of energy conservation are becoming increasingly critical, any passive system using natural ventilation to achieve its effect, offers considerable advantages both in wealthy and less developed regions. Vipac's generous research on how windtowers perform has provided a mass of data, which is already improving our detailed understanding of the principles involved. More efficient designs could reflect more efficient aerodynamics, incorporate dust-traps and controlled openings or be combined with evaporative cooling systems. We believe that the principles behind the comfort achieved by the windtowers of the Bastakiya can continue to be developed by architects and engineers for the benefit of our future built environment. With increasing awareness of environmental issues, the use of enhanced natural ventilation wherever full air-conditioning is not essential might well come to be seen as desirable and necessary.

13

Decline & Regeneration

The final phase in the story of the windtower houses of the Bastakiya is one of blight and dramatic recovery. Modern development gained momentum through the 1970s in the wake of the first Emirate oil exports, but new regulations would soon spell the end for the traditional Arabian courtyard house. Today the surviving windtowers – once so impressive in stature – are dwarfed by the soaring skyscrapers and glinting office blocks of one of the fastest growing business districts in the world.

Left:
By the early 1980s many of the windtower houses were in a poor state of repair. In 1978 a Unesco proposal for the Bastakiya would have retained the best houses, integrated with new civic and small scale commercial development. The small house of Abdul Kadr Abdulrahman Rashidi with its distinctive wooden verandah is today the headquarters of the UAE Architectural Heritage Society.

Decline of the Bastakiya

Development accelerated rapidly in Dubai after 1969 following the first exports of oil and Sheikh Rashid's strong vision for the future of the Emirate. Prosperity brought to Dubai the opportunity to improve standards of living. Dubai was looking forward to the promises of the future, rather than backwards to the hardships of the past. People saw little value in retaining traditional buildings, which were expensive to maintain, difficult to air condition, and which after all, were not very old.

In 1954 a formal Municipality was established, and, in 1958, a Land Department to give title of land to those who could reasonably lay claim to it. Much of the old part of the town, in Shindagha, Deira, Bur Dubai and the

Above:
Crumbling and efflorescence of gypsum panels and render show the ravages of rain and damp, alongside insect ravaged timbers and rotting woven palm mats at the entrance to the vacated family home of Abdullah Mohammad Al Bastaki.

Left:
In 1975 the authors recorded that many houses were in bad structural condition: 'The weight of the masonry forming the wind-towers tends to pull them away from the main structure of the buildings. Constant thermal stress and the ravages of insects in the timber beams and ceilings have contributed to the poor condition of the houses.'

There is serious cracking in the now demolished house of the Al Attar family. Note the wooden benches of a community meeting place or *dechaa* where neighbours would come together after *I'sha* (night) prayers. It was mainly used in summer, and at the end of Ramadan.

Above:
A view of a verandah in use as a kitchen when the Majlis Gallery was rented out to migrant workers.

Below right:
A windtower is razed, and the once private interior of the house of Abdulkareem Mahmoud Hamal Barshi is briefly exposed. Dariush Zandi recorded the houses before and during their destruction.

Bastakiya was already in private ownership. Sheikh Rashid commissioned London based John R Harris Architects & Planners to prepare the first town plan in 1960. Town planning rules were introduced in 1968, including a prohibition on demolition in Shindagha or the Bastakiya, or alterations other than for minor maintenance. This should have benefited preservation of buildings in the old quarters, but it contributed to a situation over the next decade in which owners stopped spending money on maintenance, and began moving out: the regulations simply went against the spirit of change that was sweeping Dubai. Further regulations were introduced in 1971, requiring new residential buildings to be set back from plot boundaries, marking the end of the Arab courtyard house, traditionally built around the perimeter of the plot.

In 1971 John R Harris carried out a Dubai Development Plan Review, which highlighted a need for conservation. It recognised that the vernacular architecture 'has an intrinsic value, an undeniable attraction, an unquestioned harmony: none of which is measurable but all of which contributes to the fascination exerted by Dubai and its creek'. Harris called for a survey of old buildings worthy of preservation, and if necessary, restoration, if future development was to be based on a policy involving conservation. In the same year Dubai's first museum was opened in Al Faheidi Fort.

Uncertainty over the Bastakiya's future led to neglect and minimal repairs after infrequent but damaging winter showers. A combination of the incompatible qualities of modern construction using cement with traditional coral and gypsum accelerated the deterioration of the old houses. Cracks occurred through shrinkage and differential settlement, aggravating problems of water ingress through both rain and rising damp. As the crumbling buildings were vacated, they were either left to deteriorate and slowly collapse, or were rented to low income Asian labourers, at a density two or

three times that which the houses were intended to accommodate, accelerating decay. A few continued to be occupied, and at least three were let to enthusiastic Europeans who wanted to live in traditional houses, and experience their environmental and historic qualities.

In view of the impeding redevelopment of the Bastakiya, in 1976 Anne Coles and Jennifer Scarce, a specialist in nineteenth-century Islamic art with the Department of Art and Archaeology of the Royal Scottish Museum in Edinburgh, put together a proposal for a combined architectural and social survey to cover all the buildings of the Bastakiya. The proposal was turned down.

A 1978 Unesco mission to the UAE issued a report with recommendations prepared by the Shankland Cox Partnership. The Bastakiya was the main area of concern for the mission, but their terms of reference were extended to cover problems of conservation in all the Emirates. The report reaffirmed that efforts to safeguard the Bastakiya must continue but 'meanwhile the environment will continue to decline, and the houses decay. Ultimately, if no action is taken, the area will be demolished through sheer neglect'.

In 1981 Dariush Zandi, an Iranian architect with a special interest in historic buildings, joined the Municipality Town Planning Section. When it was proposed that the Sheikh Saeed House in Shindagha should be restored, as the home of the ruling Maktoums, Dariush oversaw the project. Iraqi architects Makiya Associates were commissioned to design the restoration works. Little was known about traditional coral stone construction, and the

Above:
View in 1976 from the south of the Bastakiya looking towards the windtower houses of Mahmoud Mohammad Arjumand al Bastaki (centre left) and Qasim Abdulla Al Bastaki (centre right). Later buildings in the foreground were built of sand-lime blocks. Despite restrictions, temporary structures reappeared, usually in plywood, but seen here with a gunny sack windtower.

Below:
Prior to rehabilitation, individual historic buildings were identified by a metal plaque, prohibiting unauthorised entry, modification or use.

local authority, inexperienced in this type of work, approved its demolition and complete reconstruction, although this was not in accordance with international guidelines for restoration.

In 1984, an architectural competition was held that was to prove fateful for the Bastakiya. The old Diwan bordering the Creek was by now inadequate for the scale of government business being conducted from the Ruler's office. It was not felt desirable to demolish his old offices, and a major extension was planned within the Bastakiya. John R Harris won the competition, and it became necessary to demolish a substantial portion of the historic quarter.

The Bastakiya had become an eyesore to many, especially as it was situated at the Ruler's front door. Compensation was offered to the owners, in the form of cash and new plots of land. There was no opposition, most already having moved into modern villas and apartments elsewhere. Many did not even return to remove household goods they had left behind. In February 1985 bulldozers moved in. It took less than a week to flatten the remaining buildings, including some of the oldest and finest that had been built: the palatial Farouk house, the ornate Al Arshi house, and the Bukhash house.

Construction of the new Diwan was completed in 1986, drawing architectural inspiration from the houses it replaced, its service towers designed in the form of gleaming white windtowers. Next to it, a new and considerably enlarged mosque replaced the Farouk Mosque, its tall minaret dominating the remaining windtowers in the Bastakiya.

Below:
Without any previous experience of building conservation, this first example of building preservation in Dubai, of the Maktoum family home in Shindagha, was completely re-built on a concrete frame. It was completed in 1986.

Regeneration

Dariush Zandi surveyed and made a photographic record of old buildings in Shindagha, the Bastakiya and Al Ras, and identified historic areas within the old souqs worthy of preservation. The Chief Town Planner, Abdullah Al Gaith, as well as the Director of the Municipality, Kamal Hamza, actively supported him. With Shirley Kay, he co-authored *Architectural Heritage of the Gulf*, and undoubtedly his knowledge and enthusiasm promoted a growing public interest in architectural conservation in Dubai.

Above:
Construction of the new Ruler's Diwan (centre left) continued through 1985. The eastern-most end of the Bastakiya would be retained to become Dubai's principal area of historic interest.

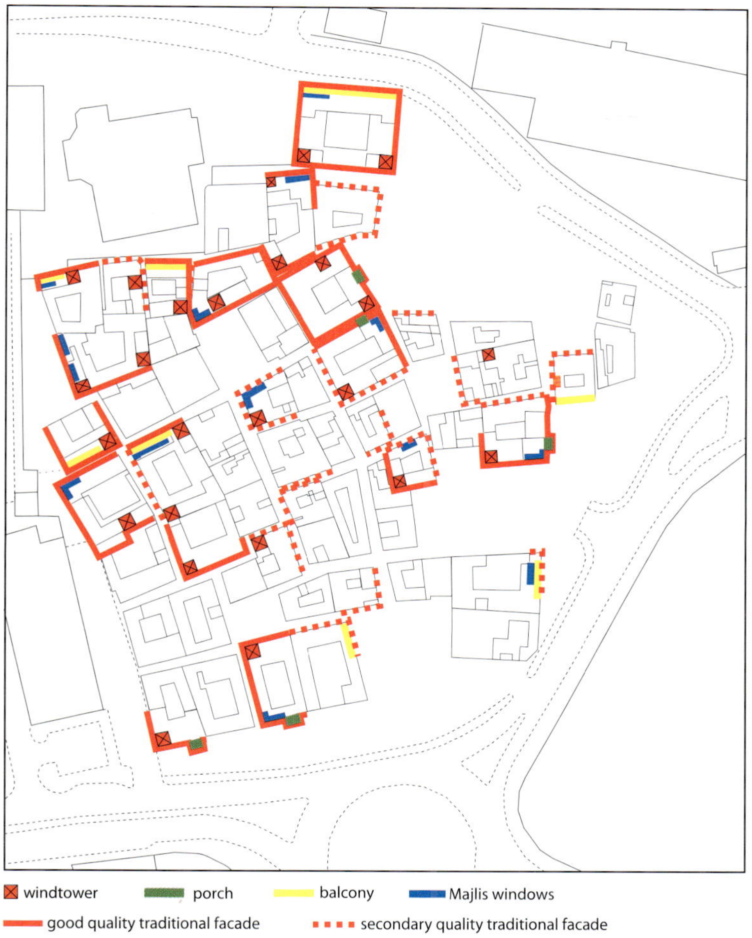

Above left:
The Llewelyn-Davies survey of 1994 highlights features of architectural merit visible externally.

Above right:
The survey also highlights courtyard features worthy of preservation.

During the 1980s Doxiadis Associates International prepared the Comprehensive Development Plan in conjunction with the Municipality and the United Nations Development Programme (UNDP). Their report, covering Dubai's Central Business District (CBD), identified the Bastakiya and Shindagha as the only traditional areas remaining within Dubai. It noted that 'historic structures in the CBD serve to add interest and flavour to CBD development, reinforce activity patterns, as well as presenting value intrinsic to the preservation of Dubai's cultural heritage'.

Two years after the demolition, a new architectural graduate, Rashad Mohammed Bukhash joined the Planning Section. Rashad had been studying in the States when his father's house was demolished. He soon became involved in a number of architectural and planning projects, but significantly for him three other restoration projects had been scheduled: the 1799 Al Faheidi Fort in need of major structural repair, Dubai's first school, Al Ahmadiya School, built in 1912 in Deira, and Hatta Village. It would be in the implementation of these projects that Rashad would develop his love for old buildings.

During an official visit by Prince Charles in March 1989, British Consul General Jolyan Kay suggested to the Prince that he might be interested to see a Bastakiya house. The Prince readily agreed. A visit to the Bastakiya was hastily slotted into the official schedule, and he was taken to the former house of Sheikh Abdulraheem Al Janahi, then rented to a British architect. That night over dinner at the Zabeel Palace, the subject of conservation was raised. Prince Charles was the final catalyst in preventing further demolition.

The Municipality sent Rashad to find out what was being done by way of conservation in Bahrain, Qatar, Kuwait, Oman, and Saudi Arabia. He visited historic buildings in each, gaining a useful overview of regional and Gulf architecture. In Jeddah he was made aware of problems created where restored buildings remained empty and unused, resulting in rapid deterioration.

With the advantage of this overview, Rashad developed an idea that the Municipality should establish a restoration unit, employing its own tradesmen and craftsmen, and building with traditional materials. His report in 1990 led to the establishment of a Historic Buildings sub-section within the Planning Section, with six labourers, an engineer, a mason and a photographer, all based in a temporary site office at Al Faheidi Fort.

In 1991, the government ordered the demolition of old Al Shindagha. Two demolition contractors were instructed to complete demolition within 15 days. Together with Dariush Zandi, Rashad commandeered a number of street cleaners and streetlight maintenance vehicles, and proceeded to work ahead of the contractors to rescue gypsum panels, doors and windows, and take photographs. This had to be done extremely quickly, as the next day the houses would be gone. They managed to survey a few of the buildings before their demolition, including the Sheikh Juma Al Maktoum and Sheikh Obaid Bin Thani houses, and six mosques.

Sadly, the demolition of Shindagha took place against a growing public awareness of the importance of Dubai's historic buildings. It would still be a few years before the potential economic benefit of heritage conservation in promoting tourism were to be more widely appreciated. In 2005 the Government ordered the reconstruction of the demolished historic buildings in Shindagha.

The restoration of Al Faheidi Fort was successfully completed and in 1994 the sub-section was upgraded to become the Unit for Historic Buildings and Exhibitions. By 1995, having expanded to a staff of 240, and with its own fabrication workshops, the Unit became the Historic Buildings Section within the General Projects Department of the Municipality.

The Municipality then commissioned British planning and architectural consultants Llewelyn-Davies to prepare a conservation plan for the area. Their substantial proposals in the 'Bastakiya Conservation Preliminary Study' were to form the basis for restoration and reconstruction of 55 buildings in the Bastakiya.

The recommendations were developed to provide a 1997 Ten Year Restoration Plan encompassing all historic buildings in the Emirate, but in particular those of the Bastakiya. At the same time a programme was put into place for their regular maintenance.

The importance which Dubai now places on its architectural heritage is illustrated through its initiative in hosting its first international Architectural Conservation Conference in 2004. A second Conference was held in 2007. Largely due to the vision of Rashad Bukhash, 'heritage' has become a part of the business of Dubai, a very far cry from the bulldozers of 1985 and 1991.

Dubai is now both looking forward to its future development, as well as to its past, reinforcing identity and celebrating history.

Above:
The Sheikh Mohammed Centre for Cultural Understanding welcomes all visitors to the Qasim Abdullah Al Bastaki House, and invites non Muslims to participate in their cultural programme, the Iftar meal that breaks the Ramadan fast, each day at sunset. It also conducts guided tours of the Bastakiya, describing aspects of traditional life.

Below:
A popular café now occupies the former home of Abdulraheem Al Attar bringing back life and colour to the old quarter.

Windtowers as Symbols

Windtowers live on in the architecture of the Emirates – no longer elegantly and efficiently fulfilling their original purpose but rather as decorative symbols of the national heritage. In origin the masonry windtowers of Dubai were a reflection of the cosmopolitan, mercantile society that grew up in the late nineteenth and early twentieth centuries. They were adopted by Arab rulers and members of the Arab elite, partly for practical purposes but also as a sign of status. Windtowers came to represent power, wealth and also a policy of openness to international commercial activity that has continued for a hundred years.

But windtowers were also more broadly based in the social fabric. Their use on *areesh* houses had brought comfort to a large proportion of the ordinary people, both local and immigrant, and were a sign of a settled urban existence. It was not surprising, therefore, that in the early 1980s the Dubai Municipality incorporated windtowers within its logo. Modern windtowers represent a link with the past, expressing continuity in a landscape of rapid urban and social change. They demonstrate a sense of 'belonging', and a memory of a former way of life. Developers use them to add regional style to modest town houses and as features on apartment blocks. With tourism as a major new industry, the most striking examples of modern windtowers are in tourist complexes, in hotels and shopping malls. The windtower has become a key international symbol of Dubai in the early twenty-first century.

Above:
Evoking the *Arabian Nights*, the hotel and souq complex of Madinat Jumeirah provide a tourist fantasy.

Below:
Windtower forms on townhouses in the suburb of Mirdif camouflage water tanks and air conditioning units while providing a harmonious contribution to buildings they adorn.

The Bastakiya restored

The restoration of the Bastakiya is now nearing completion. While it has only been possible to retain half of the original, this is still much more complete than was originally recommended in the 1978 Unesco report. There has been no demolition of what were then considered to be second or third grade structures, and no infill with new commercial or civic buildings. The high boundary wall of the 1986 Diwan has been softened by an accretion of traditional facades which will serve as market stalls.

The former sandy lanes are now all stone paved, though a stabilized sand finish might have been more appropriate to their original character. Reconstruction of an entire quarter over a relatively short period of time has resulted in some repetition of pattern book details. An inevitable smoothness in the reconstructed surfaces, which should mellow with time, has replaced a textual roughness which gave variety and intimacy to the former exteriors.

In its new guise as a cultural heart within Dubai, the Bastakiya is no longer residential in character, which while a criticism, does mean that the majority of houses have become publicly accessible. Most buildings are today either restaurants, galleries, or are planned to become museums.

It would be wrong however to give an impression that there is no longer any sense of the original community within the Bastakiya. There is a daily evening *majlis* of men who grew up together in the Bastakiya. Its origins go back to the early 1970s when they formed Al Shibl (small lions) Club, an informal football team whose members played, climbed trees, fished and swam together in the Creek. A powerful bond was forged between them. During the 1980s, as the last residents moved out of the district, they moved their premises between the abandoned houses, eventually combining their pocket money to rent a small corner house. One Ramadan, they built a *khaimah* next to it as a place to sit and socialise.

Above:
One house has been rented since 1995 by an expatriate. He successfully resisted being moved out of his home, having invested two years' hard work in its renovation, and creating a glazed roof over the courtyard, allowing the original loz tree to pass through.

Below left:
On the edge of the Bastakiya, the men's *majlis* gives an idea of the character of traditional palm frond construction, though considerably larger than a traditional room and air-conditioned. It is framed by three old trees, a subaar (*Manilla tamarind*) and two sidr trees.

Eventually, the boys went their various ways to study, but all returned. While they watched others turn their back on their old homes, they kept their club and football team together.

A small part of the original Bastakiya community lives on at this 'Areesh Majlis'. They meet daily at their clubhouse, where they dine together, play cards and dominoes, dance to the traditional local bagpipes (*habban*), and a few smoke the *qalyoon*. From here it is only a few minutes' walk to the mosque, where they pray together. Most importantly the club sits adjacent to the main access to the Bastakiya from the creek, and visitors who care to stop are made very welcome. The club takes pride in the restored area, sharing tea and coffee in traditional hospitality. Their presence maintains a tangible link with the historic community that was the Bastakiya.

Below:
An exhibition of traditional dancing in front of the UAE Architectural Heritage Society headquarters. A crisp white tower on the Diwan can be seen behind, with the new mosque to the right.

Appendix

Key to plan on p.20 showing house owners of the Bastakiya in 1978.

Preserved buildings

5	Abdulrazaq Abdulrahim Aminai
13	Abdulrahouf Abdulrahman Al Awar Al Bastaki
14	Dr Mohammed Shareef Abdulla Al Mullah
15a-e	Ahmed Qasim Al Sadiqi
19	Mir Abdulla Amiri
21	Mohammed Ali Al Zarawni
25	Mohammed Abdulkareem Haji (only family still resident here)
32	Farouk Ahmed Al Awar Al Bastaki
40	Shk Abdulrahim Mohammed Janahi (Al Abassi)
40/1	Mohammed Noor Janahi
41	Amain Hassan Al Awadi
42	Abdulrahim Darwish Al Bastaki
42/1	Shk Abdullah Shareef
43	Qasim Abdulla Al Bastaki
47	Ibrahim Jengaan
56	Abdulrahman Al Shaibani
58	Abdul Razaq Abdulaziz Al Mullah
59	Qasim Abdulla Al Bastaki
63	Abdulraheem Al Attar
64	Moyeedin Abdulla Al Bastaki with Abdul Samad Mohammed Al Bastakia
67	Abdulrahman Yousuf Al Khoory
68	Mohammed Tayeb Al Khoory
69	Abdullah Mohammed Al Bastaki
71	Mohammed Saleh Mohammed Fikree Al Bastaki
70	Makiya Abdullah Tawfiqi
74a/b	Khaja Reza Al Bastaki
79	Mahmoud Mohammed Ostadi
79/1	Abdulrazaq Mohammed Ostadi
84	Abdul Kadr Abdulrahman Rashidi Al Bastaki
87	Mir Ahmad Abdulwahad Amiri
88	Ahmad Zainal Al Bastaki
89	Sultan Moyeedin Al Bastaki
90/1	Abdulrahman Mohammed Shafea Al Bastaki
90	Ismail Abdi Al Bastaki
91	Abdul Rahman Ali Al Bastaki
92	Ghloom Ali Al Harangi
98	Mahmoud Abdulla Al Khoory
100	Mahmoud Mohammed Arjumand al Bastaki
105	Shk Mustafa Al Janahi
107	Abdulla Yousuf Al Khoory
108-9	Abdulrahman Al Sharafi
110	Abdulla Yousuf Al Khoory
111	Abdulla Yousuf Al Khoory
113a/b	Al Ostad Mohammed Al Bana Al Bastatki
118	Yousuf Jengaan
121	Shk Mohammed Shareef Abdulrahman Al Ulama
122	Abdulrahman Farouk Al Bastaki
126&126/1	Al Haja Fatima Zaya (wife) Farouk Al Bastaki

Demolished houses

d1	Haji Baqr Fakhr
d2	Abdulrahman Falakhnaz
d3	Sediq Kazim
d4	Mohammed Aqeel Kazim
d5	Abdul Kareem Farouk
d6	Haji Ahmad Arshi
d7	Haji Mohammed Falakhnaz
d8	Abdul Kareem Farouk
d9	Mirza
d10	Mohammed Saleh Kazim
d11	storerooms of Haji Mohammed Falakhnaz
d12	Mohammad Saleh Abdul Kareem Darwish
d13	Sheikh Khalifa (later Mahdi Tajir)
d14	Sheikh Khalifa bin Saeed Al Maktoum
d15	Mohammed Shareef Bukhash
d16	Abdullah Qasemi
d17	Haj Mahmoud Bastaki
d18	Haji AbdulRahman Abdullah Abbas
d19	Mohammed Shareef Bukhash
d20	Mohammed Ahmad Bukhash
d21	Ahmad Bukhash
d22	Shk Saeed bin Maktoum Al Maktoum
d23	Abdulkareem Mahmoud Hamal Barshi
d24	Haji Qaed Ahmad Al Attar
d25	Haida Jahromi
d26	Mohammad Saleh Kamelpoor
d27	Haji Mohammad Bukhash
d28	Mohammad Abdullah Abbas
d29	Farouk Ahmed Al Awar Al Bastaki
d30	Haji Ali
d31	Sheik Mosa bin Saeed – provided to the Shola Club
d32	Yousuf Abdul Kareem
d33	Haji Abdullah Kamalpoor
d34	Mullah Mohammed Yousuf Al Khatib
d35	Haji Nasrullah Anwahi
d36	Ismael Mohammed
d37	Tayeb Abdullah Haji Kazim
d38	Abdulkarem Mohammed Abdulkarem Haji Karem
d39	Mohammed Noor Fikree

Glossary

Abbreviations:

A = Arabic
LA = Local Arabic
P = Persian
B = Bastaki

abaya	(A)	outer robe worn by women, usually black
abra	(LA)	small boat to ferry passengers across the Creek, originally rowed, later fitted with a diesel motor
ajami	(A)	foreigner; *eemi* (LA). In Dubai the word is often used to refer to those from the Iranian coast
areesh	(A)	woven date palm fronds used for building. Generally used for houses built of palm fronds; specifically used for houses made for summer living
baadgir	(P)	Literally 'wind-catcher'. In Dubai these take the form of windtowers. The word has been locally Arabicised to become *barjeel*
baadkash	(B)	literally 'wind-puller', windscoop; thin offset masonry panels in external wall providing complete privacy; locally known as *maskat*
baaghcheh	(P)	garden
baalak	(B)	lower recessed alcove
baawer	(B)	unfinished room
baaweree	(B)	upper or high room
barasti		generic term for structures made of date palm fronds, particularly used by foreigners
Bastak		inland town in southern Iran
Bastakiya		quarter in Dubai settled by Bastaki merchants and their families
Batinah Coast		the north-east facing coastal plain bordering the Indian Ocean. It extends from the Emirates into Oman
bon	(B)	roof terrace used for sleeping
Buraimi		an inland oasis bordering Abu Dhabi and Oman
Bur Dubai		the old commercial centre of Dubai
chaah	(P)	well, a word seldom used today; *towi* (LA); *bir* (A)
chandal	(B)	imported (round) mangrove pole used in building; *shandal* (LA)
chebab	(LA)	type of bread
dahleez	(P)	entrance gate, lobby
daraj	(A)	wooden ladder
dareecha	(B)	window; *dareesha* (A)
dechaa	(LA)	literally 'high place' – a raised area for sitting/meeting
dehleez	(P)	entrance gate, also used for entrance lobby, *dehreez* (B)
Deira		commercial and former residential district of Dubai to the north of the Creek
dhow		wooden seafaring sailing vessel with a lateen (triangular) sail; also use more generally by foreigners in Dubai for any local craft. The word is probably of Indian origin
diwan	(A)	government department, official reception chamber
dustandaaz	(B)	high timber louvred screen *shorbaak* (LA)
Eid al Adha	(A)	Muslim festival of sacrifice 70 days after the end of Ramadan which coincides with the *Haj*
Eid al Fitr	(A)	Muslim festival at the end of Ramadan
farkha	(B)	wicket – small door within the entrance doors
farush	(B/LA)	shellstone conglomerate used for building
fesht	(LA)	coral building stones
gadou	(LA)	hubble-bubble pipe with aromatic tobacco; *qalyoon* (B)
gateya	(B)	wash room; *zaweeya* (A)
gulmeekh	(B)	pegs for hanging lanterns/pictures (lit. flower nails). Locally known as *mealaaq*
habban	(LA)	traditional 'bagpipes' made from goatskin
halva	(A)	sweetmeat based on *tahini* (sesame paste) or semolina, sweetened with sugar or honey
Hamriya		former name of the area that became the Bastakiya
haraam	(A)	forbidden

Hatta		village enclave of Dubai territory in the mountains near Omani border
horeed	(LA)	game of hide and seek
iftar	(A)	meal taken after sunset to break the fast during Ramadan
jaadumee	(B)	inner sleeping room
jedhae		split palm logs used in building
Jumeirah		suburb of Dubai, formerly a fishing village
jus	(LA)	pronounced 'yus', gypsum, used as plaster
khaimah	(A)	literally tent; also the specific name for houses made of date palm fronds that had a tight weave and pitched roofs for winter living
khatib juma	(A)	Friday preacher
kherocho	(B)	timber gargoyle; *merzab* (LA)
khoona peyah	(B)	mezzanine onion store (literally 'olive room')
kowskhan	(P)	lobby; literally, where shoes are removed
Khudmooni	(B)	Bataki, the language from Bastak, 'of ourselves'
laban	(A)	Middle East soured and set milk product very similar to yoghurt.
Lingeh		Iranian port on the Gulf serving Bastak and the interior
loz with	(B/LA/A)	Indian almond tree (*Terminalia catappa*), with a small edible fruit
madanee	(B)	mezzanine store
maghasat	(A)	pearl banks or pearling fields
majlis	(A)	reception room, or meeting place, (usually for men), council
maktab	(A)	office; here a Qur'anic school for young children, usually in a house
Maqbarat Al Shoyookh	(A)	Sheikhs' graveyard near the Bastakiya, formerly Maqbarat Bur Dubai
masjid	(A)	mosque
matbakh	(A)	kitchen
minsera	(B)	courtyard, *howi* (LA), *hosh* (A)
mistaa	(B)	children's game played with bat and ball
mostaraab	(B)	latrine
muezzin	(A)	the person who calls Muslims to prayer
mullah	(P)	religious leader
murabah	(B/LA)	sawn timber (literally, square)
nokhada	(LA)	captain of a boat
oud	(A)	sandalwood, incense
panjara	(B)	decorative perforated screen made of gypsum plaster
panjdari	(B)	room with five doors
pella	(B)	masonry staircase
Qajar	(P)	Persian dynasty that ruled from 1794 to 1925
qandeel	(B)	store for dates; *madbas* (LA)
Qibla	(A)	direction towards Makkah, to which Muslims turn when praying; a recess in a mosque indicating the direction of Makkah
qors	(B)	raised *dais* or platform
raahrow	(P)	passage
Ramadan		Muslim month of fasting, a holy month requiring abstinence during daylight hours
rolla	(LA)	banyan tree; Bengal fig (*Ficus benghalensis*)
saaj	(LA)	teak wood
saapela		landing, literally 'head of the stair'
sabaat	(B)	verandah
sabkha	(A)	saltflat, salt marsh
Safavid	(P)	Persian dynasty that ruled from 1501 to 1736, which established Shi'a Islam as the official religion and united its provinces under a single ruler
salafa	(B/A)	flat laminar stones, cut from sedimentary deposits found in estuaries
sandokhoona	(B)	lobby
sarood	(LA)	large round dining mat
sarooj	(LA)	type of building clay imported from Oman
shamal	(LA)	north-westerly wind that blows down the Gulf in winter (*shamal* means 'north' in Arabic)
sheikh	(A)	ruler, elder, chief, religious leader, widely used as a title

Shindagha		former residential quarter in Dubai at the mouth of the Creek
shorbaak	(LA)	decorated perforated gypsum balustrade; *panjara* (B)
sideri	(B)	room with three doors
sidr	(A)	thorny tree, 'crown of thorns', (*Zizyphus spina christi*)
sikka	(A)	lane, path or narrow street
sohoor	(A)	meal taken before dawn during Ramadan
Souk al Kabeer	(A)	the grand market, the main souq on the Dubai side of the creek. Originally known as 'Souq Banyan'
subaar	(A)	tamarind tree (*Manila tamarind*)
taakheechah	(B)	upper recessed alcove
tabuk	(A)	building blocks, refers here to sand-lime hand-pressed blocks, but can also refer to modern cement blocks
talli	(LA)	gold and silver thread embroidery work, usually done in bands
takhee	(B)	rear entrance door
teedumee	(B)	outer day room
teela	(LA)	game of marbles
ulama		scholars, often learned in religious matters
windtower		see *baadgir*

Bibliography

General

Cantacuzino, S and Browne, K, 'United Arab Emirates' *Architectural Review* Special Issue, June 1977.

Coles, A and Jackson, P, 'A Windtower House in Dubai', Monograph for Art and Archaeology Research Papers, 1975.

Coles, A and Jackson, P, 'Bastakia Windtower Houses' in the *Architectural Review*, July 1975, pp.51-53

Facey, W and Grant, P, *The Emirates by the First Photographers*, Stacey International 1996

Heard-Bey, F, *From Trucial States to United Arab Emirates*, Longman 1982, (latest edition Motivate Publishing, Dubai 2004).

Chapter 1: Historical Development

Anon, 'Persian Gulf' Handbooks prepared under the direction of the Historical Section of the Foreign Office, HMSO London 1920.

Avery, P, Hambly, G and Melville, C (Eds), 'The Cambridge History of Iran' Vol. VII, Cambridge University Press, Cambridge, 1991.

Bosworth, E and Hillenbrand, C (Ed), *Qajar Iran: Political Social and Cultural Change 1825-1925* Edinburgh University Press 1983.

Curzon, G N, *Persia and the Persian Question*, Longman 1892.

Hawker, R, 'Reflections on the Wind Tower House: Architectural Style & Historical Context on the Trucial Coast' in *Tribulus* Autumn/Winter 2001 (Bulletin of the Emirates Natural History Group).

Hawker, R, 'Tribe, House Style and the Town layout of Jazirat al-Hamra, Ras Al-Khaimah, UAE' unpublished manuscript 2006.

Hawker, R, 'The Windtower House of Iran and the Arabian Gulf', A paper specially prepared for this project, 2006.

Hawley, D, *The Trucial States*, Allen & Unwin London 1970

Kelly, J B, *Britain and the Persian Gulf*, Oxford 1968.

Lorimer, J G, 'Gazetteer of the Persian Gulf, Oman and Central Arabia', Government of India, Calcutta 1908 and Archive Editions 1986.

Ministry of Overseas Development, 'The First Population census of the Northern Trucial States March/April 1968', Middle East Development Division Beirut 1969.

University of El Ain, The National Atlas of the UAE, University of El Ain, 1993

Department of Civil Aviation, Annual Climate and Weather of Dubai, Dubai up-dated 2006.

Chapter 2: House Form & Architecture

Al Rostamani, A H, *Dubai and its Architectural Heritage*, Al Safeer Publishing & Advertising, 1991.

Ardener, S, (Ed), *Women and Space: Ground Rules and Social Maps*, Croom Helm, London, 1981; revised edition, Berg, Oxford and New York, 1993.

Bukhash, R M, 'Managing Restoration Projects in Dubai, United Arab Emirates' thesis for doctorate, University of Manchester, 2000.

Kay S, and Zandi, D, *Architectural Heritage of the Gulf* Motivate Publishing 1991

Kazerooni, F, *Gulf Islamic Architecture*, Farry Kazerooni, Bahrain 2002.

Michell, G, (Ed), *Architecture of the Islamic World*, Thames & Hudson 1978.

Mortada, H, *Traditional Islamic Principles of Built Environment*, Routledge 2003.

Omer, M, *Traditional Architecture of Dubai*, Arts & the Islamic World Special Supplement 27 & 28: 1998.

Ragette, F, *Traditional Domestic Architecture of the Arab Region*, American University of Sharjah, 2003 (Edition Axel Menges).

Rapoport, A, *House Form & Culture*, Prentice Hall, 1969.

Yarwood, J R, 'Al Muharraq, Architecture of a Traditional Arabian Town in Bahrain' special issue of Arts & the Islamic World no. 36, 1999.

Chapter 3: Everyday Life

Benham, M, *Heirloom: Evening Tales from the East*, Enlarged edition, SAMA, Karachi 2005.

Benham, M, *Zelzehlah: A Woman Before her Time*, Motivate Publishing, Dubai 1994.

el-Gurg, E S, *The Wells of Memory*, John Murray, London 1998.

Iddison, P, 'Food bibliography with Particular Reference to the United Arab Emirates', Al Ain 1999 and other papers on Abu Dhabi emirate.

Scarce, J, *The Evolving Culture of Kuwait*, Royal Scottish Museum Edinburgh, 1985.

Scarce, J, 'Domestic Culture in the Middle East; and Exploration of the Household Interior', National Museums of Scotland, 1996.

Wheeler, J, and Thuysbaert, P, *Telling Tales, An Oral History of Dubai*, Explorer Publishing 2005.

Chapter 11: Construction

Afshar, F, Cain, A, and Norton J, 'The Climatic Influences on Regional Architecture' in *The Architecture of Oman*, Garnet Reading, 1998 pp.17-36.

'Elements of Traditional Architecture in Dubai', Dubai Municipality Historic Buildings Section, 1996, reprinted & updated 2000 & 2005.

Yarwood, J R, 'Traditional Building Construction in an Historic Arabian Town', (Bahrain) in Construction History, Vol. 15, 1999 pp.57-77.

Chapter 12: Windtowers

Cain A, Afshar, F, and Norton, J, 'Indigenous Building and the Third World', Architectural Design, Vol. XLV No. 41975, pp.217-235, April 1975.

Fathy, H, 'Natural Energy and Vernacular Architecture' University of Chicago Press 1986.

Hawker, R, Hull D, and Rouhani, O, 'Windtowers and Pearl Fishing: Architectural Signals in the late 19th and early 20th Century', Antiquity, forthcoming.

Roaf, S, 'Windcatchers' in E Beasley and M Harverson *Living with the Desert*, Aris and Phillips 1982 pp57-72.

Roaf, S, 'The Windcatchers of Yazd', unpublished doctorate thesis, Dept. of Architecture, Oxford Polytechnic, Council for National Academic Awards 1988.

Vipac Engineers & Scientists Ltd 'The Bastakia Windtowers of Dubai Windtunnel Study, with CFD Results', unpublished report, Melbourne, 2006.

Chapter 13: Decline & Regeneration

Boussa, D, 'The Bastakia Historic District in Dubai: From Survival to

Revival', paper for the First International Conference Architectural Conservation between Theory & Practice, Dubai 2004.
Harris, John R (Architects and Planning Consultants), 'Dubai Development Plan Review', 1971.
Harris, John R, 'Proposed Bastakia Re-Development Project, Dubai' 1991.
Harris, M, 'Selected Research Extracts Relating to the Windtower Houses of the Bastakia, Dubai, United Arab Emirates' unpublished thesis for M. Arch U D Harvard 1980.
Llewelyn-Davies, 'Bastakia Conservation preliminary Study', Volumes 1 & 2, Report on behalf of Dubai Municipality 1994.
Roberts, J and Zandi, D, 'Dubai Town Walk Map' Dubai 1994.
Shankland Cox Partnership, Unesco Mission to the UAE study: 'Conservation in the United Arab Emirates' 1978.

Index

Italicised page numbers refer to illustrations; references in **bold** indicate subject boxes.

A

Abass, Abdullah Abass, *13*, 24
Abassi families, 13
Abdul Kadr Abdulrahman Rashidi house, *174-5*, *185*
Abdulkareem Mahmoud Hamal Barshi house, *25*, *33*,*177*
Abdullah Mohammed Al Bastaki house, 39, *176*
Abdullah Yousuf Al Khoory house, *39*
Abdulraheem Al Attar house, *182*
Abdulraheem Al Janahi, Sheikh, 65
Abdulrazak, Ahmed, 58, 59, 62
Abdulrazak family, 58-60, 63-4
Abdulrazak, Sharif, 58, 63
abras, 9, 15, 16, 108
Abu Dhabi, 5, 6, 8, 20, 151
Aden, 13, 27, 69
Afghanistan, 164
Ahmed, Mahmoud Ahmed, *115*
Ahmadiya school, 181
air conditioning, 4, 7, 157, 165
Al Abassi, Sheikh Abdul-Raheem Mohammed Janahi, 139-43, *141*, 145
Al Arshi house, 179
Al Attar house, 55, *176*
Al Awadhi house, 137
Al Awir, 20
Al Banna, Ostad Aqeel, *151*, 159, 167
Al Banna, Ostad Mohammed, 15, 70
Al Banna, Ostad Mohammed Saleh, 110
Al Barsha, 110
Al Bastaki, Abdulrazak Abdulrahim Aminai, 112
Al Bastaki family, 118, 120, 127
Al Bastaki, Mahmoud Ahmed, 145
Al Bastaki, Mohammed Abdulrazak, 58, *58*, 63, *64*, 65
Al Faheidi fort, 3, 20, 47, 177, 181-2
Al Gaith, Abdullah, 180
Al Maktoum, Sheikh Juma, 141
Al Maktoum, Sheikh Rashid bin Saeed, 12, 17, *17*, 18, 21
Al Maktoum, Sheikh Saeed bin Maktoum, 13, 16, *16*, 17, 141
Al Mankhool, 145
Al Qoz, 127
Al Ras, 180
Al Shibl Club, 184-5
Al Ulama, Abdullah Mohammed, 106, *107*, 114-5
Al Ulama, Mohammed Shareef Abdulrahman, 140
Al Ulama, Sheikh Mohammed Ali Sultan, 140
Ali, Ostad Ghlum, 110
Aminai family, 58
Aminai, Mohammed Amin, 58
Amiri, Ali, 132
Amiri family, 100
Amiri, Mir Abdullah, 131
animals (domestic), 44, *44*, 47, 112, 122, 123, 136
areesh (palm frond) housing, 14, 15, 17, 50, 148-150

B

Bag-e Dawlatabad, *161*, 162
Bahrain, 12, 15, 132, 163, 165, 182
Bam, 162
Bander Abbas, 10, 11, 162-3
Bani Yas, 8, 47,
Bastak, 10-15, **22-3**, 31, 46, 48, 54, 68, 118, 140, 165
  architecture, *22-3*
  history, **22-3**
Bastaki, Dr Eesa Mohammed, 59, 60, 62-3, 64, *64*
Bastakiya, the, 19-*20*, *180*
  conservation, 177-80, *181*, 182, 184
  form, *26*, 29, *30*, 30, 32, *35*, 36-37, *181*
  demolition, 20, *179*, 182, 184
  immigration, 8, 14-17, 21, 49
  map of, *20*
  ownership, *20*, 121
  pioneers, **13**
  souq, 5, 9, 14, 15, 180
  tourism, 182-3, **185**
Batinah coast, 10, 47, 52, 55, 148
bedouin, 141, 142
Bombay, 10, 55, 65, 68, 69
British Bank of the Middle East (BBME), 18, 120
British Political Agency, 141
Bukhash house, *33*, 39, 40-1, *47*, *55*, 179
Bukhash, Rashid M, 181-2
Buraimi, 69
Bushire, 11, 163

C

Cairo, 162
Caspian Sea, 164
childbirth, **50**, 54, 60
childhood, *43*, *54*, *55*, *59*, *63*, 65, 106, 131, 137
climate, 162, 164, 165-73
Collins, Alison, 131, 136-7
crafts, 54, 63

D

Dar Al Nadwa, 62, 110
Deira, 4, 18, 19, *48*, 58, 151, 176, 181
desert, 5
Dubai, 181
  Creek, *3*, 3, *9*, *14*, 14-18, *21*, 29, 37, 48, 110, 111, 113-5, 141, 184-5
  Development Plan Review, 177
  history, 8-9, 14-21
  tourism, 4
  trade, 10-13, 15, 21
Dubai Municipality, 64, 137, 144, 149, 176, 178, 180, 182, *183*
  Historic Buildings Section, 182

E

East African coast, 153
education, 53-5, 57, 58, 62-3, 100, 101, 106, 110
Eid, 25, 47, 68

F

family welfare, 52-5
Farouk, Abdul Kareem, *12*
Farouk mosque, 26, 29, 179
fire, 18-19, 121
food, 17, 35, 41, 45-7, *46*, 49, *52*, 102, 112, 123
Friday mosque, 29
fuel, 46
furniture, 41, 47-8, 51

G

Great Britain, 6, 10, 17, 21, 55, 144
Gulf, region, 10, *11*, 31, 46, 148, 162-3, 165
  coast, 36
  climate, 5-7, 15, 25, 32, 36-41, 48, 50, 55
  fishing, 5, 10, 15
Guy, Lt J N, 8

H

Hajar mountains, 5

Haji Ahmed Arshi house, 27
Haji Mohammad Falakhnaz house, *12*
Haji Qaed Al Attar house, *15*
Hamriyah, 9, 14
Hatta (village), 181
Heat Stress Index, 172
Historic Buildings Section, 111, 115
Hormuz, 162
Hyderabad, 163, 164

I

India, 6, 10, 11, 13, 46, 148, 153, 154, 165
Iran, 10-12, 15, 31, 15, 55, 99, 148, 154, 156, 162-4
Isfahan, 162
Islam, 25, 28-36
  art (Islamic), 178
  prayer, 29, 30, 63, 166, 176
  Ramadan, 25, 41, 68, 77, 134, 176, 184

J

Janah, 140
Janahi, Mohammed Noor, 140-1
Jazirat Al Hamra, UAE, 165
Jebel Ali, 21, 151
Jeddah, 27
John R Harris (architects), 177, 179
Jumeirah, 50-51, 64, 103

K

Kalba, 69, 75
Karachi, 55, 69, 106-8
Kashan, 162, *162*
Kerman, 163
Khamir, 15, 46
Kish Island, 164
Kuwait, 12, 13, 55, 100, 142, 182, 165

L

labour (migrant), 177
Lamu, 27, 153
Lar, 162
Larestan, 11, 12
Lingeh, 10-14, 48, 58, 69, 74, 106, 132, 140, *163*, 163-4, *164*
Llewellyn-Davies (planning consultants), 182
London, 100

M

Madagascar, 69
Mahmoud Mohammed Arjumand Al Bastaki house, *178*
Majlis Gallery, 100, 121, 127, 130, 131, *132*, 137, *137*, *177*
Maktoum bin Hasher Al Maktoum, Sheikh, 58
Maktoum Bridge, 63
Maktoum family, 13, 179
Maktoum Hospital, 108, 115
maritime trade, 5, 15, 17, 21
marriage, 13, 118
  weddings, **49**
Maybod, *163*
merchants, 118, 120
Minab, 15
Mohammed Sharif Bukhash house, 67-95
Musandam peninsula, 5, 75
Muscat, 10, 27

O

oil, *17*, 20, 21, 175, 176
oilfields, 5
Oman, 27, 132, 142, 143, 148, 182

P

pearling, 5, 9-13, 15-16, 58, **65**, 140, 106, 165
Persia, *see* Iran
Polo, Marco, 162
Prince of Wales, the, 144, 181

Q

Qajar era, 163
Qatar, 13, 182, 132, 165
Qasim Abdullah Al Bastaki house, *178*, *184*
Qawasim, 8, 10, 12
Qazim, Ahmed bin Mohammed Aqil, *13*
Qeshm, 165
Qur'an school, **53**, 54-55, 112, 139, 141-2, 143

R

Ras Al Khaimah, 8, 12, 21, 165
Rashid Hospital, 108
Red Sea, 10, 13, 27
Reza Shah, 15
Royal Scottish Museum, 178
Ruler's Diwan, new, 179, *180*, 184-5
  old, 179

S

Salalah, 27
Saudi Arabia, 182
Scarce, Jennifer, 178
Second World War, 17, 28
Shankland Cox Partnership, 178
Shareefi, Bibiya, 105, 106, 111-15
Shareefi family, 107, 112-3, 114, 115
Sharjah, 8, 12, 16, *162*, 165
Sheikh Juma Al Maktoum house, 182
Sheikh Mohammed Centre for Cultural Understanding, *182*
Sheikh Obaid bin Thani house, *9*
Sheikh Rashid's palace, *15*, 17, 29, 100
Sheikh Saeed house, *9*, 15, 178, *179*
Sheikhs' graveyard, 115
Shia, 12
Shindagha, *9*, 15, 47, 62, 140-1, 176-182
Shiraz, 11, 162
Sunnis, 11, 12, 152
Symbolism, 32, 35-6, 183

T

Tabriz, 162
Teheran, 52, 163
temperature, 5-7, 37, 38, 40, 41
Thesiger, Wilfred, 147
trade routes, 163
Trucial States, 8, 12, 17, 21

U

UAE Architectural Heritage Society, *174-5*, *185*
UAE University, 100
Umm Al Qawain, 12
UNDP, 181
Unesco, 175, 178, 184
United Arab Emirates, 5, 21
United States, 10, 16, 63

V

Vipac Engineering, 169, 173

W

wind-catchers, early, 161-3
  uni-directional, 161-3
windscoops, 27, 40, 41, 60, 103, 130, 134, 144, 145, 161-2
windtower houses, 15, 17, *38*, 165
  air conditioning in, 4, 7, 102, 103, 134
  arches, 37, 39, 67, 76, 77, 104, 105, 112, 113, 114
  architectural survey, 80-95
  balconies, 27, 32, 41
  beams, rafters, 153, 153, 155
  commercial use, 130, 137
  preservation of, 130, 159
  construction, *150*, *151*, *155*, 159
    framed, 27-8, 28

materials, 19, 27-28
areesh, 100, 141, 142-3, *146*, 146-150, 156
cement blocks, 71
concrete, 102
coral stone, *28,* 64, *152*
lime, 151-2, *154*
sand-lime blocks, 147, 151, 152
sarooj, 152-3, *153*
sea-stone, 27, 41, 147, 151-2, 154-5
shellstone, 27, *28*
timber, *chandals*, 28, 69, 147, *153*, *157*
methods, 155
measurement, **155**
tools, **155**
courtyards, 3, 13, 15, *38*, 44-45, 52, 70, 77, 100, 103, 108, 110, 111, 115, 116, 117, 122, 131, 132, *134*, 135, *135*, 166, 170, 173
decoration, 27, 32, 35-36, *40*, 72, 73, 117
screens,
gypsum, 35-6, 40, 60, 71, 72, 75, 76, 97, 100-103, 110, 111, 112, 114
stencilled, 35
timber, 67, 71, 104, 107, 112
defence, 31
demolition, 78, 79
deterioration, 137
doors, entrances, 25, 27, 32, 33, 58, 59, 70, 72, 74, 76, 101, 103, 112, 120, 122, 136, 137
foundations, 28, 64
furniture, 102, 112-13, 115
gardens, 26, 32, 39, 40, 45, 122, 130, *134*
gargoyles, *105*, *131*
majlis, 100, 102, 103
summer, 100, 102, 102, 103
modernisation, 102
particle pathway modelling, *171*
reconstruction, restoration, 56, 60, 64, 111, 115, 137, 144-5
roofs, 47, 48, 51, 59, 62, 77, 102, 114, 131, 134, 144, 155, 156
servants, 46, 47, 48, 49, 74
staircases, 64, 102, 114, 155, 156, 157
storage, 39, 44, 58, 70, 76, 77, 78, 100, 102, 107, 112, 113, 114, 123-4, 132, 134
summer migration, 50-52, 60, 68, 74, 75, 97, 101-2, 114, 141
summer rooms, 26, 29, 37, 60, 71, 72, 101, 125, 126, 134, *144*
verandahs, 28, *39*, 40, 51, 101, 110, 112, 113, 115, *116*, *122*, 123, 166, *177*
visitors, 31, 46, 49-50, 100, 102
washrooms, 39, 74
weathering, 137
windows, 27, 68, 69, 114, 127, *136*, *137*, 143, 157
wells, 114, 115, *135*
windtowers, *5*, *9*, 131, *139*, 143, *144*, 145
characteristics, 66, 72-4, 75, 110, 111, *166*, 166
construction, 166
decoration, *160*
height, *161*, 166-7
Iranian, 161-5
lack of, 63
multi-directional, 163, *164*
orientation, *167*, 170, 172
seasonal, 51
symbolism, **183**
uni-directional, 161, 162, *163*
use of, 102, 103, 113, 132, 165-6, 173
wind tunnel model, 169, 170, *170*
working of, 165-73
Computational Fluid Dynamics (CFD), 169, *171*, *173*
women, 47, 49, 50, 54, 63
Women's Society, 108, 110

Y

Yazd, 11, 161, 163
Yemen, 27, 141

Z

Zagros mountains, 22, 23
Zandi, Dariush, 78, 137, 177, 178, 184
Zanzibar, 27, 69, 153